RECKLESS

ROBERT K. BRIGHAM

RECKLESS

HENRY KISSINGER
and the
TRAGEDY *of* VIETNAM

PUBLICAFFAIRS
NEW YORK

PublicAffairs
Hachette Book Group
1290 Avenue of the Americas
New York, NY 10104
www.publicaffairsbooks.com
@Public_Affairs
Printed in the United States of America
First Edition: September 2018

Published by PublicAffairs, an imprint of Perseus Books, LLC, a subsidiary of Hachette Book Group, Inc. The PublicAffairs name and logo is a trademark of the Hachette Book Group.

The Hachette Speakers Bureau provides a wide range of authors for speaking events. To find out more, go to www.hachettespeakersbureau.com or call (866) 376-6591.

The publisher is not responsible for websites (or their content) that are not owned by the publisher.

Print book interior design by Jouve.

Library of Congress Cataloging-in-Publication Data has been applied for.

ISBNs: 978-1-61039-702-5 (hardcover); 978-1-61039-703-2 (ebook)

LSC-C

10 9 8 7 6 5 4 3 2 1

For Monica and Taylor

"It either works or it doesn't, and it doesn't matter."

—Richard M. Nixon

CONTENTS

PREFACE

THIS BOOK CHRONICLES Henry Kissinger's management of the Vietnam War. It focuses on his efforts to combine military strategy with diplomacy to extricate the United States from Vietnam with honor. Kissinger inherited a weak bargaining position on Vietnam, but he still believed that he, and he alone, could deliver a favorable peace agreement.

When Henry Kissinger entered the White House in 1969 as President Richard Nixon's national security adviser, there were over 500,000 US troops in Vietnam. American combat deaths were about two hundred each week, a number that was likely to grow as Communist forces increased their assault on South Vietnam. The cost of the war to US taxpayers was $30 billion per year. Kissinger believed that these conditions demanded a negotiated settlement to the war. There were simply too many explicit constraints on US power to make a military victory likely. "However we got into Vietnam," he observed, "whatever the judgment of our actions, ending the war honorably is essential for the peace of the world."[1]

An honorable peace, according to Kissinger, had to meet several essential conditions. First, there had to be a lasting cease-fire between North Vietnam and South Vietnam. This cease-fire had to include the neighboring countries of Laos and Cambodia, both of which had been caught up in the conflict. Second, there must be a mutual US–North Vietnamese troop withdrawal from South Vietnam. North Vietnamese forces operating in Laos and Cambodia also had to be redeployed to North Vietnam. Third, North Vietnam had to recognize the Demilitarized Zone as an international boundary. Fourth, with the signing of a peace agreement, all prisoners of war had to be released. Finally, Kissinger argued that any negotiated settlement had to leave the Saigon government in full political control in South Vietnam. He initially rejected North Vietnam's proposals for a coalition government in South Vietnam, which he feared would "destroy the existing political structure and thus lead to a Communist takeover." His goal, therefore, was to negotiate a final peace agreement in Paris that traded an American exit from Vietnam for political guarantees for Saigon. "We were determined," Kissinger wrote in his memoirs, "to do our utmost to enable Saigon to grow in security and prosperity so that it could prevail in any political struggle. We sought not an interval before collapse, but lasting peace with honor."[2]

To accomplish his strategic "peace with honor" goals, Kissinger promoted a tactical "war for peace" in Vietnam. But where has there ever been a successful "war for peace"? It's a theorist's concept, possible only if one is very distantly removed from the actual business of killing and dying and the aftereffects that produces. Still, with the arrogance and hubris of someone new to power, he confidently assured Nixon that he could pressure Hanoi to accept concessions it had routinely rejected during Lyndon Johnson's presidency by combining great power diplomacy with savage military blows against North Vietnam. He also advocated attacks against North Vietnamese sanctuaries inside Laos and Cambodia and the mining of North Vietnamese ports. "I can't believe that a fourth-rate power like North Vietnam doesn't have a breaking point," Kissinger told his aides during his first weeks at the White House. "Hit them," he told Nixon, and Hanoi would beg "for private talks."[3]

Finding that delicate balance between military strikes and skillful negotiations was exactly what Kissinger believed was his specialty. In over five decades of telling and retelling his role in the Vietnam

War, Kissinger has carefully constructed a narrative that is detailed, somewhat self-effacing, and on the surface, balanced. He has skillfully mixed criticism of the Nixon administration's policies with disdain for its critics. He has both downplayed the war's expansion on his watch and celebrated it. He blamed Kennedy-style idealism for the US entry into the war and championed his own realism for ending it. Kissinger gave the United States an honorable withdrawal from Vietnam, he claims, by linking Hanoi's geopolitical desires to security guarantees for the United States' South Vietnamese allies. In the end, Kissinger argues that Watergate and a weak-kneed Congress had made it impossible to defend South Vietnam, not his failures as a negotiator or strategist.

The Vietnam War remains Kissinger's most enduring foreign policy legacy. No war since the American Civil War has seared the US national consciousness like Vietnam. The controversies surrounding it tore the nation apart, and its legacies continue to shape US foreign relations today. Kissinger's role in this war has been studied in detail, but this book is the first to hold his record to a scrupulous account based on his own definitions of success and the evidence provided by recently released material in the Richard Nixon Presidential Library, Kissinger's papers at Yale University, and South Vietnamese sources contained in the National Archives in Ho Chi Minh City, Vietnam. On the strength of that it is clear that the national security adviser's war for peace was more than oxymoronic: it was a total failure. Kissinger failed in each of his stated goals to achieve "peace with honor." He failed to end the diplomatic deadlock in Paris or to negotiate a political settlement in South Vietnam that left the Saigon government a reasonable chance to survive following the American withdrawal. He failed to use great power diplomacy or military force to compel Hanoi to make compromises in the Paris negotiations. He failed to force a mutual North Vietnamese troop withdrawal from South Vietnam. He failed to neutralize Laos and Cambodia. He failed to secure a lasting cease-fire. He failed to obtain an international border at the Demilitarized Zone. He failed to link the release of all political prisoners to a lasting cease-fire. He failed to consult the Saigon government about its future until it was too late to change course in Paris.

At home, Kissinger also did much more harm than good. He failed to build a coalition of supportive allies for his "war for peace" within the Nixon administration or in Congress. He failed to contain US domestic opposition to his policies. He failed the president by overstating progress in Paris and the likelihood of success following US military escalation. Each of these disappointments narrowed his future options and shortened the time he had to achieve "peace with honor."

Kissinger's voluminous writings on the subject have obscured his failures in Vietnam, and perhaps that is the point of them. Like the Internet, Kissinger provides huge amounts of apparent information, not all of it reliable. He's a conspiratorially minded theorist, and he often wanders far from the facts. But facts are stubborn things, and it is possible, I think, to examine the historical record in detail to offer a more complete picture of Kissinger and his failed "war for peace." This research has been made easier now that his monopoly on the actual historical documents has ended. Scholars now have access to hundreds of thousands of pages of National Security Council files, the verbatim transcripts of the secret meetings in Paris, and over twenty thousand pages of Kissinger's taped telephone conversations. Utilizing this new material, this book is the first to analyze the cumulative effect of Kissinger's strategic and diplomatic failures on the final peace agreement. It demonstrates how Kissinger's misplaced faith in his own abilities to secure an honorable peace prolonged the war unnecessarily and sealed South Vietnam's fate. For all his faults, Kissinger (no matter what) could not change reality on the ground. He made a bad situation worse, however, with his reckless assumptions about the use of force and diplomacy.

ACRONYMS

ARVN   Army of the Republic of Vietnam (South Vietnamese Army)

COSVN   Central Office Southern Vietnam, Communist Party's headquarters for South Vietnam

DMZ   Demilitarized zone separating North Vietnam and South Vietnam

DRV   Democratic Republic of Vietnam (North Vietnam)

GVN   Government of Vietnam, also known as RVN (South Vietnam)

JCS   US Joint Chiefs of Staff

MACV   US Military Assistance Command Vietnam

NLF   National Liberation Front, Communist front organization in South Vietnam

NSC   National Security Council

NVA   North Vietnamese Army, also known as PAVN

PAVN   People's Army of Vietnam (North Vietnamese Army)

PLAF   People's Liberation Armed Forces, military arm of the NLF, derogatorily called Viet Cong

POW   prisoner(s) of war

PRG   Provisional Revolutionary Government, NLF's government-in-waiting

RVN   Republic of Vietnam, also known as GVN (South Vietnam)

RVNAF   Republic of Vietnam Armed Forces (South Vietnam's armed forces)

KEY PLAYERS

Creighton Abrams   MACV commander, 1968–1972, US Army chief of staff, 1972–74

Nguyen Thi Binh   PRG/NLF foreign minister

Mai Van Bo   Head of DRV's commercial legation in Paris

Leonid Brezhnev   General secretary of the Communist Party, Soviet Union, 1964–1982

David Bruce   Special ambassador to Paris negotiations

McGeorge Bundy   National security adviser to presidents Kennedy and Johnson, 1961–1966

William Bundy   Assistant secretary of state for the Far East, 1964–1969

Ellsworth Bunker   US ambassador to South Vietnam, 1967–1973

Anna Chennault   Member of the "China lobby," vice president of Flying Tiger Line and secret contact to the Saigon government

Frank Church   US senator (D-ID), cosponsor of the Cooper-Church Amendment

Charles Colson   Special counsel, Nixon administration

John Sherman Cooper   US senator (R-KY), cosponsor of the Cooper-Church Amendment

Bui Diem   South Vietnam's ambassador to the United States, 1965–1972

Ngo Dinh Diem   President of the RVN, 1955–1963

Anatoly Dobrynin   Soviet ambassador to the United States

Pham Van Dong   DRV prime minister

Le Duan   Secretary-general of the Vietnamese Communist Party, 1960–1986

John Ehrlichman   Counsel and assistant to the president for domestic affairs under Nixon

Daniel Ellsberg   RAND analyst who leaked the Pentagon Papers

Zhou Enlai   Premier of the People's Republic of China

Vo Nguyen Giap   General and minister of defense, PAVN

Barry Goldwater   US senator (R-AZ) and 1964 Republican nominee for US president

Alexander Haig   Deputy national security adviser, Nixon administration

H. R. Haldeman   White House chief of staff for President Richard Nixon

Mark Hatfield   US senator (R-OR), cosponsor of the Hatfield-McGovern Amendment

Hubert Humphrey   Vice president of the United States under President Johnson

Lyndon Johnson   President of the United States, 1963–1969

Nikita Khrushchev   Premier of the Soviet Union, 1958–1964

Henry Kissinger   National security adviser, Nixon administration, 1969–1973

Alexei Kosygin   Premier of the Soviet Union, 1964–1980

Nguyen Cao Ky   Vice president of South Vietnam, 1967–1971

Melvin Laird   Secretary of defense in the Nixon administration, 1969–1974

Anthony Lake   National Security Council staff member under Kissinger

General Hoang Xuan Lam   South Vietnamese general who led 1971 invasion of Laos

Henry Cabot Lodge Jr.   US ambassador to South Vietnam, 1963–1964, 1965–1967

Winston Lord   National Security Council staff member; accompanied Kissinger to Paris

George McGovern   US senator (D–SD) and Democratic Party US presidential nominee, 1972, cosponsor of the Hatfield–McGovern Amendment

Robert S. McNamara   Secretary of defense for Presidents Kennedy and Johnson, 1961–1967

John McNaughton   Assistant secretary of defense, 1961–1967

Mike Mansfield   US senator (D–MT)

Duong Van Minh   Former South Vietnamese general and politician

Ho Chi Minh   President of the DRV, 1945–1969

John Mitchell   US attorney general in Nixon administration and chair of the Committee to Re-Elect the President (CREEP)

Thomas Moorer   Chairman of the Joint Chiefs of Staff, 1970–1974

Edmund Muskie   US senator (D–ME) and US presidential candidate, 1972

John Negroponte   US Foreign Service officer; participated in Paris peace talks

Richard Nixon   President of the United States, 1969–1974

General Lon Nol   Led coup against Prince Sihanouk in Cambodia

William Porter   US delegate to the avenue Kléber/Paris Peace Talks

Nelson Rockefeller   Governor of New York, US Republican presidential candidate, 1964

Peter Rodman   National Security Council staff member; accompanied Kissinger to Paris

William Rogers   Secretary of state in the Nixon administration, 1969–1973

Jean Sainteny   French politician; served as messenger for Nixon with Ho Chi Minh

Norodom Sihanouk   Head of state of Cambodia, 1960–1970

Ray Sitton   US Air Force colonel who gave Kissinger bombing targets for secret attacks on Cambodia

William Sullivan Coordinated avenue Kléber/Paris peace talks for Nixon

Nguyen Van Thieu President of the GVN

Le Duc Tho DRV Politburo member; negotiated with Kissinger in Paris

Xuan Thuy DRV diplomat; negotiated with Kissinger in Paris

General Co Van Vien South Vietnam's defense minister

General Vernon Walters US military attaché at the embassy in Paris

General Earle Wheeler Chairman of the Joint Chiefs of Staff, 1964–1970

Mao Zedong Chairman of China's Communist Party

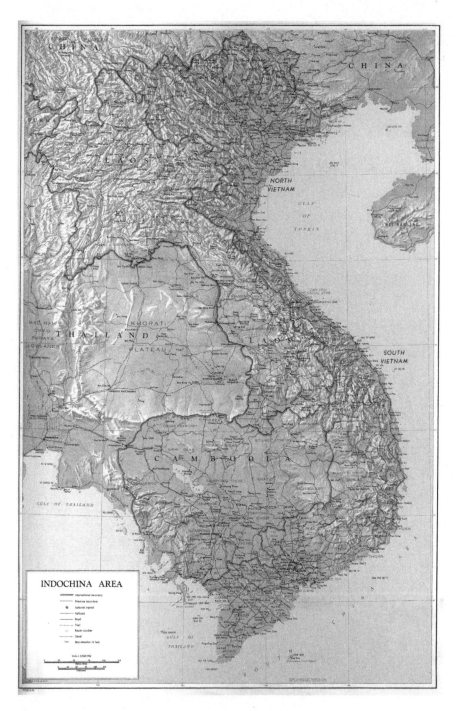

Courtesy of the University of Texas Libraries, the University of Texas at Austin

CHAPTER ONE

THE APPRENTICE, 1965–1969

IN THE EARLY MORNING of November 25, 1968, Henry Kissinger, a Harvard professor and longtime foreign policy adviser to perennial Republican presidential hopeful Nelson Rockefeller, walked into the Pierre Hotel at the intersection of Fifth Avenue and Sixty-First Street in Manhattan, and took the elevator to the thirty-ninth floor to Richard Nixon's transition headquarters. Nixon had just narrowly defeated Democrat Hubert Humphrey in the 1968 US presidential election and was wasting no time putting his new administration together. The Pierre was an unlikely place for the president-elect to have his transition headquarters, given its ties to the East Coast establishment that Nixon so despised. Kissinger, however, had spent much of his adult life trying to gain entry into that world, courting Rockefeller and others who saw democratic collapse as one of the century's most pressing concerns. Yet Kissinger and the president-elect held many views in common. Both were classical realists who believed the world needed strong leaders that acted without passion to restore order and stability to the international system. They placed great

1

emphasis on what Kissinger called "consequential diplomacy"—the role of great men in advancing the interest of the nation and in shaping political outcomes.[1] They thought that the United States alone was strong enough to defeat fascism, communism, and other forms of tyranny. They also considered themselves self-made men. Neither was born to the upper class. Each had achieved great heights because of talent, not patronage.

Kissinger later claimed that he was surprised by the invitation to the Pierre. He had spent much of the 1960s supporting other Republicans at Nixon's expense. He had declared that Nixon was "unfit to be the president" and thought the president-elect was "a hollow man" who had a dangerous "misunderstanding of foreign policy."[2] He recognized Nixon's personal insecurities, and they worried him. Haunted by the inconsequential life his father had led, Nixon was a striver and a loner, someone who demanded loyalty and wanted to be admired. Kissinger saw these characteristics as potentially damaging in the nuanced world of foreign affairs. But Nixon had power, something Kissinger had been seeking without much luck for over a decade.

Nixon was well aware of Kissinger's "disparaging comments." He knew that Kissinger had challenged his "competence" in foreign policy, but he expected this "from a Rockefeller associate" and "chalked it up to politics."[3] Others saw something more sinister behind Nixon's willingness to overlook Kissinger's comments and contact him. Journalist Seymour Hersh claimed that Nixon ignored Kissinger's remarks because the Harvard professor had given the presidential campaign team secret information about the Johnson administration's negotiating position during the Vietnam peace talks in Paris.[4] "There is a better than even chance that Johnson will order a bombing halt at approximately mid-October," Kissinger wrote to the Nixon campaign shortly after his September 1968 trip to Paris.[5] With this information, Hersh claimed, the campaign could move behind the scenes to block progress in any negotiations that might surface.

As Kissinger predicted, on October 31, just five days before the 1968 presidential election, a desperate Lyndon Johnson publicly pledged to stop all US bombing and shelling of the Democratic Republic of Vietnam (DRV, or North Vietnam) for the first time since Operation Rolling Thunder, the sustained bombing of North Vietnam, had begun in February 1965. Johnson also announced that he would expand the peace talks to include the South Vietnamese government and its sworn enemy, the National Liberation Front (NLF, derogatorily called the Viet Cong). He hoped that his October surprise would allow the Democratic nominee, his vice president, Hubert H. Humphrey, to close the narrow gap in the race with Nixon. On the eve of the election, Johnson's plan seemed to have worked. There were only a few percentage points separating the two candidates, and momentum was in Humphrey's favor—until the South Vietnamese president, Nguyen Van Thieu, announced that he would not send a representative to Paris and that his government would never negotiate with the NLF without political guarantees.[6]

There was much speculation in the press at the time that Kissinger had not only told the Nixon campaign secret information about Johnson's negotiating position in Paris, but had also used Anna Chennault, a longtime friend to Republicans and anti-Communists in Asia, to deliver a message to the South Vietnamese government telling it not to agree to negotiate in Paris. The implication was that Saigon would get a much better deal from the Nixon administration.[7] In his 1987 memoir, *In the Jaws of History,* Bui Diem, who at that time was South Vietnam's ambassador to the United States, has confirmed contact between Chennault, the Nixon campaign, and the Saigon government, but he has downplayed its influence, claiming that Thieu had already decided that he would not negotiate with the Communists.[8]

Newly released documents from Trung tam luu tru quoc gia II (National Archives II) in Ho Chi Minh City support Diem's claim.[9] The Saigon government was incensed by rumors that Anna Chennault influenced the decision not to negotiate. It was true that she had hosted many dinners at her Watergate apartment along the banks of the Potomac River in Washington that had included several top South Vietnamese officials, but Saigon's leaders claimed that these events were seen as a way to convince the Americans to continue to support South Vietnam, not opportunities to listen to advice from Chennault. Having lost over 100,000 troops and an equally high number of civilians, and facing increased military pressure from Hanoi's People's Army of Vietnam (PAVN), Saigon government officials claimed that they did not need a dilettante to tell them how to deal with the Communists, no matter how many friends she had in Washington.[10]

But Anna Chennault was no dilettante. She was the widow of Lt. General Claire Chennault, the American leader of the Flying Tigers, who defended China against Japanese invaders during WWII. Born Chen Xiangmei, Anna was a war correspondent in China when she met her future husband. After the war, the two founded the Civil Air Transport that operated on mainland China until Mao's victory. Fleeing to Taiwan, the Chennaults became fixtures of the "China Lobby," an alliance of conservative Americans and Chinese nationalists who blamed the Truman administration for "losing" China. In the late 1950s, after her husband's death, Chennault moved to America and took over the running of the Flying Tiger Line, then the biggest freight airline in the world.[11] She became a steadfast supporter of Republican politics and politicians, and as one Nixon official observed, she was a "very shrewd operator."[12] She would have been a very likely go-between had Saigon not so readily dismissed this claim.

The idea that Kissinger was somehow behind a secret plan to convince Thieu not to negotiate with the NLF because Saigon would get a better deal from Nixon was even more preposterous. "Kissinger was totally irrelevant to our [South Vietnamese] deliberations," one former South Vietnamese official later claimed. "We had been uneasy with the Johnson administration's discussion of negotiations at our July 18 meeting in Honolulu and had long planned to back out of any talks that the White House was using to score political points during the 1968 presidential election. We did not need a college professor from Harvard telling us how to solve our diplomatic problems."[13]

Kissinger, too, has always downplayed his role in the 1968 presidential campaign. In the first volume of his massive memoirs, *White House Years*, he argues that he had only met Nixon once prior to November 1968, and he repeatedly denies having had any direct contact with the Nixon team during the campaign. "During the national campaign in 1968," Kissinger writes, "several Nixon emissaries—some self-appointed—telephoned me for counsel. I took the position that I would answer specific questions on foreign policy, but that I would not offer general advice or volunteer suggestions."[14] Nixon certainly had other sources of information inside the Johnson White House who were close to negotiations. But much of the evidence suggests that Kissinger did intervene on Nixon's behalf, even if his meddling did not influence decision making in Saigon as much as Hersh and others claim.

It was not access to information that made Kissinger so appealing to Nixon. It was in equal measures Kissinger's understanding of power—Nixon believed that he needed Kissinger to shape and implement his broad foreign policy designs—and his willingness to make difficult decisions in the face of public pressure. Nixon liked what Kissinger thought about the exercise of power. He had read Kissinger's early scholarly work on foreign policy in a nuclear world and was impressed. He also believed that Kissinger shared his belief that domestic politics (not elections) was merely fixing "outhouses in

Peoria."[15] Both men relished the arena of foreign affairs, and Nixon thought that Kissinger would be useful in creating the stable world order that he envisioned. Furthermore, Kissinger seemed to understand that Nixon's foreign policy background made bold moves possible. He confided to close friends that Nixon might just be able to make huge inroads in bringing Moscow and Beijing in from the cold.[16] By reorienting American power and prestige following a necessary withdrawal from Vietnam, Kissinger thought a Nixon presidency could tackle larger and more important foreign policy problems. In short, Nixon liked Kissinger as a potential junior associate in foreign policy and Kissinger admired Nixon's willingness to hire someone for his expertise rather than for patronage. Kissinger and Nixon were two self-made men who would take on the world together.

When Nixon and Kissinger finally met at the Pierre, the president-elect did not talk about grand strategy or the war in Vietnam; rather, he outlined the massive organizational problems he faced. He had very little confidence in the State Department. He also thought that the Johnson administration had ignored the Joint Chiefs of Staff on most issues dealing with Vietnam at its peril. He thought that the CIA was staffed by "Ivy League liberals who behind the facade of analytical objectivity" were usually pushing their own agenda.[17] Nixon also believed that the Johnson White House was run too informally, with key foreign policy decisions made over lunch.[18] All of these concerns, and his personal insecurities, left Nixon with the desire to run foreign policy from the White House. He needed a strong national security adviser to help him centralize power and to develop a robust and credible foreign policy.

Despite his concerns about Nixon's character and capabilities, Kissinger agreed with the president-elect's reorganization plan. He told Nixon that he should set up a strong National Security Council staff in the White House and then sideline the State Department.

By cutting out the State Department completely, Nixon could control foreign policy discussions and limit the influence of career professionals who had snubbed him when he was vice president under Dwight Eisenhower. Like Nixon, Kissinger had a profound disdain for bureaucracy, going well beyond the usual carping that went on in Washington. He thought the seasoned experts at the State Department tended their own gardens but were incapable of broad strategic thought. Zhou Enlai, the Chinese prime minister, once told Kissinger, "You don't like bureaucracy." Kissinger replied, "Yes, and it's mutual; the bureaucracy doesn't like me."[19] After sharing their mutual suspicions and ideas about governmental reorganization, Nixon awkwardly showed Kissinger the door, making some vague references about continued conversations on these matters.

After his meeting with Nixon, Kissinger returned to Harvard that afternoon to teach his foreign policy seminar. The next day he received a phone call from John Mitchell, a senior member of Nixon's campaign staff, asking him to return to New York for a follow-up meeting. When he arrived at the Pierre Hotel, Mitchell asked him, "What have you decided about the National Security job?"[20] Kissinger had had no idea that he had been offered it—during their discussion the previous day, Nixon had never mentioned a specific job for him in the new administration. Once Nixon confirmed that he wanted him as his national security adviser, Kissinger uncharacteristically asked for some time to consider the offer. It now seems clear that his own insecurities caused him to ask permission from his Harvard colleagues and his former boss, Nelson Rockefeller, to join the president's staff. Most agreed that Kissinger had a duty to accept the position, but some felt that working for Nixon was beyond the pale. No one questioned Nixon's rationale in selecting him. As historian Robert Dallek has noted, both "were outsiders who distrusted establishment liberals" and both had "grandiose dreams of recasting world affairs."[21] They also shared an obsession with secrecy. One week later, Kissinger accepted the offer. He was the first of Nixon's national security team to be announced, a telling statement of the new president's desire to ignore the foreign policy establishment.

Kissinger was an able ally in pushing the State Department aside. He believed that the department was filled by "probably the ablest and most professional group of men and women in public service," but the "reverse of their dedication is the conviction that a lifetime of service and study has given them insights that transcend the untrained and shallow-rooted views of political appointees."[22] Nixon was a little blunter: he wanted to take power "from the bureaucrats and place it where it belonged, in the White House."[23] Accordingly, Nixon appointed William Rogers, a lawyer and former attorney general, as secretary of state precisely because he lacked foreign policy experience. Nixon told Kissinger that he "considered Rogers's unfamiliarity with the subject an asset because it guaranteed that policy direction would remain in the White House."[24] He also wanted a secretary of state who was a good negotiator rather than a policy maker—"a role he reserved for himself" and his national security adviser.[25] Rogers was a skilled manager of people, Nixon explained, so the "little boys in the State Department" had to watch themselves, because he would not tolerate their nonsense.[26]

Kissinger, however, saw Rogers as an unqualified rival. Shortly after they met, he concluded that Rogers proved the old adage that "high office teaches decision-making, not substance."[27] He did not believe that Rogers would grow more perceptive about the intricacies of foreign policy simply by being on the job a long time. Rogers thought tactically, like the lawyer he was, but he did not possess a strategic or geopolitical mind. "The novice Secretary of State," Kissinger wrote disparagingly of Rogers, "thus finds on his desk not policy analyses or options, but stacks of dispatches which he is asked to initial and do so urgently, if you please."[28] Kissinger himself treated Rogers like a petty clerk. He later explained that once Nixon had appointed "a strong personality, expert in foreign policy, as the national security advisor, competition with the Secretary of State became inevitable."[29] (Talking in the third person was a favorite way of Kissinger to insert objectivity into any conversation.) Throughout his time at the White House, he did what he could to undermine Rogers in the eyes of the president.

Melvin Laird was Nixon's inspired choice as defense secretary. Laird (R-WI) was a longtime member of the House of Representatives and had considerable expertise in defense matters. On the surface, Laird was an odd choice for a president who wanted to consolidate power because of his years of experience in Congress, but Nixon thought he was reliable and did not crave the spotlight the way Robert S. McNamara and Clark Clifford, Johnson's two secretaries of defense, had. Laird knew how Congress worked and how to count votes, two qualities that Nixon admired. Laird was also willing to mend fences between the White House and the Joint Chiefs, something the president strongly encouraged. Unlike Kissinger, Laird had sensitive political antennae and understood the political need to withdraw US forces from Vietnam. He came to the Nixon administration determined to rescue the prestige and capabilities of the American military, which he thought had suffered during the four years of war in Vietnam. Laird and Kissinger disagreed on most matters relating to the war, and their outsized personalities often led to clashes inside the Nixon administration. Kissinger saw Laird as a skilled policy maker, though he thought he "acted on the assumption that he had a constitutional right to seek to outsmart and outmaneuver anyone with whom his office brought him into contact."[30] Laird challenged Kissinger on Vietnam policy repeatedly, often getting the best of his more educated colleague.

Nixon liked his new triad, and he skillfully played Laird and Kissinger off each other to achieve his objectives and to satisfy his need for respect, attention, and power. But when it came to foreign affairs, Kissinger was his most trusted confidant. Nixon's very first meeting on January 21, 1969, his first day in office, was with his national security adviser, cementing Kissinger's role. Kissinger treasured Nixon's confidence, and he would use his trusted role with the president to shape and influence the administration's response to the war in Vietnam.

From his very first day in the White House, Kissinger plotted to overturn the bureaucracy and to control decision making. While others in the administration attended inauguration ceremonies, Kissinger was busy implementing Nixon's radical bureaucratic revolution. Most important, three National Security Decision Memorandums (NSDM 1, 2, and 3) restructured the machinery of government, making the NSC the center of policy making and relegating the State Department to a secondary role in diplomacy. Kissinger also required that his NSC clear all policy cables before they were sent overseas, thus marginalizing the State Department from most foreign policy matters. Without informing Rogers, Kissinger then sent letters under Nixon's name to heads of state around the globe, telling them of this important change. Relishing the speed and secrecy with which Kissinger carried out his plans, Nixon allowed the NSC to double in size, and he tripled its budget during his time in office. One of Kissinger's most trusted aides, Lawrence Eagleburger, later noted that Nixon and Kissinger "developed a conspiratorial approach to foreign policy management"[31] with the government's reorganization. "It was a palace coup," declared William Bundy, a former State Department official, "entirely constitutional but at the same time revolutionary."[32] Historian George Herring observed, "What had been created in 1947 as a coordinating mechanism [the NSC] became a little State Department."[33]

But Nixon and Kissinger did more than just agree on process and the need for secrecy. They also generally agreed on key strategic issues. Both were rather pessimistic about the war in Vietnam and wanted to move on to what they considered more important foreign policy issues, such as arms limitations with the Soviets. Nixon told Kissinger that he did not want to devote all of his foreign policy time and energy to Vietnam, as Johnson had done, because the war was really a short-term problem.[34] Nixon was more than willing to let Kissinger handle the task of developing policy options for Vietnam as long as he left the decision making up to the president. Kissinger agreed, stating that the general problem in Vietnam had been that military operations and diplomacy had been divorced. He believed that negotiations could provide a favorable, or at least acceptable, outcome for the president if the government's various programs in Vietnam were studied carefully. The war could then be managed, coordinated, and "the whole puzzle put together."[35]

Prelude: Designing a Policy

Kissinger had actually begun putting the whole puzzle together years before he joined the Nixon administration. While at Harvard, he used his prerogative as director of the Defense Policy Seminar to invite to campus experts who dealt closely with Vietnam. He understood that the conflict in Vietnam was the most pressing foreign policy issue of the day and that to gain influence in Washington, he would have to develop expertise on the war.

One of his first guests in early 1965 was John McNaughton, Defense Secretary Robert S. McNamara's assistant and an expert on counterinsurgency. McNaughton had come highly recommended by Kissinger's Harvard colleague Roger Fisher, who taught at the law school and was a specialist on international negotiations. Fisher would later write, "McNaughton did more sustained thinking about the benefits of both escalation and withdrawal [from Vietnam] than any of the advocates for either position."[36] Kissinger had also heard that McNamara relied thoroughly on McNaughton to develop policy options on Vietnam, so McNaughton became a source of information and a model for Kissinger.

At Harvard, McNaughton spoke about the military problems that the United States faced in Vietnam and was incredibly pessimistic about the Saigon government's capabilities. He did not believe that the Johnson administration could defeat the Communists through air power alone, and he was not in favor of a major escalation in the number of American ground forces. McNaughton summed up his remarks by making six observations about why the United States should withdraw from Vietnam. To begin with, he did not believe that Vietnam was in America's "sphere of influence." He also felt that the Vietnamese revolutionaries had taken up arms because they had no other path to political power. He thought that the high morale of Communist forces presented the Saigon government with significant obstacles. He thought that the Saigon government was corrupt, elite, and "full of slobs." He believed that the weak and poor in Vietnam should ultimately prevail over the social elite. And, finally, he believed in an all-Vietnamese solution for South Vietnam.[37] McNaughton ended his remarks by asking, what would happen if South Vietnam collapsed? He believed that the United States could then walk away from Vietnam with its prestige intact.[38]

McNaughton's comments caught Kissinger by surprise. He stated publicly that he thought McNaughton's pessimism was unwarranted and showed poor judgment. He said as much to his former Harvard colleague National Security Adviser McGeorge Bundy in a letter dated March 30, 1965, assuring him that he believed Johnson's "present actions in Vietnam are essentially right." Kissinger concluded his letter by expressing his "respect for the courage with which the administration is acting."[39] Privately, however, he shared McNaughton's skepticism about American prospects in Vietnam. Since the Kennedy administration, Kissinger had had grave doubts about Washington's commitment to the war. "All history proves that there is no cheap and easy way to defeat guerilla movements," he wrote in 1962. "South Vietnam has been plagued by Communist Viet Cong attacks ever since it became independent in 1954. Their defeat can only be accomplished by adequate military force." Kissinger concluded, "I hope that we...have made the internal commitment to ourselves to see that a sufficient military effort is made to end the guerrilla attacks; we cannot be content with just maintaining an uneasy peace."[40] Of course, an uneasy peace is exactly what he agreed to in 1973. For Kissinger, the purpose of having power himself was to help develop policies that overcame what he perceived as the Kennedy administration's tentative reaction to crises. If Kennedy had demanded reforms from the Saigon government and gotten them, he could have backed South Vietnam from a place of power.

Kissinger sharpened his critique of America's Vietnam policy during the last months of the 1964 presidential race. Lyndon Johnson was seeking election in his own right after Kennedy's assassination in November 1963, and he was running against a host of Republicans who had sharp differences on foreign affairs. Kissinger believed that Nelson Rockefeller, whom he was advising on foreign policy, needed to distance himself from Johnson and from the rest of the Republican field, especially front-runner Barry Goldwater, a conservative senator from Arizona. Goldwater had a scorched-earth policy when it came to Vietnam. He wanted to carry the war to North Vietnam and advocated massive bombing raids against Communist troops and supply lines.[41] He also lamented that the fact that the United States had not used nuclear weapons against North Vietnam. Johnson, in Kissinger's mind, was simply carrying out Kennedy's timid plans to support South Vietnam without the use of American troops.

Kissinger believed that Rockefeller should make the presidential race a contest over Vietnam.

Rockefeller never grasped the subtleties of Kissinger's Vietnam policy papers, however. Kissinger suggested that Rockefeller force Johnson to admit that the war was going badly, that the NLF controlled much of the countryside, and that the war was now a region-wide conflict also involving Laos and Cambodia. The Soviets and the Chinese sponsored the insurgents fighting the South Vietnamese government, and Kissinger argued that Rockefeller should make sure that the American people understood that this all had begun on Kennedy and Johnson's watch. Moreover, the Johnson administration's "hesitancy to be firm and unwavering in the face of Communist advances in Laos and Vietnam," Kissinger wrote in September 1964, "has increased the trend toward neutrality in our SEATO allies." He urged Rockefeller to link American failures in Vietnam to larger foreign policy issues: "Isolated problems or states no longer exist. Single, simple remedies are no longer available. Every event has worldwide consequences."[42]

But Rockefeller could never find his footing on Vietnam. He often ignored Kissinger's recommendations, instead staking out policy positions that were similar to Lyndon Johnson's. Rockefeller and Kissinger also underestimated the amount of public support for Goldwater and his recklessly clear positions.

At the Republican National Convention in San Francisco, where Goldwater easily won the Republican Party's 1964 presidential nomination, Rockefeller saw his desires to moderate his party's foreign policy positions evaporate. As he gave his convention speech, Rockefeller was booed so loudly he could barely be heard over the crowd. All of Kissinger's work to create a nuanced Vietnam position was lost on an angry mob. For Kissinger, the experience was terrifying. According to his official biographer, Niall Ferguson, "Time and again Kissinger was reminded ominously of the politics of his

German childhood."[43] In Goldwater and those who supported him, Kissinger saw a movement that was "similar to European fascism."[44]

When the Republican Party rejected Rockefeller's ideas in San Francisco, Kissinger decided to vote for Lyndon Johnson and see whether he could influence the Democrats and maybe hit the reset button on his government experience. However, as historian Robert Dallek has noted, it was a Republican, not a Democrat, who secured Kissinger his first government job dealing directly with the Vietnam War.[45]

In the spring of 1965, Kissinger rekindled his friendship with Harvard colleague George Lodge, the son of Republican presidential hopeful Henry Cabot Lodge Jr. Johnson had recently appointed the elder Lodge ambassador to South Vietnam, a position he had also held in the Kennedy administration. Kissinger had supported Lodge's appointment enthusiastically, and their relationship led the ambassador to hire Kissinger to conduct a strategic assessment of the American position in Vietnam. Kissinger jumped at the chance to participate in policy making, even if he was only reporting to the ambassador.

In preparation for his October 1965 visit to Vietnam, the first for Kissinger, he made a list of experts to consult and books to read. He wrote to several US military leaders who had spent time in Vietnam and found that most were optimistic about the Army of the Republic of Vietnam (ARVN) but were less positive about the Saigon government. Most of Kissinger's energies, however, were devoted to understanding the American position. He sent a letter to Colonel John "Mike" Dunn, Lodge's former military attaché in Saigon, who had a rather bleak view of American personnel in South Vietnam. Dunn told Kissinger that the American military in Vietnam was "the most professional in their viewpoint" but the CIA was the best informed, though "not always objective." The embassy people, Dunn warned, were "seldom either professional in their attitudes or particularly well informed."[46] This last statement stuck with Kissinger. He was, after all, making his report to the ambassador and the embassy staff.

Kissinger also called on experts in Cambridge. On August 4, 1965, he joined fifteen others for an intense meeting at Harvard in Seminar Room 2 of the International Legal Studies Center. Kissinger chaired the session, asking a series of questions that would help inform him of the problems facing the United States in Vietnam. Although he had long advocated a more forceful American military response there, his questions, taken from the transcript of the meeting, focused almost entirely on negotiations to end the war. Kissinger asked:

(a) Should negotiations await some change in the military situation?
(b) Can military operations be geared to support the object of bringing about negotiations?
(c) What non-military measures can we take during military operations to support the objective of negotiations? (What do we do if the Saigon regime collapses?)[47]

After addressing several queries about process, Kissinger then asked his colleagues to address a number of pressing questions under the heading "The Substance and Purpose of Negotiations":

What are we trying to achieve? To show that wars of national liberation won't work? To curb Chinese expansion? To exploit Sino-Soviet conflict? Johnson and Rusk say we are trying to preserve free choice for the people of Vietnam. Are we fighting against a certain method of change (wars of national liberation) or the fact of change? Can we give content to the phrase "a free and independent South Vietnam"? Would South Vietnam alone be the subject of negotiation or should other problem areas be included?

What guarantees are needed? Who must participate in the guarantees?[48]

In hindsight, the questions and the answers were rather naive. Lucian Pye, MIT's leading China scholar, suggested that the first objective really was "to get North Vietnam to cease their aid of the insurgency."[49] He spoke as if this was something that the Johnson administration had inadvertently overlooked, and something that was easy to accomplish. Harvard political scientist Samuel Huntington, who would later play a pivotal role in Saigon, suggested that the Johnson administration should try to "separate the Viet Cong from Hanoi and negotiate with them on the creation of a government in Saigon with Communist participation but not domination."[50] But Hanoi had already made clear that the total reunification of Vietnam was its first priority. Some at the meeting supported creating protective enclaves, walling off South Vietnam with seven or eight US military divisions.[51] This suggestion carried no weight in the Johnson administration, and the president had been clear that there would be no enclave strategy. The last speaker of the day was MIT political scientist Norman Padelford, who concluded that Vietnam was the "wrong war at the wrong time in the wrong place."[52]

It now seems clear, however, that one important lesson Kissinger took away from the Harvard seminar was that the "frame of reference of American discussion of Vietnam has been too narrow."[53] John King Fairbank, Harvard's leading historian of China, offered this observation. After making several somewhat reductionist arguments about the place of China in Vietnamese history, Fairbank said that the United States needed to "enlarge our conception of what the US interest is." He concluded, "The main thing is to try to get China into the act, to give her the idea that she has a responsible role in the world, to get her into the United Nations, and to establish

17

contact with her at as many levels and in as many ways as possible."[54] Fairbank's suggestion intrigued Kissinger. He would draw on this formulation when he joined the Nixon administration, linking China's desires to improve relations with the United States with Nixon's desire to end US involvement in Vietnam.

Even though he was intrigued by Fairbank's reframing the Vietnam problem to include China, Kissinger's focus on this day was squarely on negotiations. He argued that the United States could not enter into negotiations "unless we know what our objectives are, at least within broad limits." He concluded that the administration must know what is "desirable from our point of view" and "what is bearable."[55] Kissinger, it seems, was embracing some of what John McNaughton had said during their April seminar. The Johnson administration had no idea how this war was going to end, Kissinger feared, because it had no idea what it wanted. What could Johnson live with in regard to the future of South Vietnam? What would be the price of that future? No one in Cambridge was asking those questions, and Kissinger suspected that few in Washington were, either.

Nonetheless, on the eve of his first trip to Vietnam in October 1965, he decided to arrange one last set of meetings with Washington officials. He met with William Bundy, Johnson's assistant secretary of state for East Asian and Pacific Affairs, who warned that optimistic reports from the CIA masked the reality.[56] He then visited CIA officials, including William Colby, who was the former Saigon station chief. Colby assured Kissinger that the South Vietnamese forces were more than capable of handling the People's Liberation Armed Forces (PLAF), and that new recruits had allowed the government to expand its pacification programs aimed at destroying the NLF's infrastructure in rural provinces.[57] A later meeting with CIA director Admiral William Raborn, who was also rather optimistic about America's chances in Vietnam, revealed that the top intelligence officer knew little about the particulars of the war and was often confused about Saigon officials. Kissinger concluded that Raborn, despite his optimism, "was amazingly badly informed" on Vietnam.[58]

Walt Rostow, an economist now working at the State Department, also offered a positive picture. He believed that the Saigon government was faring well against the guerrillas and that the limited pacification program had shown some positive early results. Rostow told Kissinger that the war could be won if the "main forces of the Viet Cong" were "smashed" and if the United States could make the "North Vietnamese...cease their direction and supply" of the PLAF.[59] A short visit with McNaughton exposed that Kissinger's Harvard seminar guest had not softened his position on withdrawal in the last six months and that he lacked Rostow's enthusiasm for the war. After showing Kissinger several internal Defense Department studies that indicated very little probability of success, McNaughton told him, "Let's face it...At some point on this road we will have to cut the balls off the people we are now supporting in Vietnam." He suggested that if Kissinger really wanted to help Lodge out with his study, he should "address [himself] to the question of how we can cut their balls off."[60]

Kissinger came away from these meetings more disillusioned about American tactics in Vietnam but not about its wartime aims. He still believed that the United States was fundamentally correct to challenge Communist expansion in South Vietnam, but he feared that the Johnson administration's tactics were flawed—that the slow squeeze it had committed itself to in Vietnam was not going to push Communist forces into the sea. Without the complete commitment to a military victory, Kissinger believed, the administration was going to have to find a political settlement to the war. But how could it find a political settlement if Johnson had not defined what was acceptable? Kissinger thought that the problems in Vietnam were strategic, not necessarily tactical. The goal, therefore, was simply to develop an overall strategic outlook for the war that cemented the United States' geopolitical objectives with its modes of operation.

Kissinger outlined this problem in a preliminary report to Lodge submitted on the eve of his trip, where he challenged some fundamental American assumptions about the war. He argued that Johnson had been wrong in applying gradual military pressure against the Communists. He told Lodge he believed the president had erred when he announced on April 7, 1965, in a speech at Johns Hopkins University, that he was "prepared to enter into unconditional discussions" with Hanoi.[61] Kissinger thought that using terms such as "unconditional negotiations," "cease-fire," and "tacit mutual concessions" was "demoralizing to our friends."[62] He also wondered where talk of negotiations with Hanoi would lead. "It is true that we cannot know all the elements of a negotiating position in advance," he wrote Lodge. "But we do know that we will have to adopt an attitude towards the NLF: we must know whether we will strive for an all-Vietnamese or simply South Vietnamese solution; we must have ideas on how to police an agreement. We must be precise on these issues, there is grave danger that negotiations will primarily concern the extent of our concessions. Our Vietnamese allies may lose confidence. The Communists, in short, could repeat the pattern of previous successful civil wars."[63] Lodge called Kissinger's report "a remarkable contribution from someone who has never been here."[64]

During his three-week trip to Vietnam in October 1965, Kissinger met with several senior US military leaders, including General William Westmoreland, commander of Military Assistance Command in Vietnam (MACV), who assured him that the war was going well. Westmoreland informed him that it would take nineteen months to pacify about half of the country and another eighteen months after that to control nearly 80 percent of South Vietnam. Everyone on Westmoreland's staff had the same rosy predictions. Kissinger told

Lodge, "If I listened to everybody's description of how we were succeeding, it is not easy for me to see how the Vietcong are still surviving."[65] Kissinger met other Americans who had similarly optimistic predictions. After one briefing at the Second Corps headquarters, Kissinger concluded that "the Army has degenerated. They have produced a group of experts at giving briefings whose major interest is to overpower you with floods of meaningless statistics and to either kid themselves or deliberately kid you."[66] He grew increasingly skeptical about US tactics in Vietnam during his visit, but still fundamentally believed in its war aim of challenging Communist expansion.

Kissinger left Saigon in early November 1965, and hidden away in his diary entry of November 2 is the birth of the Nixon administration's "peace with honor" formulation, based on his own analysis of the situation: "We have to come out honorably in Vietnam."[67] Later, as national security adviser and secretary of state, with the largest national security assessment capabilities in the world at his disposal, Kissinger still relied most heavily on his own calculations. He thought that his strategic compass pointed truer than most, so why not depend upon his own virtues? He also considered himself an action-intellectual. He was bored grading papers and giving lectures. Even before Harvard granted him tenure, Kissinger was a regular in Washington. One of his great frustrations was that Kennedy and Johnson had not relied more heavily upon his expertise.

Ending the War on Acceptable Terms

On the eve of Nixon's inauguration in 1969, Kissinger's views on Vietnam were further clarified in a now-famous *Foreign Affairs* article. Niall Ferguson has called this essay "one of the most brilliant analyses of the American predicament in Vietnam that anyone has ever written."[68] Hyperbole aside, Kissinger's insights are intriguing. He argued that the United States had a conceptual problem in Vietnam, which was its tendency "to apply traditional maxims of both strategy and nation-building to a situation which they did not fit." The Johnson administration, aided by General William Westmoreland, who was in charge of all allied military operations as commander of the MACV, had lost sight of one of the "cardinal maxims of guerrilla warfare: The guerrilla wins if he does not lose. The conventional army loses if it does not win."[69] Westmoreland had pursued a conventional strategy of attrition against the insurgents, Kissinger argued, following "the classic doctrine that victory depended on a combination of control of territory and attrition of the opponent." Westmoreland believed that defeating the NLF's main forces "would cause the guerrillas to wither on the vine."[70] He spoke of a future crossover point in the war when Hanoi would find its substantial losses in support of the southern revolution unacceptable and would quit the fight.[71] Westmoreland's tactics were more complicated than Kissinger's quick visit to Vietnam revealed, but this did not stop the Harvard professor from making quick judgments about what was needed to win in Southeast Asia.

Westmoreland's crossover point proved illusory. "Military successes," Kissinger wrote in the *Foreign Affairs* article, "could not be translated into permanent political advantage."[72] He doubted that the Johnson administration understood the fundamental conception of the war from Hanoi's point of view: "We fought a military war; our opponents fought a political one. We sought physical attrition; our opponents aimed for psychological exhaustion."[73] Kissinger thought that the Communists had achieved their objectives while diminishing the American will to continue aiding South Vietnam.

He also believed that the Johnson administration had severely mishandled the peace negotiations. Harking back to his 1965 trip, Kissinger again argued that Johnson did not understand that "our diplomacy and our strategy were conducted in isolation from each other."[74] As Kissinger had noted in his report for Lodge back in 1965, Johnson's major mistake, an unforced, self-inflicted wound, was to announce that he would go anywhere and meet with anyone to discuss peace in Vietnam. The president initially made this announcement during an April 1965 speech at Johns Hopkins University, but he repeated it often. Kissinger believed that this gave a distinct advantage to Hanoi, allowing its leaders to determine where and when to engage in diplomacy. How could the United States enter into unconditional negotiations with Hanoi "unless we know what our objectives are, at least within broad limits?" Most important, Kissinger believed— as he'd first argued back in the August 1965 Harvard seminar—that Washington must know what is "desirable from our point of view" and "what is bearable."[75] The Johnson administration had no idea how the war was going to end because it had no idea what it wanted. Kissinger concluded that Nixon did not have to repeat these same mistakes.

The way forward was to combine military pressure with careful diplomacy based on the national interest. Kissinger ruled out a unilateral withdrawal, noting:

> The commitment of 500,000 Americans has settled the issue of the importance of Vietnam. For what is involved now is confidence in American promises. However fashionable it is to ridicule the terms "credibility" or "prestige," they are not empty phrases; other nations gear their actions to ours only if they can count on our steadiness. The collapse of the American effort in Vietnam would not mollify many critics; most of them would simply add the charge of unreliability to the accusation of bad judgment. Those whose safety or national goals depend on American commitments could only be dismayed.... Unilateral withdrawal, or a settlement which unintentionally amounts to the same thing, could therefore

lead to the erosion of restraints, and to an even more dangerous international situation. No American policymaker can simply dismiss these dangers.[76]

Remaining steadfast in support of the Saigon government did not mean that the war would go on forever. Kissinger maintained that the Communists could not win the war militarily and that therefore they would be forced to negotiate a mutual withdrawal from South Vietnam. He had no evidence to support these claims, but they certainly found fertile ground among Johnson's critics. Kissinger argued that negotiations could be influenced by military strikes at key times and places that would make it more difficult for the Communists. If Washington and Hanoi could agree on a mutual troop withdrawal caused in part by the pain of these military strikes, it would then be up to the South Vietnamese themselves to figure out their own political future. Such an approach would also allow the United States to more closely coordinate its military operations with diplomacy. Kissinger felt strongly that separating military issues from political issues in negotiations could also help the United States avoid a direct confrontation with its South Vietnamese allies if differences of opinion cropped up during peace talks. This was his general framework for the negotiations he would soon lead secretly in Paris, where he met with high-ranking North Vietnamese officials for four years to hammer out an acceptable peace. These first principles never changed, but Kissinger would eventually surrender them one by one. In fact, his requirement that military and political be separated eventually granted Hanoi a free pass in South Vietnam after an American troop withdrawal.

Of course, Hanoi thought that Kissinger's proposals were naive and preposterous. Having fought the French for decades and having committed untold thousands to the southern revolution, Communist Party leaders were not about to separate military issues from political ones. For the Communists, the war had always been about the political future of Vietnam south of the seventeenth parallel. Reunification of the country under the socialist banner was the party's first principle and this would not be negotiated away, no matter how elegantly Kissinger claimed that it could be. As *Nhan Dan*, the party's daily newspaper, later declared, "The military and political aspects of the issue are inseparable because the underlying cause of the war is the American imposition of a stooge administration on the South Vietnamese people."[77] As one former foreign ministry official offered, "The military is the bell, but diplomacy is the sound of the bell."[78] Kissinger misread Hanoi's intentions and capabilities perfectly.

From his first days at the White House, however, Kissinger believed that it was possible to end the war on acceptable terms. This required a sophisticated strategy based on linkage and leverage. He had no doubt that he was the only one in the Nixon administration who could handle this difficult assignment. It is not entirely clear why Kissinger had such self-confidence in his ability to negotiate an end to this deadly conflict. He had no experience in serious negotiations before joining the White House. In fact, much of his approach in Vietnam was based on outdated theories about cold calculations of power. He did not understand how to negotiate peace because he ultimately thought he could force the enemy to bend its knee through military force alone.

His first order of business along this torturous path was to develop a strategy for the Vietnam War in the midst of serious military and political constraints. To that end, in December 1968, before he actually took up his office in the White House, Kissinger hired the RAND Corporation, a think tank with strong ties to the Defense Department, to prepare a study outlining contingency options in Vietnam. This was more than an academic exercise. Kissinger had been a consultant at RAND and respected its work. He had heard that RAND was now "dovish" on the war, but he also knew that it would explore all options, including those he would outline in his *Foreign Affairs* essay. Fred Kiel led the RAND team and Daniel Ellsberg, a former marine, was its top analyst. Kissinger had some history with Ellsberg. Shortly after the 1968 election, he told a RAND seminar audience that he had "learned more from Dan Ellsberg than anyone else in Vietnam."[79] Ellsberg did have considerable wartime experience, and he had just finished a detailed secret history of American involvement in Vietnam for the Pentagon. Two years later, he would leak this study to the *New York Times*, much to Nixon's dismay.

Ellsberg wrote the first draft of the RAND study and presented it to Kissinger and a few close associates on December 20, 1968. Kissinger wondered why there was no "win" option listed among the various potential policy choices. Ellsberg later recalled telling Kissinger, "I don't believe there is a win option in Vietnam."[80] Kissinger also noted that there was no mention of coercive power, no threat option. Ellsberg agreed to revise the paper to include these two options. Just before the inauguration, he sent a new draft to Kissinger that described a full spectrum of possibilities. At one extreme was "military escalation aimed at negotiated victory." Military options under this category could entail "air and ground operations in Cambodia," "unrestricted bombing of North Vietnam including Hanoi," and the mining of Haiphong harbor. Any combination of these options would be a purposeful escalation of the war. The paper argued that "the threat or onset of higher levels [of escalation] is likely to bring major concessions from DRV, perhaps sufficient for a satisfactory settlement." The overall goal of this option was to "destroy the will and capability of North Vietnam to support the insurgency."[81] This option clearly appealed to Kissinger.

At the other extreme was "unilateral withdrawal of all U.S. forces."[82] Kissinger quickly denounced the withdrawal option, claiming that it was not a viable choice. He did not want this idea presented to the president, so it was deleted from the final list of options discussed by the full NSC on January 25, 1969. The fallback extreme position was a "substantial reduction in U.S. presence while seeking a compromise settlement."[83] This option involved gaining approval from Saigon to slowly begin a phased reduction of US troops to about 100,000 by the end of 1971 while building up South Vietnamese military forces. There were other options in Ellsberg's paper, but none of them was taken seriously.

In addition to the four outcomes outlined in Ellsberg's paper, the January 25 NSC session heard a range of military strategies. The Joint Chiefs wanted to build up the South Vietnamese armed forces without withdrawing US forces, but Laird and Nixon chafed at that idea because it would add significant costs to an already expensive war with no promise of success. The Chiefs countered that at its current pace, it would take two to three years to modernize the South Vietnamese forces to the point that it could cope with the Communist military threat. The modernization scheme was not intended "to build an RVNAF [Republic of Vietnam Armed Forces] capable of dealing with an external (North Vietnam) threat."[84] Kissinger worried that any "escalation of force might suggest to the other side that our staying power has been compressed."[85]

When the long NSC meeting ended, Nixon had not made a concrete decision on any of these options. By default, then, the two extreme options were now unofficial Nixon administration policy. No one present at the NSC meeting could have predicted that the administration would pursue military escalation and troop withdrawals simultaneously. Ellsberg later agreed that it was difficult to imagine trying to bomb Hanoi into submission while at the same time supporting a policy of unilateral US troop withdrawals.[86] Just what was the United States supposed to negotiate at Paris? What leverage did it have? How could US negotiators demand a mutual withdrawal of US and North Vietnamese troops from South Vietnam if the United

States was going to withdraw its troops anyway because of domestic political pressure? How would Hanoi respond to an escalation of the war? Would it put more military pressure on the Saigon government? Was the Saigon government ready to take over the war militarily? Answers to these questions remained elusive. This strategic confusion, caused in part by Nixon's refusal to be pinned down on a specific policy option, was exacerbated by a confrontation between Kissinger and Defense Secretary Melvin Laird.

Kissinger and Laird disagreed on some fundamental aspects of Vietnam policy, especially the redeployment of US forces. Their tactical disagreements turned into a personal rivalry that played out during key meetings of the NSC. In early March 1969, Laird presented Nixon with a concrete plan to unilaterally withdraw US forces from Vietnam. Citing political pressures at home, Laird had requested specific plans to turn the war over to Saigon. He also pressed General Creighton Abrams, the US forces commander, to draw up firm plans (with hard numbers and dates) for the withdrawal. Some military reports suggested that increased funding for the RVNAF, first implemented in late 1968, had paid off, resulting in considerable progress.[87]

During an NSC meeting on March 28, 1969, General Andrew Goodpaster, who had served on Nixon's transition team, declared that "the caliber of the force [South Vietnamese armed forces] has improved. There can be no question about their improvement.... We are, in fact, closer to de-Americanizing the war."[88] Goodpaster had been a trusted military officer during the Eisenhower years and Nixon had come to respect his opinion while serving as vice president. Nixon often responded to complex military programs with a great deal of skepticism, but he liked Goodpaster and this helped Laird sell the program of an American withdrawal.

Nixon was encouraged by Goodpaster's comments. "We need a plan," the president declared. "We must get a sense of urgency in the training of the South Vietnamese. We need improvement in terms of supplies and training."[89] Just as Kissinger was about to intervene, Laird interrupted and told the president, "I agree, but not with your term 'de-Americanizing.' What we need is a term 'Vietnamizing' to put emphasis on the right issue."[90] Nixon agreed with the semantic and policy change, cutting Kissinger out of one of the most important strategic decisions of the war.

"Vietnamization," as Laird's plan was unfortunately called, had been tossed about by the Johnson administration for years. Johnson had once famously said, "We are not about to send American boys 9 or 10,000 miles away from home to do what Asian boys ought to be doing for themselves."[91] Laird now thought that the Saigon government and its forces were capable of taking over more responsibility for the war, because the latest reports showed considerable progress on the military front.[92] He wanted to reduce the combat role of US troops and begin the phased US withdrawal, while at the same time pressing ahead with new military supplies for South Vietnam. Even Abrams, who had been generally cool on Saigon's progress, reported in March 1969 that the South Vietnamese performance had improved substantially. But Abrams thought "Vietnamization" should move forward only if three indicators were favorable: (1) progress in the pacification program designed to eliminate the top Communist cadres, (2) continued improvement in the South Vietnamese army, and (3) a reduction in the direct threat to the Saigon government from North Vietnam.

Laird was well aware of Kissinger's objections and Abrams's conditions, but he pressed forward anyway with a plan to withdraw fifty to seventy thousand American troops in 1969 alone and the drafting of a long-range plan for the total withdrawal of US forces. Laird was no dove, but he had concluded long ago that a total military victory in Vietnam was unlikely at acceptable cost and risk and that a continued force presence there was doing more harm than good. He was especially critical of Westmoreland and Abrams for their handling of the South Vietnamese army. He thought the military responsibility was being transferred painfully slowly under Abrams and that this had created dependency in Saigon. President Thieu, of course, hated to see the US troops leave, but if a withdrawal had to happen, Thieu hoped it was joined by increased American aid for South Vietnam. Abrams and Thieu also thought that the US withdrawal would be accompanied by a withdrawal of all North Vietnamese troops from South Vietnam. Laird suffered no delusions that Kissinger was likely to win this point through negotiations, nor that the military could expel Communist forces from South Vietnam. He also understood that the American people would remain skeptical about claims of Saigon's substantial military progress. The only way forward seemed to be troop withdrawals and a substantial buildup of the South Vietnamese military, significantly above 1968 levels.

Laird's plan appealed to Nixon. He could satisfy the doves by withdrawing US forces, and at the same time, the hawks would be pleased that the US was actually increasing its aid to the South Vietnamese government. He also credited Laird's "enthusiastic advocacy" of Vietnamization as the basis for his decision, further alienating his national security adviser.[93] Kissinger was apoplectic. He argued that Vietnamization would ultimately weaken the US bargaining position in Paris, because a US withdrawal would convince Hanoi that the United States no longer cared about the political outcome in South Vietnam. How could Laird take away one of the most important levers that the United States had in Paris—the presence of a large number of American troops? As Kissinger put it in his memoirs, he had had "great hope for negotiations," but the administration now risked "throwing away our position in a series of unreciprocated concessions. At home, the more we sought to placate the critics, the more we discouraged those who were willing to support a strategy for victory, but who could not understand continued sacrifice for something so elusive as honorable withdrawal."[94] Throughout the negotiation process, Kissinger complained that domestic political considerations were putting too many constraints on the US negotiating team in Paris. It was impossible to implement his broad strategic plans in the face of such obstacles.

A frustrated Kissinger warned the president that Laird's plan had many pitfalls. "Our main asset," he wrote to Nixon in late March 1969, "is the presence of our troops in South Vietnam. Hanoi has no hope of attaining its objective of controlling the South unless it can get us to withdraw our forces." He assured the president that the DRV could not force the United States to withdraw its forces "by military means." The implication was clear: why would Nixon agree to Laird's plan when he did not have to? There was no military pressure for the United States to withdraw. He also believed that the South Vietnamese forces would not be ready to take over the war for a number of years. Kissinger appealed to Nixon's need to appear strong in light of domestic political pressure, stating, "Our liabilities are the domestic opposition in the United States and the continuing weak base of the Saigon government."[95] Nixon remained unconvinced by Kissinger's appeals.

A week later, Kissinger tried a different approach. He suggested that Hanoi had used its forces "the way a bullfighter uses his cape: to keep us lunging in strategically unproductive areas and to prevent us from grinding down the guerrilla forces." The major problem now facing the United States if Nixon accepted Laird's Vietnamization plan was that "de-escalation would amount to self-imposed defusing of our most important asset....All this suggests that we should not agree to de-escalate now." Kissinger begged the president to hold firm, to not give in to the political temptation of withdrawing forces. He doubted that troop withdrawals would have much political meaning if they were not accompanied by a major escalation in military strikes. The planning of the two had to be carefully coordinated, and Kissinger assured Nixon that he was very close to having "the overall game plan" in place.[96] The president worried, however, that public opposition to the war was growing and that if he did not show progress in ending the war by the 1970 midterm political elections, protests would increase and Congress would cut funding for the war, exactly at the time when new resources were needed to support the Saigon government and its forces. "If we had no elections, it would be fine," Nixon told Kissinger and the rest of the NSC.[97] But time was now another enemy in the Vietnam War. Domestic politics mattered to Nixon. Elections mattered to Kissinger, too, far more than he has been willing to admit, but Nixon did not think he understood electoral pressures.

Nixon announced his administration's Vietnamization plan on April 1, 1969. Rather than implementing a unilateral withdrawal, he tied the redeployment of American forces to the other side's actions. The plan called for the complete withdrawal of US troops six months after Hanoi completed its own withdrawal from South Vietnam. Nixon erroneously believed that he could simply outlast Hanoi if he piled on the military pressure. "The key point," he claimed, was not "the timetable but rather getting Hanoi to comply with the conditions for withdrawal."[98] The following week, Nixon had Laird draw up the formal withdrawal plans (National Security Study Memorandum 36), complete with timetables for transferring the US combat role to South Vietnam. Ironically, NSSM 36 (and another report, NSSM 37) assumed that the war would drag on for years in South Vietnam, that Saigon would face increased military pressure from the Communists, and that there would be no mutual troop withdrawal. This report eventually proved reliable as the final peace agreement signed between North Vietnam and the United States allowed ten North Vietnamese infantry divisions to remain in South Vietnam following the complete US troop withdrawal.

The mutual troop withdrawal would be the subject of many hours of negotiating in Paris. Kissinger would continue to press for a mutual withdrawal, but he did so as thousands of US troops were leaving Vietnam. Nixon would periodically reassert his steadfast determination to see a mutual withdrawal. Kissinger complained to anyone who would listen that Nixon and Laird had tied his hands in negotiations.

During the battle over troop withdrawals, Kissinger turned his interest to military strikes. He believed that the United States had to increase its military pressure on Hanoi if it was unilaterally going to withdraw its own forces from South Vietnam. He envisioned a major escalation in the bombing and an expansion of the war's parameters to send Hanoi the message that troop withdrawals did not mean that the United States was in full retreat. Attacks against North Vietnamese assets would also buy Saigon time, now that American troops were being withdrawn. Kissinger also wanted to ensure that Laird would never be able to outmaneuver him at another NSC meeting. Accordingly, he devised a questionnaire, now known as National Security Study Memorandum 1 (NSSM 1), on the war's progress for all departments and agencies, which would keep them busy compiling massive studies while he tried to regain the president's confidence. Kissinger recalled Ellsberg to the White House to collate the answers to the questions. The study took months and was totally inconclusive, just what Kissinger wanted. "I'm tying up the bureaucracy for a year," he explained to an aide shortly after Nixon's inauguration, "and buying the new president some time."[99]

Part of Kissinger's strategy was to use that time to convince Nixon that Laird's troop withdrawals were not going to help end the war on favorable terms. Kissinger appealed to Nixon's interest in increased military strikes against the Communists when he asked Laird and the chairman of the Joint Chiefs, General Earle Wheeler, what tactics could be used to signal to Hanoi that there was "a new firm hand at the helm."[100] The key issue for Kissinger was how to apply enough military pressure to coerce the Communists to make some concessions in Paris. Wheeler thought that carrying out air attacks against the DRV could signal that the Nixon administration was more formidable than its predecessor. Lyndon Johnson had refused to bomb near Hanoi, and he never launched offensive military operations against North Vietnamese sanctuaries inside Laos or Cambodia, operations that Kissinger would soon insist would be essential in the US effort to buy Saigon time to stand on its own feet militarily. He also thought military operations in Laos and Cambodia against Communist havens would send the right message to Saigon. Laird, however, warned Kissinger that new attacks against North Vietnam, or in Laos and Cambodia, would create political nightmares for the administration.[101]

Laird's warning was prophetic. He was always more conscious of the political repercussions of policy, but Kissinger pressed on, telling Laird and Wheeler that their suggestions were not bold enough. Kissinger wanted Wheeler to "find ways to ratchet up the military pressure that did not risk breaking the negotiations."[102] He disagreed with Laird when the defense secretary claimed that MACV was doing everything possible to keep the military pressure on Hanoi and the PLAF. Laird understood, however, that stepping up military operations went against public demands that the war be brought to a close. If Kissinger was going to force options on the rest of the administration that included military escalation, he was going to have to do so without Laird's full support and out of the public view.

This impasse led to one of the most fateful choices of the war, the decision to bomb Cambodia. The decision did not come lightly, but it was fully embraced by Kissinger. Years later, Kissinger claimed that the decision to attack North Vietnamese sanctuaries along Cambodia's border with South Vietnam was in direct response to a Communist military offensive that began on February 22, 1969.

He maintained that Hanoi had violated the 1968 bombing halt understanding by launching new attacks over the Demilitarized Zone (DMZ). Nixon called the attacks "small-scale but savage" and thought the offensive was a "deliberate test, clearly designed to take measure of me and my administration at the outset."[103] In typical Nixon fashion, the president said, "My immediate instinct was to retaliate."[104] Kissinger agreed: "If we let the Communists manipulate us at this early stage, we might never be able to negotiate with them from a position of equality, much less one of strength."[105]

But even before the Communist offensive, Nixon and Kissinger had been studying how to destroy North Vietnamese sanctuaries in Cambodia. During the 1968 presidential race, both had challenged Johnson's decision not to strike Cambodia. In early January 1969, before his inauguration, Nixon asked for reports on North Vietnamese strength in Cambodia and on what Abrams was doing "to destroy the build up there."[106] The president concluded, "I think a very definite change of policy toward Cambodia probably should be one of the first orders of business when we get in."[107]

Years later, Kissinger claimed that he had asked Nixon to delay the bombing of the Cambodia base area because he wanted to "give negotiations a chance."[108] He also claimed that he had encouraged Nixon to normalize diplomatic relations with Cambodia prior to the air raids in the hopes that the Cambodian government could then pressure the PAVN to withdraw.[109]

But Kissinger's claims are disingenuous. In a phone conversation with Nixon on March 8, a week before the president approved the mission, Kissinger told him he had to act *before* private peace talks began in Paris or he would "be accused of insincerity."[110] Kissinger also made it clear to Nixon that he favored the bombings to influence the negotiations. "We have combined heavy military pressure with a deliberate pace in Paris," Kissinger wrote to him in a memo.

"We have specifically refrained from taking the initiative on opening private talks."[111] Feeling some time pressure, therefore, Nixon asked Kissinger to consult with Abrams on the bombing missions.

The general had been studying this problem for months. He replied that enemy strength in Cambodia included "11 known base areas, 3 divisions, and perhaps 5 to 7 regiments" along the border with South Vietnam.[112] Abrams insisted that he now had credible evidence of where these PAVN forces were and, more important to Nixon, where the secret Communist headquarters for the southern revolution (Central Office South Vietnam, or COSVN) was located. The intelligence on the targets "appeared to be very accurate and sound" and there "was every reason to believe there would be no Cambodians in the target area."[113]

The BREAKFAST Bombings

On February 18, over breakfast in the secretary of defense's conference room at the Pentagon, Kissinger, Wheeler, and Laird met with two of Abrams's staff (no representative from the State Department was present), who briefed them on the Communist buildup in Base Area 353 inside Cambodia. One of the aides took notes, referring to the meeting as "the breakfast group."[114] From that moment on, the mission to attack PAVN sanctuaries in Cambodia was given the unfortunate code name BREAKFAST.

Following the breakfast meeting, Kissinger ordered Colonel Ray Sitton, known in the Pentagon as "Mr. B-52," to develop a list of bombing options that would form the backbone of the BREAKFAST attacks. As he was completing his assignment, Sitton got a call from another colonel, Alexander Haig, who told him that they had to fly to Brussels to brief Nixon on the Cambodian target list. Nixon was on his first trip abroad as president, shoring up the European alliance that had been badly shaken during the Johnson presidency. Before the briefing, Sitton asked Wheeler whether he was "selling something" or simply providing the president with information.[115] Wheeler responded that he trusted Sitton to know what mood the president was in and to act accordingly. Kissinger suggested that the briefing take place on the short flight from Brussels to London, but Nixon was so busy practicing his remarks that he did not meet with Sitton. Instead, Kissinger took the briefing.

Sitton assumed that he had traveled all that way in vain until he got a cable from Kissinger approving the target list. Kissinger demanded that Sitton keep the mission a secret, however, even from the pilots. With Kissinger's help, Sitton devised a plan to use phony logbooks to cover up the illegal attacks. "There are valid targets right along the border [inside South Vietnam] adjacent to that," Sitton explained. "We will merely show in the record that we flew a mission to this area."[116] The intrigue continued with each new set of targets. Sitton described going to the White House basement entrance, where Kissinger would meet him: "Dr. Kissinger would look at it [the sortie target], approve it or amend it, whatever he felt like doing."[117] Later it was revealed that the air force chief of staff knew nothing of the Cambodian bombing missions. It was Kissinger, and Kissinger alone, who accepted and approved the bombing targets. Even Sitton later questioned this practice: "I don't know what he was using or his reason for varying them." Wheeler told Sitton that the reason for selecting certain targets did not matter, "because it seemed to be working."[118]

On March 15, Nixon used the pretext of Communist rocket attacks against Hue and Saigon to order the immediate implementation of the BREAKFAST plan. Nixon told Kissinger that the order was "not appealable" and that he should keep Henry Cabot Lodge Jr., now head of the Paris delegation, and Ellsworth Bunker, ambassador to South Vietnam, in the dark about the attacks.[119] No one in Saigon was to make any public statement about the Communists' attacks until after the US planes hit their targets, and then only after Nixon himself gave approval. "I mean it," the president declared, "not one thing is to be said to anyone publicly or privately, on or off the record, about this new attack on Saigon."[120] He also ordered that the State Department not be notified about the attacks inside Cambodia until "only after the point of no return."[121] Rogers was not to be trusted with information about the bombing, Kissinger told Laird in a phone call later that day, because some senior State Department officials had previously gone public in opposition to raids in neutral Cambodia.[122]

After Nixon's order, Kissinger forwarded an approved target list to Sitton, who sent the coordinates on to Saigon. From there a courier passed them along to the appropriate radar stations and control sites. After the normal mission briefing, pilots and crews received secret instructions from a ground radar station in South Vietnam just after takeoff. According to journalist Seymour Hersh, who gained access to Sitton's secret target lists through the Freedom of Information Act in the 1980s, "The radar sites, using sophisticated computers, would in effect take over the flying of the B-52s for the final moments, guiding them to their real targets over Cambodia and computing the precise moment to drop the bombs."[123] When the mission was complete, the officer in charge burned all evidence of the real target. Then, he wrote up a fake report showing that the sortie scheduled to hit a target in South Vietnam was actually flown. He included a full accounting of everything used in the mission to complete the deception. This process was repeated with every new target list.

The first BREAKFAST strike at two p.m. on March 17, 1969, Washington time, launched a secret fourteen-month nighttime bombing campaign, known as Operation Menu, which hit the same six PAVN base areas in Cambodia until the end of May 1970. During Menu, American B-52s dropped 108,823 tons of ordnance and flew 3,875 sorties. Laird later confirmed that between March 1969 and March 1970, the Menu bombing amounted to "nearly one-fifth the tonnage dropped by U.S. forces in the Pacific theater during all of World War II."[124]

Despite this destruction, by March 1970, the primary strategic objective had not been met. The bombing campaigns actually drove the North Vietnamese troops deeper into Cambodia, not into South Vietnam, as planned. Although thousands of North Vietnamese troops were killed during the entire Cambodian intervention, Hanoi replaced these troops without melting its strategic reserve. Nixon's obsession with finding the secret Communist headquarters, reported to be just inside the Cambodian border, near what US officials called the parrot's beak because of its geographical features, also ended in disappointment. The mobile offices for the southern revolution (COSVN) were not bound to architecture and highways as were governmental offices in the United States, so escape was relatively easy. Finally, some scholars have claimed that the US bombing raids drove rural Cambodians into the arms of the Khmer Rouge, whose genocidal program was not yet in view, destabilizing the Cambodian government, which had eventually allied itself with the United States.[125]

It took five years for the American public to find out the true scale of the secret bombing of Cambodia. Recounting these events, historian Greg Grandin concludes, "That's *how* an illegal, covert war came to be waged on a neutral country, a war run out of a basement by a presidential appointee who a few months earlier was a Harvard professor."[126]

But this does not explain fully *why* Kissinger pursued this illegal tactic so recklessly. For Kissinger, every action usually had a dual purpose. The secret bombing of Cambodia was no exception. Kissinger firmly believed that striking PAVN sanctuaries inside Cambodia would hurt Hanoi's ability to wage war in South Vietnam and that this in turn would have an impact on negotiations in Paris. From a material perspective, there is no doubt that he was right. He has always linked Hanoi's decision to escalate the conflict with his willingness to support the bombing campaign in Cambodia. In his justification for his wartime policies, *Ending the Vietnam War*, Kissinger claims that the decision to bomb Cambodia came only after the PAVN offensive in early 1969 that killed nearly two thousand Americans. Of the attacks, he writes that Hanoi understood that they had "humiliated the new President."[127]

But Kissinger also believed that he could isolate Laird and Rogers by so resolutely supporting the secret bombing in Cambodia, because he knew the president supported it, too. Laird was not necessarily against bombing Cambodia, but he thought it should be made public. He later explained, "I told Nixon you couldn't keep the bombing in Cambodia secret.... It was going to come out anyway and it would build distrust.... I was all for hitting those targets in Cambodia, but I wanted it public, because I could justify before Congress and the American people that these were occupied territories of the North Vietnamese, no longer Cambodian territory."[128] Rogers also warned against keeping the bombing secret, and both told the president that they disagreed with his political reasons for not going public. Kissinger knew better than to challenge the president. He supported the secret bombing of Cambodia because it served his purposes in Saigon, Paris, and in Washington, as well as his strategic imperatives.

Three days after the bombing began, on March 20, 1969, Kissinger called Nixon with good news: "Hanoi has accepted bilateral private talks." He concluded that "we now know how badly they need them."[129] The implication, of course, was that there was some correlation between the Cambodian bombing campaign and the DRV's willingness to resume peace talks in Paris. Nixon and Kissinger thought that added military pressure on Hanoi could end the war on favorable terms within the year, and they were delighted to learn that Hanoi wanted to meet again. They were both eager to move on to what they considered more important foreign policy issues, such as thawing relations with the Soviet Union and "opening" China. Kissinger fed that part of Nixon that believed that "a little fourth-rate country" like Vietnam "had to have a breaking point."[130] He also encouraged the president to think that acts of toughness—such as bombing Cambodia—could substitute for tactical and strategic disadvantage in Vietnam.

Nothing could have been further from the truth. Although Nixon did not make the official announcement of his plans to withdraw American troops from Vietnam until April 1, 1969, Hanoi understood much earlier that this was the policy that he would be forced to support. DRV negotiators hoped to use the Paris talks to speed up the withdrawal process.[131] They understood that Nixon would need to wind down the war through troop withdrawals if he wanted to win reelection. Therefore, it was not the bombing of Cambodia but, rather, the withdrawal of American troops that rekindled Hanoi's desire to meet with Nixon's representatives in Paris. Party leaders concluded that if the DRV endured the American bombing campaigns, they could destroy Washington's staying power. Ultimately, DRV leaders would concede nothing short of a unilateral American withdrawal. This negotiating position should have been clear to Kissinger in 1969. He later admitted that he had underestimated Hanoi's willingness to accept enormous sacrifices to reach its geopolitical goals.

For all his machinations to coordinate military strikes with diplomacy, Kissinger never fully understood that Nixon's domestic

political needs were also a major driving force behind US negotiations. Nixon had to agree to Laird's Vietnamization plan because
there was no path to reelection without following through on his
campaign promise to end the war. He thought that bringing troops
home could actually bolster public support for continuing the war
by sending massive arms shipments to South Vietnam and using US
air power to cripple Hanoi's military capabilities. The escalation of
the war in neighboring Cambodia also had a strategic imperative: to
gain time for South Vietnam to build its armed forces in preparation
for battle against North Vietnam.

Kissinger felt no moral qualms about escalating the war. The fact
that the bombing did not destroy COSVN, force the PAVN from
Cambodia, or lead Hanoi to the bargaining table seemed not to faze
him. Despite all evidence to the contrary, he and the president believed that the bombing had worked. Nixon was so pleased with the
news that the North Vietnamese wanted to negotiate in Paris that he
allowed Kissinger to take over the peace talks completely. This was
a mistake for the usually politically astute Nixon. It gave his national
security adviser what he wanted most, consolidation of the war decision making in his office, but it led to some imprudent choices. By
the end of Nixon's first six months in office, Kissinger had perfectly
melded strategic imperatives with personal politics. He had taken a
risk by supporting the secret bombings, but in his mind the attacks
had succeeded. Now Hanoi had agreed to meet secretly in Paris and
Kissinger was in complete control of those negotiations.

CHAPTER TWO

THE LONE COWBOY, 1969

"THE MAIN POINT STEMS from the fact that I've always acted alone," Kissinger told Italian journalist and war correspondent Oriana Fallaci, in a revealing 1972 interview. "Americans admire that enormously. Americans admire the cowboy leading the caravan alone astride his horse, the cowboy entering a village or city alone on his horse. Without even a pistol, maybe, because he doesn't go in for shooting. He acts, that's all: aiming at the right spot at the right time."[1] Smelling a huge story, Fallaci pushed Kissinger: "You see yourself as a kind of Henry Fonda, unarmed and ready to fight with his bare fists for honest ideals. Solitary, brave." He replied, "Not necessarily brave. This cowboy doesn't need courage. It is enough that he be alone, that he show others how he enters the village alone and does everything on his own." Kissinger concluded this interview, which he later described as one of his biggest public mistakes, by stating, "I want to be where the action is."[2]

In much of his academic writing, Kissinger argues that men of action, like Austrian diplomat Klemens von Metternich, are not bound by convention or even hard facts. He had long admired Metternich, whose cool calculations had tied Europe together and raised Austria's fortunes following Napoleon's defeat in the early nineteenth century. Metternich was a man of action, not prone to sentimentality or morality in foreign affairs. Like Metternich, men of action were driven to ignore the restraints of reality and the advice of experts so as to lead effectively. Kissinger took a dark view of humanity, and this led him to see international politics as characterized by an unending collision of interests: you settled one problem only to have another surface. He was particularly drawn to the role of history, contingency, and uncertainty in diplomacy. But he also believed that leaders needed to act to control these forces; too much information can weaken resolve, as he claimed had been the case with Kennedy and Johnson in Vietnam. Kissinger was a careful reader of Spinoza and Kant, and he learned from both that history is tragedy, but that men of free will can bend history toward a new reality. He also believed that each generation had the freedom to decide for itself what, if anything, from the past "is analogous" to the present.[3] History teaches by analogy, not by a strict reconstruction of cause and effect, he concluded. Writing in 1963, while still a Harvard professor, Kissinger suggests that "there are two kinds of realists: those who manipulate facts and those who create them. The West requires nothing so much as men able to create their own reality."[4] This belief allowed him to insist that the best one could hope for was to establish a world of order and rules.

Among the most important of these rules was that the world needed policing and American power. While other intellectuals, such as Arthur Schlesinger Jr., George F. Kennan, and Reinhold Niebuhr, eventually questioned the imperial presidency created by the postwar expansion of American power, Kissinger never once doubted America's exceptional role in the world. Yet he criticized the crusading impulse in US history, claiming that this compulsion had led John F.

Kennedy unnecessarily to Vietnam. However, Kissinger also despised overzealous crusading's crude twin—isolationism—that surfaced in the United States from time to time. He believed that powerful states had an obligation to create a world order based on stability and promotion of the national interest above such abstract ideals as democracy and human rights. He was not the idealist that his official biographer, Niall Ferguson, claims him to be. He was instead a classical realist who ironically acted with great emotion and personalized much of his effort to secure America's place in the international system. As a lone actor, an instrument of free will, he was determined to shape history.

Kissinger naturally thought, therefore, that Moscow could easily influence events in Hanoi because he believed that the powerful do what they want and the weak suffer, as they must. He did not understand that for Moscow, forcing Hanoi to concede its first principles carried with it unacceptable costs and risks. Nonetheless, he sought to link Moscow's desire for progress on strategic arms reductions with Washington's desire for an honorable peace in Vietnam. This linkage was one of Kissinger's most ambitious plans to end the war on honorable terms. He would continue to use the coercive power contained in the US threat to escalate the war against Hanoi, but he would also enlist Soviet help to influence the Democratic Republic of Vietnam (DRV) to accept some compromises in Paris. Nixon approved this approach and made it the cornerstone of a doctrine that would bear his name. This complex strategy was pure Kissinger, however. The Soviet ambassador to the United States, Anatoly Dobrynin, was his unwilling partner in the plan. Neither would be happy with the result.

"In all my conversations with Dobrynin...," Kissinger wrote in his memoirs, "I had stressed that a fundamental improvement in U.S.-Soviet relations presupposed Soviet cooperation in settling the war."[5] Even though Secretary of State William Rogers wanted to move quickly on a strategic arms limitation treaty with the Soviets,

Kissinger insisted that Moscow "should be brought to understand that they cannot expect to reap the benefits of cooperation in one area while seeking to take advantage of tensions or confrontation elsewhere."[6] Kissinger rather naively believed that the war had to be settled sooner rather than later and that the road to peace went through Moscow. He and Nixon held out hope that serious negotiations would be under way by November 1, the anniversary of the cessation of the bombing of the DRV. The time was right to involve the Soviets because, according to Kissinger, the bombing of Cambodia had created a panic in Hanoi, which had led to the DRV's decision to renew talks in Paris. He thought that the Johnson administration had made a mistake by not putting enough pressure on the Soviets to influence events in Vietnam, believing instead that the Soviets needed to take a stronger interest in a settlement and that the only way to convey this message to Moscow was to threaten further escalation of the war. Nixon agreed: "We have to say [to the Soviets], 'Look, if you go on supporting North Vietnam, we will have to act dramatically...' On the other hand, we have to say, 'If you are willing to give ground and help us out of this morass, it could mean lots of good things.'"[7]

Kissinger was keen on linking Soviet cooperation on the Vietnam War with trade talks, arms limitations treaties, and progress in the Middle East—all issues of great importance to Moscow—because he wrongly believed that he alone understood the "connections and motivations that linked far-flung events."[8] Like his hero, Metternich, he envisioned a world that depended on a complex network based on a balance of power. He thought that he could construct such a world from the Nixon White House if the president gave him the power to do so. Kissinger created a small foreign policy empire inside the National Security Council by cutting Defense and State out of most important foreign policy issues. Even in his own office, he concentrated power. His subordinates were denied direct access to the press, to diplomats, and, most important, to the president. Once his realm was established, Kissinger used his keen intellect to create a grand strategy that relied upon linkage, back channels—contact with foreign officials outside of official government protocol, usually conducted in great secrecy—and coercive diplomacy. These efforts fit his personality well and supported his desire to conduct foreign policy outside of the usual channels.

In Nixon, Kissinger found a willing partner, one who favored back-channel communication and bold action over the slow-moving national security bureaucracy. Nixon saw the value in linking Soviet cooperation on Vietnam to larger foreign policy issues. The two men did not like each other personally, but both understood and appreciated that linkage was based on a realistic view of the world. Both were also attracted to the necessary secrecy and slightly conspiratorial nature of the strategy. Over time, however, Kissinger complained that Nixon was less trusting than he needed to be to have sustained success linking Soviet behavior to superpower negotiations on vital national security issues. The president progressively closed the door to outsiders, including Kissinger, making grand strategic moves almost impossible. Kissinger described how this process worked: "Nixon increasingly moved sensitive negotiations into the White House where he could supervise them directly, get the credit personally, and avoid bureaucratic disputes or inertia that he found so distasteful,"[9] explaining that "these extraordinary procedures were essentially made necessary by a President who neither trusted his cabinet nor was willing to give them direct orders."[10] But it was not the president but Kissinger who first pushed State and Defense away from decision making on Vietnam.

No one suffered more from Kissinger's desire to formulate policy alone than Secretary of State Rogers. From their first days in the new administration, Kissinger did all that he could to isolate Rogers from the president. He often used Nixon's desire for back-channel communication as a reason to cut Rogers out of the loop, but Kissinger also challenged Rogers's competence and understanding of complex foreign policy ideas, such as linkage. He also complained to Nixon that Rogers was out to get him. White House chief of staff H. R. Haldeman wrote in his diary that Kissinger was "obsessed with discussing" every detail of Rogers's effort to undermine his foreign policy initiatives.[11] When it came to dealing with the Soviets on Vietnam, Kissinger was especially harsh in his criticisms of Rogers.

On March 8, 1969, Rogers met with Dobrynin to discuss the Soviet role in the Paris negotiations, as instructed by Nixon. According to Kissinger, the meeting ended in disaster because Rogers "unilaterally abrogated the two-track approach of separating military and political issues."[12] Rogers, Kissinger claimed, had proposed renewed talks in Paris to discuss both political and military matters, representing a "major change in U.S. policy with serious consequences both for our posture at the Paris peace negotiations and our relations with South Vietnam."[13] Kissinger argued at the time that since taking office in January, the Nixon administration had "undertaken a basic shift in our policy."[14] The White House now believed that "the political future of South Vietnam must be settled by the South Vietnamese themselves" and therefore that political matters should not be negotiated with Hanoi or the National Liberation Front (NLF) in Paris.[15] Kissinger was especially enraged that Rogers did not see that discussing political matters was exactly what the Communists wanted, and that such discussions "could only lead to acrimony with the South."[16] The White House, Kissinger told the president, "will be under great pressure to force [Saigon] not to prevent successful negotiations."[17] Finally, Kissinger warned Nixon that Hanoi's "strategy was to get us: (1) to engage in talks about political subjects, (2) to talk with the NLF, and (3) into talks on de-escalation." According to

Kissinger, Rogers "gave Hanoi the first 2 of its 3 objectives, did not rebut the third and did so without getting anything in return."[18]

Nixon took Kissinger's criticism of Rogers seriously. The president routinely complained about Rogers and the "little State boys" who always "start squealing" when tough decisions had to be made.[19] Toughness was one quality that Nixon and Kissinger admired, and both agreed that Rogers was not tough. Kissinger reminded the president that Rogers had waffled during discussions over bombing Cambodia, and he questioned the secretary's loyalty.[20] By constantly bombarding the president with examples of Rogers's incompetence, disloyalty, and lack of toughness, the national security adviser helped marginalize the State Department. He also satisfied whatever emotional or strategic need he had to control the foreign policy process, especially the back channel to Moscow.

Kissinger had moved quickly to create the back channel to Moscow. Only weeks into the new administration, he had arranged a meeting between Nixon and Dobrynin, purposely excluding Rogers. The job of informing Rogers that he would not be attending the first meeting between the new president of the United States and the Soviet ambassador—while Kissinger would, a major breach of diplomatic protocol—fell to Haldeman, who blamed it all on Kissinger. Nixon cemented the back channel, however, by telling Dobrynin that he should discuss any sensitive issues privately with Kissinger rather than with the State Department. Kissinger applauded the president's approval of the back channel with Moscow because he believed that "our best course would be a bold move of trying to settle everything [with Hanoi] at once. Such a move should...attempt to involve the Soviet Union."[21]

Kissinger met regularly with Dobrynin, usually at least once each week. During one of their first encounters, he presented Dobrynin with a three-point statement on peace in Vietnam initialed by the president. In point one, Nixon confirmed "his conviction that a just peace is achievable." In point two, the president reaffirmed his willingness to "explore other avenues other than the existing negotiating framework," including direct meetings between US and DRV officials to "discuss general principles of a settlement," with the technical details to be handled in Paris. Finally, Nixon claimed that "all parties are at a crossroads and that extraordinary measures are called for."[22] Kissinger warned Dobrynin that the president favored a quick settlement to the war and that "we might take measures that would complicate the situation" if Hanoi did not agree to compromise on its insistence that the South Vietnamese government had to be dissolved prior to any agreement or that it had the right to keep its troops in South Vietnam after the November 1 deadline.[23] Dobrynin was evasive in his reply, explaining to Kissinger that "Soviet influence in Hanoi was extremely limited."[24] He did ask Kissinger, however, to clarify what measures the United States might take if Hanoi refused to cooperate. Kissinger never responded.

Nixon was pleased with the initial meetings between the two, so he empowered Kissinger to make a formal proposal to the Soviets, the first of its kind since the Vietnam War had started. Without informing Defense Secretary Melvin Laird or Rogers, the president had Kissinger tell Dobrynin that he was prepared to send a high-level US delegation to Moscow, headed by Cyrus Vance, who had been part of the US negotiating team in Paris. Vance would be empowered "to agree immediately on principles for a negotiation on strategic arms limitations."[25] In exchange, Nixon expected the Soviets to tell Vance how they would help in Vietnam. Vance would also be given the authority to meet with North Vietnamese officials to discuss both political and military matters outside of the formal Paris talks. This was the first time that Nixon placed value on a parallel negotiation track in Paris outside the avenue Kléber negotiations. It would not be the last. There was nothing new in the proposal for Moscow on military matters. The United States still insisted on a cease-fire and a mutual troop withdrawal from South Vietnam, even though the Laird plan for American troop withdrawals was already in progress. But on the political side, there was a significant change, at least in Kissinger's mind. The United States would accept the political participation of the NLF in a coalition government in South Vietnam if it renounced violence and if it would accept an agreement on an independent South Vietnam that would last five years, after which "there would be negotiations for unification" with North Vietnam.[26] Kissinger underscored that this was a rare opportunity for North Vietnam, and the White House expected Hanoi to respond within two months. He clearly understood, however, that Hanoi was not likely to take the bait. Of course, the Communists were not about to renounce political violence, so essentially his conditions were meaningless.

Months passed before Dobrynin eventually told Kissinger that Hanoi had not responded positively to Nixon's proposal. At the time, Kissinger wondered whether Dobrynin had even sent the message to Hanoi, because no official reply "was ever received from Moscow."[27] It now seems clear that Soviet officials did pass the proposal along to DRV prime minister Pham Van Dong, who simply rejected it outright in early May 1969. Dong explained that there was nothing new in the American proposal, that it settled no political questions, and that it did not include the DRV's demand for a unilateral US troop withdrawal on a fixed timetable.[28] Anything that needed to be said, the prime minister concluded, could be said in Paris. He then pointed the Nixon administration to the NLF's Ten-Point Overall Solution, announced on May 8, 1969. The plan called for (1) a unilateral US troop withdrawal from South Vietnam, (2) South Vietnamese elections that included NLF candidates on the ballot, and (3) the "reunification of Vietnam" through an agreement "between the two zones without foreign interference."[29] There was no mention of North Vietnamese troops at all. The statement concluded with the controversial declaration that the NLF was the only true representative of the people of South Vietnam, implying once again that the Saigon government had to be replaced before any agreement could be signed.[30] The front had once promoted a coalition government, but now it insisted that it alone held political legitimacy. It appeared as if the NLF's negotiating position was actually hardening at the exact same time that Kissinger and Nixon were trying to use Moscow to influence events in Vietnam.

Partially in response to the NLF's peace proposal, Nixon tried one more approach with Moscow, this time on his own, by publicly stating that he was serious about resuming the bombing of North Vietnam and widening and intensifying the war if there was not a settlement soon. "I must also make clear, in all candor," the president warned in a May 14 televised speech, his first to the nation on the Vietnam War, "that if the needless suffering continues, this will affect other decisions."[31] He also added that he wanted "to end this war" and that the "time had come for some new initiatives."[32] Among those new initiatives was a proposal to withdraw all US forces from South Vietnam if the People's Army of Vietnam (PAVN) also withdrew from South Vietnam, Laos, and Cambodia. Both sides were to stick to a strict twelve-month timetable. Kissinger considered this a major improvement over Lyndon Johnson's insistence that North Vietnamese troops retreat across the Demilitarized Zone (DMZ) six months before the last residual American troops were withdrawn. Always focusing on domestic politics, Nixon thought that such a withdrawal plan would play well in the 1970 midterm elections. Again Hanoi rejected Nixon's proposals outright, partially because they knew that US public opinion was forcing the president to make American troop withdrawals his top priority.[33]

As Nixon was delivering his address, Kissinger was explaining to Dobrynin that if the Soviets did not "produce a settlement," the United States would "escalate the war."[34] Kissinger always assumed that Moscow wanted to end the Vietnam War as much as the United States did, so as to move on to bigger and more important issues. This was partially true. But it is also true that the Soviet Union gained significant power and prestige inside the Communist camp from its close relationship with Hanoi. The outgoing US chief negotiator in Paris, Averell Harriman, tried to tell Kissinger as much. "They're going to take Hanoi's side in these negotiations," Harriman warned. The Soviets might help smooth over some of the finer details of the peace talks, he suggested, but "they won't take our side in supporting the Thieu government, for instance."[35] Tommy Thompson, former US ambassador to the Soviet Union, echoed Harriman's caution. He claimed that the Soviet state-controlled media was "vocal and un-equivocal" in its support for the DRV negotiating position and that it was "unlikely that the Soviets will go far in pressing Hanoi toward concessions unless the talks are near breakdown."[36]

There were multiple reasons that Moscow was a difficult partner for the United States in ending the Vietnam War. For one, the Soviets desperately needed to combat China's claims, with an occasional echo from Hanoi, that the Soviet Union was a revisionist state. The rift between China and the Soviet Union had intensified shortly after the Soviets' 20th Congress in 1956 when Nikita Khrushchev, first secretary of the Communist Party of the Soviet Union, denounced Joseph Stalin's abuses and excesses against the party. Khrushchev criticized Stalin for having failed to make adequate defensive prepa-rations before the Nazi invasion of the Soviet Union in June 1941, for purging many high-ranking and experienced Red Army offi-cers during the Second World War, and for his attacks against po-litical rivals within the party. He then claimed that the transition from capitalism to socialism could be accomplished by parliamentary means and not just through a bloody revolution. All this criticism of Stalin and the suggestion that socialism could come about peacefully was interpreted by the Chinese as a gesture toward peaceful coexistence with the West, a fundamental challenge to China's self-proclaimed role as the vanguard of continuous revolutions in the southern world.

The rift grew when Beijing's party-controlled press published essays criticizing the Soviets for their "Maoist pretentions to ideological and policy leadership of the Communist world."[37] Mao Zedong's bold claims about surviving a nuclear war so enraged Moscow officials that Red Army contingency plans now included a clash with Communist China. Mao boasted, "If war breaks out, it is unavoidable that people will die. We have seen wars kill people. Many times in China's past half the population has been wiped out.... We have at present no experience with atomic war. We do not know how many must die. It is better if one-half are left, the second best is one-third.... After several five-year plans [China] will then develop and rise up. In place of the totally destroyed capitalism we will obtain perpetual peace. This will not be a bad thing."[38] Writing in 1960, Deng Xiaoping, general secretary of the Chinese Communist Party, claimed, "The Soviet party is opportunist and revisionist; it lacks any deep knowledge of Marxism; its ideas about disarmament are absurd; peaceful coexistence could mean nothing, except as a tactical weapon to deceive the enemy; the Soviet idea of a division of labor among the countries of the socialist camp is wrong; and China must go her own way."[39] By the end of 1960, the Soviets had pulled all of their advisers out of China and Moscow was looking for ways to prove its credentials in the socialist camp by supporting what it called "wars of national liberation." Following the October 1962 Cuban missile crisis, the war in Vietnam was at the top of Moscow's list.

The Soviet Union was in a difficult position, therefore, when Kissinger asked for Moscow's help in ending the war. It had to choose between its leadership of the Communist world or improved relations with the United States and the benefits that would surely follow. Of course, he underestimated how much the Soviet Union needed to be a champion of the southern world. Besides, the Soviet Union had already cashed in on its relationship with Hanoi. The DRV had backed Moscow after its 1968 invasion of Czechoslovakia and had pledged neutrality in the Sino-Soviet dispute. Aid from the Soviet Union to the DRV had increased steadily since 1964, and in March 1966, at the Soviet Union's 23rd Congress, Le Duan, the secretary-general of the Vietnamese Communist Party (VCP), called the Soviet Union "a second motherland."[40] Perhaps no incident showed Hanoi's move toward Moscow more vividly, however, than the damage to the Chinese cargo ship *Hongqi* (Red Flag) in Haiphong harbor. The *Hongqi* had a cargo of war materiel for delivery to the DRV but was asked to anchor outside of the port while priority was given to a Soviet ship that was arriving later in the day. During the delay, the *Hongqi* was damaged by an American air strike, causing considerable outrage in Beijing.[41] All of this points to a complicated but complementary relationship between the DRV and Moscow, one that could not easily be put aside for larger foreign policy objectives. The Harvard professor who championed realism and linkage did not understand the basic political needs of his major adversary.

Soviet prime minister Alexei Kosygin set the record straight at the end of May 1969, rejecting Kissinger's threats outright. On May 27, he sent Nixon a letter explaining that Moscow would only solve mutual problems with the United States on a case-by-case basis and that linkage was dead.[42] Kissinger remained unconvinced. He asked to meet with Dobrynin on June 11 for one more round of discussions.

During the meeting, Kissinger reiterated the US position on the war: both sides must agree to a mutual troop withdrawal and the South Vietnamese must settle the political questions themselves. Dobrynin asked about a coalition government in South Vietnam. Kissinger replied, "We are both realists." To bring about a coalition government in South Vietnam, Kissinger continued, "we would have to smash the present structure of the Saigon Government while the NLF remained intact." This, he concluded, "would guarantee an NLF victory sooner or later. We would never accept that."[43] Kissinger then turned the conversation to Moscow's influence in Hanoi. "Hanoi was very difficult," Dobrynin explained. The DRV leadership believed that they "knew their own requirements better than the Soviet Union."[44] A frustrated Kissinger reminded the Soviet ambassador that Moscow provided the DRV with 85 percent of its needed military equipment and therefore had built-in leverage in Hanoi. A subdued Dobrynin asked Kissinger about the state of US–Soviet relations. Kissinger then voiced the sentiment that the Soviets had been hoping not to hear again: "A really massive change [in the relationship] depended on the settlement of the Vietnam War." Dobrynin ended the meeting complaining to Kissinger that Americans "always seem to link things."[45]

Just two days later, on June 13, Prime Minister Alexsei Kosygin announced the final Soviet response to Kissinger's linkage ploy. In a statement of fraternal socialist solidarity, Kosygin pledged Moscow's support for the Provisional Revolutionary Government (PRG), created by the NLF in 1969 as a government-in-waiting, and praised it as "the legal government and the true representative of the people of South Vietnam."[46] Moscow had been discussing the creation of such a front government with Hanoi for a number of months. As the Nixon administration announced that it would begin pulling American troops out of Vietnam, North Vietnamese leaders decided to follow that move with a small troop withdrawal of their own. The Soviet Union and the North Vietnamese then launched a joint diplomatic offensive, insisting that the creation of the PRG was the most encouraging prospect for peace in Vietnam in a number of years and rejecting US attempts to drive a wedge between Hanoi and Moscow.[47] The same day that the Soviets officially recognized the PRG, Andrei Gromyko, Moscow's minister of foreign affairs, cabled the PRG's new foreign minister, Nguyen Thi Binh, pledging the Soviet Union's full support and confirming that the peace talks in Paris were the only place that discussions on Vietnam should take place.[48] The secret idea of using Moscow to force Hanoi into a quick negotiated settlement by the Nixon administration's November 1 deadline was allowed to die of natural causes shortly after Kosygin's announcement. Kissinger would have to try another path to end the war on honorable terms.

Back Channels

Frustrated by Moscow's unwillingness to aid the US cause in Vietnam, in June 1969 Kissinger created a back channel directly to Hanoi outside of the Paris talks. This was entirely against protocol and was unknown to most in the Nixon administration. Kissinger opened the back channel through Raymond Aubrac, a French scientist who had played a key role in a secret contact, now known as PENNSYL-VANIA, with Hanoi a year before Nixon came to power. Aubrac was an old friend of Ho Chi Minh, and in the summer of 1967 he'd promised to deliver a message to the aging DRV leader if the Johnson administration had anything new to say. Kissinger, who knew Aubrac from meetings in Europe of the Pugwash group, an organization of antinuclear scientists and policy officials, had referred the proposal to Secretary of State Dean Rusk, with a copy to Defense

Secretary Robert S. McNamara. PENNSYLVANIA went nowhere in late 1967, but Kissinger and Aubrac continued their conversations about Vietnam during the first year of the Nixon administration.

In mid-1969, Kissinger urged the French scientist to reach out to his Vietnamese friends in Paris again with the news that Nixon was willing to negotiate with the DRV based on the realities in Vietnam. He thought that Hanoi would notice the subtle but important distinctions between the Nixon administration's position on negotiations and the Johnson administration's insistence that the DRV withdraw all of its troops from South Vietnam before the United States did the same. Aubrac reported Nixon's willingness to negotiate to Mai Van Bo, the head of the DRV's commercial legation in Paris. On June 14, shortly after the Moscow channel dried up, Aubrac cabled from Laos that he had just met with a high-ranking DRV official there and that Hanoi seemed to be responding positively to a message from Kissinger that read, "The president would like to explore channels outside the current framework of the negotiations."[49] The message proposed that "delegates from the United States and Vietnam could meet outside the Paris framework" to discuss "the general principles of a solution." Once agreement on principles was achieved, Kissinger concluded, "then the final technical negotiations could shift back to Paris."[50] Of course, he thought that he should be the one to conduct the secret talks in Paris. This would place him at the center of the most important decisions being made about Vietnam and help him keep his spot next to the president. He understood, even at this early date, that eventually Vietnam would be a secondary concern for the United States and that the president would make history by moving toward rapprochement with China and the Soviet Union. Kissinger wanted to be along on that journey.

To cement his role in the secret talks, Kissinger encouraged Nixon to follow up Aubrac's contact with a letter to Ho Chi Minh.

The letter became the topic of much conversation at the White House in mid-July. Kissinger arranged for the president to meet with Jean Sainteny, a former French military officer turned diplomat and businessman who had years of experience in Vietnam and who had built up trust in both Washington and Hanoi. In preparation for the meeting, Kissinger told Nixon that he should ask Sainteny to set up a meeting between the national security adviser and Le Duc Tho, the head of the North Vietnam's negotiating team in Paris. But Kissinger did not like being cut out of the back channel by Nixon, so he requested that he, and not his old friend Sainteny, "deliver the letter to Ho Chi Minh through Le Duc Tho."[51] The president eventually balked at Kissinger's suggestion and instead spent a considerable amount of time with Sainteny, going over the contents of the letter and the administration's position on negotiations. The two concluded that Sainteny would deliver the letter and that he would stress the administration's concern "that nothing can be gained by further delay in substantive negotiations."[52] Nixon was sticking to his November 1 deadline for substantive negotiations so as to influence the 1970 US midterm elections.

In the final draft of the letter, Nixon pledged his support to "move forward at the conference table toward an early resolution to this tragic war."[53] He claimed that his speech of May 14 had "laid out a proposal which I believe is fair to all parties." Still, he insisted, he was ready to discuss other programs, "specifically the 10-point program of the NLF."[54] He also asked Sainteny to tell Hanoi that if the present impasse in the negotiations continued beyond November 1, he would be forced to resort to military actions of "great consequence."[55]

Sainteny left for Florida the next day. Before he left, he sent the White House a letter outlining what he would say to the DRV delegates in Paris and his contacts in Hanoi. Nixon was certainly pleased by Sainteny's willingness to act on behalf of his administration and was thrilled to read that Sainteny would tell his Vietnamese friends that "President Nixon sincerely wishes to put an end to this war and he is prepared to discuss it with good will with the highest responsible authorities of the government of Hanoi on condition that he would find on their part the same real desire to reach a resolution." Sainteny concluded by telling Nixon that he would inform Hanoi that Kissinger would travel to Paris on August 4 and that Kissinger expected to learn "of Hanoi's reaction to the message of the President" while in France.[56] Sainteny delivered the letter to Xuan Thuy, North Vietnam's second-in-command in Paris, three days later, on July 18.

Nixon's letter puzzled DRV leaders. First, they were confused that it was addressed to Ho Chi Minh, the aging leader of the Communist Party in Vietnam. Ho had not been involved in the day-to-day activities of the party for nearly two years, and everyone in Hanoi knew that the party's secretary-general, Le Duan, had successfully isolated him from important decisions. In addition, Ho was very ill—in fact, he would die in his sleep only two months later. Second, the letter suggested that Nixon wanted to negotiate along the lines of the NLF's ten-point plan. If this was true, why had the US bombed Cambodia and why was it sending increased aid to the Republic of Vietnam Armed Forces (RVNAF) and the Saigon government? Third, Nixon's warning that he would widen and intensify the war if Hanoi did not negotiate soon and in good faith, carried with it the thinly veiled threat that the United States would resume bombing the DRV. But party leaders wondered, was this even possible, given the hostile reaction in Congress to such threats and the pledge by some in Congress to place restrictions on US bombing missions? Fourth, Nixon officials were still insisting publicly on a mutual troop withdrawal, but by mid-July the US was already beginning a unilateral exit. Was the troop withdrawal merely a pretext to expand the air war over North Vietnam, or had public pressure forced the president's hand? And, finally, shortly before receiving Nixon's letter, Hanoi had learned that Nixon and South Vietnamese president Nguyen Van Thieu had met at Midway Island to discuss Laird's Vietnamization program. Although Saigon had not been involved in the discussions at the Pentagon, Thieu accepted American withdrawals as a political necessity.[57] Hanoi understood this to mean that the United States was propping up Saigon for an eventual American withdrawal. Indeed, the first US troop withdrawal, eight hundred members of the Ninth Infantry Division, had already taken place in July, and more would follow. Did this mean that the United States would no longer support an open-ended military commitment to South Vietnam? In the end, Hanoi could not help but conclude that Nixon's letter did not seem to mesh with what was actually happening in Vietnam or in the United States.

Hanoi's confusion over Nixon's letter caused the party's Politburo, led by Le Duan, to approve a back-channel contact in Paris between Xuan Thuy and Kissinger to further probe the US position. Le Duan had disapproved of negotiations in general ever since the 1954 debacle at Geneva, which had divided Vietnam at the seventeenth parallel following its war with France. He was a southerner who believed that the party had surrendered at the negotiating table what it had rightfully won on the battlefield, leaving the South an occupied land in the hands of the American allies in Saigon.[58] Hanoi would not make that mistake again, according to Le Duan, but he was still intrigued to hear what Kissinger had to say. Technically, Xuan Thuy was the head of the North Vietnamese negotiating delegation in Paris, though Le Duan had sent Le Duc Tho, a much higher-ranking party official, to serve as his "special adviser" there. The meeting between Kissinger and Thuy, therefore, had approval at the highest levels of government in Hanoi, despite Kissinger's later claims that Thuy "was not a policymaker but a functionary."[59]

Few Nixon administration officials at the time knew how important this initial back-channel contact was, or perhaps they would have insisted on more involvement in Kissinger's planning for the meeting.

The first secret meeting took place in Paris on August 4 at Sainteny's house on rue de Rivoli. Kissinger seemed eager to hear North Vietnam's response to Nixon's letter to Ho Chi Minh.[60] Thuy evaded giving that response for much of the three-hour meeting. Instead, he laid out North Vietnam's position. Hanoi wanted the Saigon government dissolved and a coalition government that included the NLF put in its place. Hanoi also insisted on an unconditional and unilateral withdrawal of American troops on a fixed timetable. "We wonder why the U.S. could bring its troops rapidly and it could not pull them out rapidly?" Thuy asked Kissinger. "Why don't you propose 5 or 6 months for the complete withdrawal of troops from SVN [South Vietnam]."[61] For the remainder of the secret negotiations, getting a fixed deadline on US troop withdrawals was one of Hanoi's first principles. Kissinger then repeated a formulation he would make again and again in negotiations: troop withdrawals were a result of reaching an agreement, not an unconditional move on the part of the Nixon administration. Hanoi had not anticipated Kissinger's design, but North Vietnamese leaders smelled weakness in the proposal. Nixon had already announced that twenty-five thousand US troops would be withdrawn from Vietnam by August 31, withdrawal of a further thirty-five thousand would be announced in September, and eventually he would order that another fifty thousand troops be redeployed by April 1970. What Hanoi wanted, however, was a US commitment to withdraw all of its troops, including residual forces, as quickly as possible without a mutual withdrawal of North Vietnamese troops. "You can adjust the speed of our troop withdrawal," Kissinger told Thuy, "by that of yours [from South Vietnam]."[62]

Kissinger did not expect Thuy to agree to a mutual troop withdrawal. He understood that the North Vietnamese representative was there to accept concessions, not make any. "They were specialists in political warfare," he later wrote of Thuy and his associate, Mai Van Bo. "They pocketed American concessions as their due, admitting no obligation to reciprocate moderation."[63] He was also well aware that Hanoi was counting on "the nervous exhaustion" of the United States.[64] Kissinger believed that North Vietnam had no intention of making progress in Paris at this time, even in back-channel talks, because it might slow the momentum of US troop withdrawals. In the years to come, Hanoi would use the secret contacts to try to speed up the process, but for now, North Vietnam seemed intent to let the US withdraw at its own pace. There was nothing he could say to Thuy in August 1969 that would convince him that the United States might "stop bringing soldiers home."[65] It was not a credible threat, and Hanoi understood this fully. Kissinger concluded that after the first US troop withdrawals, Hanoi "was on the verge of achieving the second of its objectives without reciprocity [the first was the bombing halt] . . . a US unilateral withdrawal.[66]

Kissinger then outlined the Nixon administration's program to get a settlement on the war by November 1, one year after the cessation of US bombing of North Vietnam. He claimed that the United States had made a series of "unreciprocated gestures" in the previous year, including the announcement of the unilateral withdrawal of twenty-five thousand American troops; the acceptance of the NLF in national elections in South Vietnam as long as it renounced violence; the commitment to finding common ground between the NLF's ten-point program; and the recognition of the existing balance of political and military forces. He finished with a warning: "If by November 1 no progress has been made, the United States would have to consider steps of grave consequence."[67]

Thuy sat patiently and without expression as he listened to what Kissinger would later call "the most comprehensive American peace plan yet,"[68] phrasing Kissinger introduced in all his secret meetings in Paris. When Thuy finally responded, he reverted to Hanoi's long-held position that the United States needed to dismantle the Saigon government and settle the political questions in South Vietnam according to the NLF's ten points. A coalition government made up of the PRG and remnants of the Saigon government would help solve all political questions, Thuy suggested, but the NLF was not to be dissolved as the Johnson administration had demanded. As to military problems, the United States needed to provide a concrete timetable for the unilateral withdrawal of all American troops. The political and military issues were linked, he explained: "One could not be solved without the other."[69] He then suggested that Kissinger had said that the United States had launched a partial and then total bombing halt against the DRV and then it had announced plans to withdraw twenty-five thousand US troops. Kissinger agreed, stating that this was a sign of goodwill, but he added that he "had found no goodwill by the DRV."[70] Thuy explained that this was not true, that Hanoi had responded with "great goodwill."[71] North Vietnam's original position was that no talks would take place before a total US bombing halt. The act of goodwill was meeting with US representatives in Paris before a total bombing halt was in place. He implied that the United States had not seen this gesture as a sign of goodwill.

Since Kissinger and Thuy were restating positions that had already been expressed repeatedly in Washington and Hanoi, nothing substantial came of the August 4 meeting. Neither side was yet ready to concede any key point. Detecting the diplomatic stalemate and not wanting to come home empty-handed, Kissinger then suggested that the two agree to a secret back channel at the highest level. To accelerate the negotiations, Kissinger claimed that "the President of the

United States is prepared to open another, secret channel with Vietnam [and] to appoint a high-ranking representative of competence to have productive discussions. . . . If this channel is opened, the United States will adjust its military activities to create the most favorable circumstances to arrive at a solution."[72] Thuy accepted the back channel on the spot, without consulting Tho or party leaders in Hanoi. Kissinger then raised a practical problem. "Did they prefer Sainteny or General [Vernon] Walters as a means to communicate with [Kissinger]" when they wanted to use the back channel? Thuy said if he had anything to convey, he would say it to General Walters. Kissinger reminded Thuy that "General Walters [could] not discuss; he [could] only take messages" for him.[73] This back channel became the forum for serious negotiations for the remainder of the war. And Kissinger, of course, convinced Nixon that he alone should be the contact.

The back channel to Hanoi came at a price, however. Kissinger had shut out Defense and State, keeping them informed only through summaries of the conversations with Thuy and later with Tho. He had very little input from either department. He developed the US negotiating position with less and less consultation with anyone else in the government, including the president. Few in Kissinger's National Security Council ever fully understood where the negotiating strategy was heading, even his closest associates. Scores of transcripts of Nixon and Kissinger reliving the highlights of negotiations in Paris make it clear that Kissinger was cutting people out of the loop.[74] There is also ample evidence that Kissinger himself could not always keep up with the various proposals being put forward in Paris.[75] And of course, he did not consult at all with his allies in the Saigon government before he met with Thuy. They had no idea of the substance or character of the conversations. In other words, Kissinger had complete control of what was being said to the highest-ranking Vietnamese representatives, with little open debate or discussion with other senior policy makers in the Nixon administration or America's allies in Saigon.

In Retrospect

This way of conducting the secret talks with Hanoi may have pleased Kissinger, and it may have suited his personality, but theory and history suggest that it was the wrong way to build support for a negotiated settlement. Rather than isolating himself from the rest of the national security bureaucracy, he should have built a negotiations constituency within the government that cooperated fully in putting together first negotiating principles and mechanisms to handle the discussions in Paris. Sustainable peace agreements require big networks to be successful.[76] Kissinger practiced poor tradecraft by isolating the talks to only a few. He was trying to get the minimum number of actors necessary in a room in Paris to get the peace signed with Hanoi, but in the process he also failed to create the broadest possible support for any agreement among the South Vietnamese. He failed to grasp that the war in Vietnam had actually become a mutually hurting stalemate. High casualties had led to military exhaustion, and this was a period then that was ripe for meaningful negotiations. But Kissinger conditioned each meeting in Paris with military escalation, or at least the threat of escalation. This coercive approach paid few dividends. There was much to be explored with Hanoi and Saigon, if only he was willing. Instead, he stuck to rather outmoded views of power, violence, and peace.

One of the keys to the most successful peace agreements is "buy-in." Skilled negotiators make their adversaries understand that they will get more of what they want if they stay inside a process that guarantees political compromise and full participation in public life for most of the belligerents. Kissinger failed to examine what sources of leverage he had to move Hanoi from violence to serious negotiations.

He met Hanoi's violence with coercive threats and increased violence. Kissinger never once used the carrot of negotiations, convinced that the stick of intimidating power was the only thing that Hanoi would understand.[77] The prospect of descending into a deeper and bloodier conflict in 1969—the bloodiest year of the war—should have sparked an interest in Kissinger to spend more time exploring his negotiation options. He had done his homework on Vietnam from his first trip there in 1965, but once in the White House, he seemed to forget all that he had learned. If he was willing to be creative—and why not, since nothing else was working—he might have been able to link the most important aspects of US first principles to a cease-fire and peace agreement. Instead, he stuck to worn-out formulas that increased the violence in Vietnam for little political or military gain for the United States or its allies, formulas that Hanoi routinely objected to.

Kissinger also failed at the most basic tasks of ending deadly conflict. Rather than shutting out Laird and Rogers, he should have used them to build a coalition of supportive colleagues who could have helped develop oversight guarantees, burden sharing, enforcement mechanisms, and the governmental capacity needed to see a successful agreement finalized. Perhaps most important, Kissinger clung hopelessly to Thieu's government of South Vietnam, without consultation with or inclusion of others, but he never fully embraced Thieu, and in fact he was rather dismissive of most South Vietnamese political leaders. By cutting Saigon out of the process, Kissinger missed the opportunity to explore a potential and important asset: other political options in South Vietnam that may have garnered more support among the population than the corrupt Thieu. Non-military leaders were present in many realms of South Vietnamese civil society, but Kissinger's negotiating strategy failed to surface them. His coercive strategy in Paris lacked vision, shutting out potential allies. Altering this approach would have taken away from his privileged position within the administration, but it might have led to more expansive and coordinated negotiations to end the war.

On the American side, Kissinger did assemble what he called "The Senior Review Group," comprising high-ranking officials from the State Department, the Defense Department, the Joint Chiefs of Staff, the CIA, and his own National Security Council (NSC) staff, to discuss the secret negotiations. This group was one of six subcommittees that he established to handle national security affairs. It met infrequently, however, and rarely had access to his most detailed notes on the Paris negotiations.[78] He had also expanded his NSC staff from twelve to thirty-four in a further effort to closely control all aspects of Nixon's foreign policy by "greatly reducing the Department of State's participation" in the formulation of policy.[79] In September 1973, Nixon appointed Kissinger secretary of state, replacing Rogers, making him the first and only person to serve simultaneously as national security adviser and secretary of state. Eventually, however, Kissinger's concentration of power and his lone cowboy strategy left him frustrated and dejected. It did not do South Vietnam much good, either.

The analysis of the August 4 Kissinger-Thuy meeting reveals some of the problems with Kissinger's approach. Writing from Paris five days after the meeting, Henry Cabot Lodge Jr., the former US ambassador to Saigon, who now headed the American negotiating delegation in Paris at the avenue Kléber talks (which were separate from Kissinger's secret talks also in Paris) that focused primarily on technical issues, suggested that Kissinger drew out Thuy on the need for a mutual withdrawal, but that Thuy "was careful not to indicate in any way that they were prepared to engage in a step by step tacit withdrawal process. He left their withdrawal open, but gave no sign that it would be phased and geared to our withdrawal."[80] Lodge was well aware that belligerents usually agree to link a mutual troop withdrawal *before* either side commits to the act. When Kissinger demanded that the DRV withdraw its troops from South Vietnam as a condition for further US troop withdrawals and progress in Paris, he was pushing a rather weak reed. Kissinger had already admitted as much in memo after memo to Nixon complaining that Vietnamization was taking away one of his most important negotiating assets.[81] DRV leaders understood that the American public demanded US withdrawals and that there was absolutely no reason for them to respond to Kissinger's threats about escalation. Kissinger knew this, too, calling troop withdrawals "salted peanuts" for the American public; the more troops were withdrawn, the more withdrawals would be expected.[82]

Yet he held out some hope that he could use the steady diet of US troop withdrawals to America's advantage. He understood that he had no chance of reversing Nixon on the withdrawal issue, but now Kissinger wanted to link the withdrawals to greater military action against North Vietnam and increased aid to South Vietnam. He wrote to the president in early September, suggesting that one reason for a recent lull in PAVN infiltration into South Vietnam might be that Hanoi was waiting to see how the Nixon administration responded to Vietnamization. Kissinger suggested that Hanoi might "fear Vietnamization" if "by gradually reducing US presence and lowering casualties," the administration "could maintain American public support [for the war] while [South Vietnam] is successfully strengthened."[83] This formula would become the cornerstone of the Nixon Doctrine later in the year. Kissinger also laid out several options on what to do now that American troops were coming home, but he clearly favored "military escalation" as a "*means* to a negotiated settlement, not as an *end*, since we have ruled out military victory."[84] He wanted to end the war quickly by pushing for a negotiated settlement along the lines of the proposal advanced by the aborted Vance mission. If Hanoi refused to negotiate, the US should force the DRV into submission with "a series of short, sharp blows."[85] During an

NSC meeting on September 12, Kissinger suggested that the United States needed a comprehensive plan to end the war, "not just troop withdrawals."[86] Nixon agreed that a strategy entirely dependent upon Vietnamization would not work. He authorized Kissinger to form a small working group inside the NSC to study the problem.

Duck Hook and Pruning Knife

Kissinger's planning group met in the White House Situation Room for most of September and October, trying to piece together some military options that would give them an edge in the negotiations and lessen the negative impact of US troop withdrawals. The planning was given the name "Duck Hook." Typically, Kissinger insisted that all escalation planning be confined to his small working group, away from Rogers and especially Laird. It was also typical that his only answer to the Vietnam riddle was military escalation. Not once did the Duck Hook planning staff explore how to incentivize the negotiations by looking at what could be done to improve the political climate in Saigon to secure more support for the government.

Instead, the group explored a variety of military options against North Vietnam, each designed to achieve maximum political, military, and psychological shock at increasing levels of intensity. One action after another was put forward: mining Haiphong harbor; blasting the irrigation dikes along the Red River with iron bombs; resuming the bombing against North Vietnam and intensifying it by striking cities, roads, and bridges; and even using "the nuclear option," literally.[87] Kissinger fed Nixon each of these possibilities because the president wanted to make a bold statement on Vietnam in October or November. Nixon sent Kissinger a draft of the speech he was planning to make, outlining his new policies toward Vietnam, in late September for revisions. It appears that some on Kissinger's staff—Tony Lake, Roger Morris, and Peter Rodman, in particular—collaborated on the president's speech, at least on those aspects that dealt directly with Duck Hook.

Nixon ordered the Joint Chiefs and Creighton Abrams to conduct a study of their own on the feasibility of the escalation proposals developed by Kissinger's working group. He wondered whether Kissinger had gone far enough in his proposals and was hoping that the military brass would embrace more intensive attacks against North Vietnam. On September 25, the military planning group met with Nixon at the White House to present their findings. Operating under the name "Pruning Knife," the military group gave Nixon old wine in new bottles. Since almost every possible military option had been considered before, the Pruning Knife report really did not contain the bold or imaginative planning Nixon had hoped to see from his military experts. Furthermore, there was considerable disagreement among the top military planners on whether any of Kissinger's escalation options were even viable. Pruning Knife studied the familiar recommendations of the Joint Chiefs of Staff, but left Nixon frustrated. He told his aides that the military brass needed to think bigger. He wanted to make the DRV leadership serious about negotiations. "I was not elected to preside over the senseless attrition of American lives by a deluded foe," Nixon exclaimed.[88] Yet the president refused to endorse escalation at the meeting. Instead, he retreated to Camp David and ruminated about how Hanoi had underestimated just how tough he was.

Sensing that the chief executive was waffling, something he was prone to do, Kissinger went on the offensive. He arranged for the president to telephone when he was on the line with Dobrynin. Kissinger took Nixon's call, then returned to Dobrynin and reported, "The president just told me in that call that as far as Vietnam is concerned, the train had just left the station." Dobrynin said he hoped it was "an airplane" and not a train because "an airplane can still change its course of flight." Kissinger replied, "The president chooses his words very carefully. He said train."[89] Kissinger often used others to stiffen Nixon's resolve. He had orchestrated the call with Dobrynin to push Nixon toward action. Nixon eventually ordered Kissinger to convince Moscow and Hanoi that he was a "madman" capable of doing almost anything not to lose the war in Vietnam. Earlier in the year, the president had told an aide, "I want the North Vietnamese to believe I've reached the point where I might do anything to stop the war. We'll just slip the word to them that, 'for God's sake, you know Nixon is obsessed about communism. We can't restrain him when he's angry—and he has his hand on the nuclear button,' and Ho Chi Minh himself will be in Paris in two days begging for peace."[90] But when the Pruning Knife and Duck Hook military escalation options came upon his desk for approval in early October 1969, he balked. He thought that Kissinger, in promoting military escalation against North Vietnam, was underestimating the impact of domestic politics.

Nixon knew that there were serious problems in Congress. Senator Charles Goodell, a Republican from New York, had put forward a resolution in late September demanding that all US troops be withdrawn from Vietnam by the end of 1970. The resolution also prohibited the use of congressionally appropriated funds for Vietnam after December 1970. The resolution was defeated easily in the Senate, but Senators Mark Hatfield, Jacob Javits (another New York Republican), and George McGovern proposed similar legislation over the next three weeks. Kissinger later blamed Goodell and the antiwar movement for backing Nixon into a corner. "Having transmuted the war into a domestic conflict between good and evil at home," Kissinger wrote after the war, "the Peace Movement preferred—for reasons it viewed as highly moral—America's collapse in Vietnam to an outcome which, precisely because it might be considered 'honorable,' might also whet the government's appetite for further foreign adventures."[91]

But Kissinger would not give up. In early October, he wrote to Nixon outlining the final contingency military operations the Duck Hook planning had produced. Although he suggested that his paper did not address the "relative merits of [military escalation]," Kissinger nonetheless argued that "to achieve its full effect," military action against Hanoi had to be "brutal." He warned Nixon that once they moved toward escalation, "we should not allow ourselves to be deterred by vague, conciliatory gestures by Hanoi." There would be some pushback from the American public and Congress, Kissinger concluded, but serious problems could be avoided if "each action" against the DRV was "short and compact."[92] He thought someone with Nixon's considerable political skills could hold the country together by expertly explaining the reason for escalation. The next day, Nixon took the paper and its author with him to his retreat in Key Biscayne, Florida. With Kissinger at his side, he pondered his various options for escalating the war. As the day dragged on, it became clear that the president was increasingly uncomfortable with the path Kissinger had outlined.

The paper put Nixon on the horns of a dilemma. Encouraged by Kissinger to escalate the war in Vietnam as cover for the readily apparent US weakness in Paris caused by the American troop withdrawals, Nixon also had to consider his domestic opponents and the growing antiwar movement. He knew full well that the National Mobilization Committee to End the War in Vietnam (MOBE) was planning a massive nationwide demonstration against the war on

October 15. If he escalated the war against Hanoi before the protest, it might be an accelerant to the antiwar movement. If he waited to act until after October 15, it would look as though he was "making the tough move after the 15th just because of the rioting at home."[93] Keeping Congress in line also presented the president with enormous difficulties. Kissinger kept flattering the president, but it was only a matter of time before Nixon dismissed his strategy altogether.

As the October 15 protest neared, Nixon had one final meeting with Laird—who had finally been told of the planning groups—the Joint Chiefs, and the Pruning Knife and Duck Hook planning committees at the White House on October 11. The president set the tone early, telling the group that the purpose of the meeting was to "evaluate what we could do if it became necessary to take more military action against Vietnam."[94] Laird was the most outspoken opponent of military escalation at the meeting. He claimed that the United States had already hit all available targets and that planning any other military operations against North Vietnam "[would] take at least a year." He favored what he called the "long haul option": allowing Vietnamization to work by continuing to withdraw US troops to gain support for increased aid to the Saigon government.[95] Although Kissinger had tried to cut him out of all Duck Hook planning, Laird had used his contacts in the White House to monitor Kissinger's military planning. He even had secret tape recordings of Kissinger's White House phone conversations. Finally, Laird used the opinions of top aides involved with Duck Hook, notably Tony Lake and Roger Morris, to shore up his argument that military escalation would do little to advance the peace process.[96]

Kissinger sat quietly as Laird criticized every single escalation proposal. He was also silent, and no doubt discouraged, when General Wheeler, chair of the Joint Chiefs of Staff, delivered his report stating that Pruning Knife was not a "sound military plan" and that it had many "problem areas."[97] Kissinger had hoped that Nixon would enthusiastically embrace new attacks against North Vietnam, but the reality was that the government could not agree on the proper military path to take. Nixon feared criticism from the left and right about his Vietnam policies, and it paralyzed him during the Duck Hook debates in late October. There were no good options, and Duck Hook had simply led to strategic confusion. At the end of the meeting, Nixon kicked the can down the road again, deciding not to decide on Duck Hook's future. He would wait until after the October 15 protests to address the nation, and he would postpone military escalation.

The debate over escalation took its toll on Kissinger. He had entered the Nixon administration, according to the national press, as a breath of spring after the "tired men" of the Johnson years.[98] But nine months later, some of Kissinger's colleagues noticed that he was frustrated and discouraged because nothing seemed to be working in Vietnam.[99] He had lost the debate over Vietnamization to Laird, and now it looked like the Joint Chiefs, MACV, and the Pentagon would win once again. Adding to his troubles, several NSC staffers resigned in September over Kissinger's harsh treatment. Joe Kraft, a *Washington Post* columnist, suggested in a column that Kissinger had cut most of the NSC out of important foreign policy decision making and that this had cost his agency influence at the White House. Nixon flew into a rage, demanding that Kissinger get Kraft to write a more favorable piece on the administration.[100] The more frustrated Kissinger became, the more his famous temper interfered with his ability to influence the president, causing even more anger and frustration. Supremely aware of his carefully cultivated image as coolheaded in a crisis, after nine months of frustration over Vietnam he appeared to be "overexcited" and "over depressed" about his failures.[101]

Nixon worried that Kissinger's emotions often interfered with his ability to manage foreign affairs crises. "He's mixed up," Nixon once claimed.[102] The president suggested that Kissinger "has the inability to see that...he himself is ever wrong."[103] Nixon also noted that "Henry is very excitable, very emotional almost."[104] Kissinger's temper tantrums and his constant threats to resign upset Nixon. "He's the kind of fellow that could have an emotional collapse," Nixon once told an aide.[105] The president thought it was "ludicrous" that he spent so much of his time "propping up this guy."[106] Just months after taking office, Nixon had become so tired of Kissinger's emotional eruptions that he created a special "Henry-Handling Committee."[107] Assistant to the President John Ehrlichman, Chief of Staff H. R. Haldeman, and Attorney General John Mitchell had the job of keeping Kissinger "calm" and "on an even emotional keel."[108] Their goal was to keep him away from the president when he was upset. Ehrlichman in particular was tasked with listening to Kissinger's constant threats to resign and his tirades against subordinates and colleagues; occasionally, he would tell Nixon that they should get Kissinger "some psychotherapy."[109]

Kissinger's frustrations eventually led him to jettison Duck Hook. "As the scenario took shape," he wrote after the war, "it became apparent that there was not enough consensus in the administration to pursue such a course."[110] He failed to realize, of course, that he himself had destroyed much of that consensus by cutting Laird and Rogers out of the war planning as much as possible. Both raised strong objections to Duck Hook, convincing the president that the American public could not tolerate military escalation. Nixon eventually agreed. "I believed it would be very hard to hold the country together," he admitted after the war, "while pursuing a military solution."[111] Laird continued to argue that rallying the American people to patiently support a protracted war was the correct path to take. Polling suggested that the phased withdrawal of American troops already under way was hugely popular.[112] The withdrawal was actually gaining support for Nixon's other Vietnam policies; namely, increasing military aid to South Vietnam and using American air power when necessary to hit the PAVN now operating inside South Vietnam. Nixon liked this controlled escalation because it gave him public support, something he was always concerned about. The president worried that Kissinger did not understand politics, and that his rapid escalation plans threatened to destroy the fragile coalition that Nixon was trying to build and solidify around his Vietnam policies. Despite his best efforts, Kissinger alone could not provide the president with any guarantees that military escalation would bring Hanoi to its knees. Nixon probably would not have supported escalation so close to his original November 1 deadline anyway, but the withdrawal of Duck Hook on October 17 was certainly a momentary blow to Kissinger's credibility inside the government.

Years later, Nixon and Kissinger both agreed that it was a mistake to cancel Duck Hook. "In retrospect," Nixon confessed, "I think we should have done it [Duck Hook]. I was worried how it would affect our chances of improving our relations with the Russians and Chinese. And I didn't feel the traffic would bear it within the administration." Nixon had feared resignations by Laird and Rogers if he'd gone ahead with Kissinger's plan, and he later said, "I just wasn't ready for that."[113] Shortly after the 1973 Paris Peace Accords, which ended American military involvement in Vietnam, journalist William Safire asked Kissinger whether he would have done anything differently. He responded: "We should have bombed the hell out of them the minute we took office." Even with a Nobel Peace Prize in hand for his role in the peace negotiations, a bitter Kissinger regretted not following through on the Duck Hook threat: "We could have ended the war much sooner," he claimed, "if we had been willing to do in 1969 what we ended up doing in 1972."[114] Despite these overly optimistic reflections, Kissinger found himself at the end of October 1969 without a viable Vietnam policy.

Accordingly, it would be up to the president to cobble something together in time for his speech in early November. Nixon understood that he would have to respond directly to the Moratorium, as the antiwar protests of October 15 were now called. Hundreds of thousands of protestors gathered in cities across the country to protest America's involvement in Vietnam. Joining the young antiwar activists were members of Congress and even some returning veterans. Kissinger wanted Nixon to use his upcoming televised speech to lash out at the antiwar protestors, whom he in part blamed for Duck Hook's postponement even though he had joined Nixon in killing the proposal. He told Nixon that the protestors were "dividing the country and making it impossible to settle the problem [the war] on a reasonable basis."[115] But Nixon thought he could do even more with his speech. He believed that he could actually shore up support for increased aid to South Vietnam and new attacks against Communist troops and sanctuaries, while withdrawing US troops.

On November 3, Nixon finally went before the American public to outline his new Vietnam policy. What became known as the Silent Majority speech firmly established Vietnamization as the cornerstone of the Nixon Doctrine. The "primary mission of our troops," Nixon announced, "is to enable the South Vietnamese forces to assume the full responsibility for the security of South Vietnam." Vietnamization would allow the United States to simultaneously reduce American casualties and terminate the war on honorable terms. By withdrawing its troops and demanding that the DRV do the same, the United States was setting the stage for the South Vietnamese to settle the political issues of the war amongst themselves. Nixon believed that this policy would garner public support, allowing the public and Congress to continue to support the Saigon government until it could compete politically and militarily on its own. Nixon emphasized that the United States was withdrawing its troops from a position of "strength and not from weakness." He also spoke of the US commitment to South Vietnam and warned that antiwar activists were actually making peace more difficult. He called for support from those he labeled the "great silent majority" and concluded with a shrewd and dramatic warning: "North Vietnam cannot humiliate the United States. Only Americans can do that."[116]

Nixon's Silent Majority speech did what Kissinger could not: it reconciled the contradictory elements of American public opinion on the war. By leaving the escalation option out of the speech, the president relied almost exclusively on Laird's policy proposals, at Kissinger's expense. The national security adviser did not take this slight lightly. In what must have been a humiliating and torturous month of November, Kissinger simultaneously stroked the president's ego for his masterful handling of the November 3 speech and plotted to overturn the gains that Laird and Rogers had made inside the White House. The night of the speech, Nixon phoned Kissinger on three separate occasions for reassurance that he had done well. Kissinger assured Nixon that the speech was "great" and that "if we did not reach the people tonight, it is impossible to do so."[117] Nixon agreed that they would get a "great reaction from the average person."[118] As for Rogers and Laird, much to Kissinger's delight, the president suggested that they "should have been ecstatic about the speech" but that "neither showed that—they haven't got the guts. I think they'll have to go."[119]

Kissinger followed up the phone conversations with several memos to the president pointing out the weakness of Vietnamization and condemning Rogers's new effort to negotiate a cease-fire. In late October, Rogers had suggested extending the traditional Christmas holiday truce with a more permanent and negotiated cease-fire. The issue should have come before the NSC during a November meeting, Kissinger reported to Nixon, but the State Department tried "to circumvent this procedure and organize a bureaucratic consensus which would have limited your [the president's] ability to determine the best course on the basis of an orderly review."[120] An orderly review was rarely part of Kissinger's management of the NSC. However, he reminded Nixon that he had already informed the secretaries of state and defense that "this is a time for us to stand on what we have offered and let Hanoi take stock and give some indication it is willing to participate in genuine negotiations. I think it would be very detrimental to our overall objective if there were any dope stories that we were offering a stand still cease-fire or any other diplomatic concession at this time."[121] Even the Communists rejected the idea of a cease-fire, he wrote the president.[122] These memos aimed specifically at Rogers and Laird are unusual even for an administration known for secrecy and intrigue. Still, Nixon wanted to keep all options on the table, so he asked Kissinger to explore how all of this would play out in Paris.

Kissinger's relentless assault on Laird and Rogers, along with his fawning over the president, kept his own policy hopes and personal ambitions alive. Within three days of the Silent Majority speech, having already postponed the military escalation option Kissinger favored, Nixon met with Dobrynin and repeated all of his threats about what would happen if North Vietnam did not compromise soon. He told Dobrynin that the United States would have to "pursue our own methods for bringing the war to an end." Nixon warned, "We will not hold still for being diddled to death in Vietnam."[123] Reverting to form, Kissinger applauded the president's approach with Hanoi and the Soviets. "I wager no one has ever talked to him that way his entire career! It was extraordinary! No president has ever laid it on the line like that."[124] Kissinger followed these compliments with word that Xuan Thuy might be interested in meeting him in Paris again.[125] Nixon was delighted.

By the end of 1969, then, Kissinger and the US policy toward Vietnam had come full circle. He still supported a compromised peace arrived at by coercing Hanoi into concessions in Paris through threats of greater violence and through greater Soviet pressure on the DRV. The erratic Nixon supported both positions in private, even if he often abandoned them in public. But the president could be managed, Kissinger thought. Despite Nixon's embrace of Vietnamization, Kissinger never gave up hope that he alone could develop the winning exit strategy in Vietnam. The events of 1969 did reveal that even when Laird and Rogers won, they sometimes lost. Kissinger was able to make the future of the secret contacts the cornerstone of Nixon's end game in Vietnam. He still felt trapped by circumstances and knew that he would never be able to reverse US troop withdrawals, but he deluded himself—and eventually the president—into thinking that there was a way forward that did not involve the United States' giving Hanoi the Saigon government on a platter. Kissinger believed that he could eventually use increased US military pressure to condition the talks in Paris, forcing Hanoi to abandon some of its first principles as the price needed to get the United States to do the same. Nixon's Silent Majority speech had garnered enough public support that Kissinger believed he now had a credible threat to escalate the war over North Vietnam even while Laird continued to bring US troops home. At the beginning of the year, the administration had no clear direction or plan for Vietnam other than Vietnamization. Kissinger now saw an end game come into focus based on his earlier experience studying the war in the Johnson years.

CHAPTER THREE

BOLD MOVES, 1970

"I HAVE ALWAYS BELIEVED that the optimum moment for negotiations is when things appear to be going well," Kissinger wrote in his postwar memoirs.[1] In early 1970, he told Nixon that things were indeed going well for the United States in Vietnam. According to the latest military reports, the Army of the Republic of Vietnam (ARVN) now controlled over 55 percent of the countryside in South Vietnam, more than doubling the territory under its control from the previous year.[2] Combined US and Republic of Vietnam (RVN) bombing and shelling and Saigon's pacification program further compressed revolutionary forces into ever-smaller areas of the countryside. Nixon's "Silent Majority" speech in November 1969 had rallied public support for the president's plan to bring US troops home while simultaneously increasing aid and military material to the Saigon government. These withdrawals were being managed with care not to create public demands for an even faster retreat.

Kissinger thought that the time was right, therefore, to approach Hanoi about more secret meetings in Paris. He believed that the Democratic Republic of Vietnam (DRV) might be motivated to make some concessions, including its demand for the ouster of the Thieu government, so as to speed up an American withdrawal. Kissinger's linkage here was problematic. He wrongfully equated the DRV's desire to speed up the US withdrawal with its insistence that the People's Army of Vietnam (PAVN) be allowed to stay in South Vietnam and that the Saigon government not be given a monopoly on political control. He oversold Hanoi's willingness to embrace these US enticements, failing to see other possibilities.

Self-Stunted Strategy

For a negotiator, success comes in figuring out what you have to give that your adversary really wants. What levers can you push to condition behavior and outcomes? Kissinger understood the power of America's coercive threats, but he did not exploit Hanoi's first principles. He did not use what Hanoi wanted most for reciprocity on key issues. He also failed to properly gauge was what possible through coercion and what was possible through negotiation. North Vietnam wanted a timely US troop withdrawal, but Vietnamization was taking care of that, though not at the speed that Hanoi's leadership wanted. But North Vietnam also insisted that the United States replace the Saigon government as part of the agreement. Kissinger never fully explored what this might mean. Hanoi obviously wanted to take South Vietnam by force and unite the country under the Communist banner, but Kissinger failed to explore what might have made that task more difficult. Instead, he stubbornly clung to Thieu and Nguyen Cao Ky, South Vietnam's vice president. There is evidence to suggest that a vibrant civil society was developing in the south around what it meant to be South Vietnamese.[3] This political project was joined with enormous cultural production along these same lines. It now seems clear that the South Vietnamese population had a strong sense of cultural and political identification with the state, even if they sometimes were dubious about its leadership. There was a robust belief in a shared history and aspirational future that could have been useful in thinking about what a final peace agreement might have looked like. Could a more inclusive US negotiating effort have surfaced the names of groups or individuals that might have presented a popular third way—besides the Communists or Thieu/Ky—that could have come to power in Saigon? Even a cursory exploration of the vanguard of South Vietnamese society would have been helpful. Instead, Kissinger kept his circle of knowledge about South Vietnam and his negotiating strategy purposefully small. There may not have been a way out of the Vietnam conundrum by examining the opportunities here, but it was a path not pursued.

Likewise, Hanoi also seemed very interested in postwar reconstruction aid. Nixon and Kissinger used it like bait, but they never made it an integral part of their negotiating strategy. Not once did Kissinger explore what it would mean in Hanoi if the United States announced its willingness to underwrite the costs of achieving a negotiated settlement. There were vague references to reconstruction aid in the secret talks, but nothing concrete. Later, Nixon would offer private assurances to Hanoi that the United States would help it rebuild, but these overtures were never formally introduced in the various proposals.

These were all failures of imagination and creativity when it was needed most. Ultimately, Kissinger concluded that Hanoi was employing a strategy of waiting the United States out, and therefore the time was right to search for a breakthrough that could bring an honorable end to the war in 1970. He expected the DRV to surrender many of its first principles or pay an enormous price for its insolence. This is how he negotiated; he issued ultimatums and coercive threats, but eventually he bargained away many of America's first principles one by one. Contrary to much that has been written about the secret negotiations, Hanoi rarely conceded on their major points. This reality did not stop Kissinger from using coercive power to condition the talks, even when it diminished domestic US support for the Nixon administration's policies in Vietnam and had little effect in Hanoi.

Kissinger was not interested in "shaving salami," as he called the DRV's attempts to hold out to see what the next US concession might be.[4] Instead, he wanted to make one or two bold moves during secret negotiations with Hanoi that assured a reasonable negotiated settlement to the war as quickly as possible. This was naive at best. He always feared that he would run out of time in the negotiations. He worried that Congress would substantially cut funding for the war or that the American public would demand the total withdrawal of all US troops before he could secure a safe future for South Vietnam and resurrect US international prestige and credibility. Kissinger understood that Nixon faced an increasingly hostile Congress and that the opposition controlled both houses, the first time a US president had come to power under those circumstances since Zachary Taylor did in 1849. Since taking power, Kissinger believed that escalation and coercive diplomacy were actually the best ways to quiet domestic critics, to counter the phased US troop withdrawal, and to entice Hanoi into meaningful negotiations. He also relished the idea that supporting a harder line inside the Nixon administration brought him even closer to the president at William Rogers and Melvin Laird's expense. The expanded bombing campaigns against PAVN sanctuaries in Cambodia during Nixon's first year in office were designed to show Hanoi that the US troop withdrawals were not as important as the potential US escalation of the conflict. "A bold move" of military force, Kissinger had argued, was "the only way to end the war quickly and the best way to conclude it honorably."[5] Time would prove him wrong.

Because of his decisive action against the PAVN in Cambodia and the threat to resume the air war against North Vietnam, Kissinger assumed that Hanoi would be interested in making some compromises at the meetings in Paris. He thought that his bold moves and Nixon's Silent Majority speech had taken away one of Hanoi's most important weapons in the secret talks: US public opinion. Congress, too, had been relatively quiet. Saigon's gains against the PAVN and People's Liberation Armed Forces (PLAF) inside South Vietnam also buoyed the prospects for compromise in Paris, Kissinger concluded.

Sensing Opportunity

For once, Kissinger seems to have captured Hanoi's mood perfectly. In January 1970, party leaders gathered at the Eighth Plenum of the Vietnamese Communist Party (VCP) to assess the war's progress. Many were nervous about the military gains made by the armed forces of South Vietnam. The Cambodian bombings had also set the PAVN back considerably. Le Duan, the VCP's secretary-general, convinced his fellow party members that these new developments had created unfavorable conditions for the revolution in South Vietnam.[6] The PLAF was losing control of the countryside to the Saigon government at an alarming rate, he warned. Since the 1968 Tet Offensive, the front had lost nearly half of the population formerly under its control.[7] Increased aid and material, including new heavy artillery and tanks, had given the Saigon government a momentary military advantage, and perhaps Le Duan decided the party needed to make countermoves quickly. Heeding Le Duan's warning, the party decided that it needed to "broaden" and "diversify" its response to the war.[8] "We must answer enemy attacks not only with war and political activity," they argued, "but also with diplomacy."[9] The VCP now committed itself to serious bargaining in Paris to help buy time for its military program. There was also the issue of postwar reconstruction aid that many in Hanoi's Foreign Ministry thought might bear some fruit if the negotiations were handled delicately in Paris, an option Kissinger never fully explored.

Kissinger sensed that the window for negotiations might be open for only a brief period of time, however. He worried that once Hanoi found a way to replace cadres at a faster rate in South Vietnam; it would regain territorial losses and would no longer be interested in substantive talks. He never doubted the DRV's capacity to endure the heavy bombing, even though he publicly stated that it was crippling Hanoi. The statistics from South Vietnam were "moderately encouraging," Kissinger concluded, but he also knew "that North Vietnam's confidence was unbroken."[10] Based on a series of pronouncements from PAVN General Vo Nguyen Giap, Kissinger argued that Hanoi may have temporary difficulty "in adequately maintaining its compulsory draft system" and there was little evidence to "suggest even obliquely that any new infusion of manpower is planned from North Vietnam," but that conditions could reverse themselves quickly.[11] He also feared that the contradictions in Nixon's Vietnamization strategy were all too apparent in Hanoi. Continued troop withdrawals silenced domestic critics temporarily, but Kissinger had consistently complained that they also weakened his hand. He had hoped for the best, thinking that maybe Hanoi saw that Vietnamization had actually allowed Nixon to win public support for continuing a new phase of the war, sending massive amounts of military supplies to South Vietnam while expanding the US air war. If the Nixon administration could continue to apply military pressure, maybe he could achieve a breakthrough in Paris. Kissinger always beat the familiar drum.

On January 19, 1970, Kissinger sent the president a memo highlighting the importance of negotiations and the need to keep military pressure on Hanoi. He warned that "the North Vietnamese cannot have fought for 25 years only to call it quits without another major effort."[12] And despite all the rosy predications in Washington, he pointed out that the United States had "not seen proof that [the] ARVN has really improved."[13] Despite nearly $200 million in increased funding for the South Vietnamese armed forces, Kissinger was still apprehensive that Saigon was not able to stand on its own against Communist forces. He claimed that the ARVN looked formidable on paper, but that desertion rates remained a key problem. Without American troops by their side, he wondered whether the ARVN could ever counter the "aggressive and offensive fighting spirit" of the PAVN and PLAF.[14] The ARVN was a constant source of frustration for Kissinger, and he often let that irritation out in National Security Council (NSC) meetings. He complained bitterly about the ARVN's unwillingness to take casualties and that when it did face the PAVN, it would take "a shellacking."[15]

He was even more concerned, however, that Nixon was losing faith in the value of negotiations and might shut them down completely. "I don't know what these clowns want to talk about," the president told Kissinger during a phone conversation on January 14, 1970.[16] "The line we take," Nixon warned, "is either they talk or we are going to sit it out. I don't feel this is any time for concession."[17] Kissinger conceded that Nixon might be correct; Hanoi might be entertaining the idea of negotiations to buy time so that it could rebuild the PLAF and increase PAVN infiltration into South Vietnam. But he could not tolerate the thought of Nixon's handing the war over to the military planners at the Pentagon, especially Laird, so he continually stressed to the president that the secret talks in Paris was the place where the war would end. Kissinger told Nixon that if he could meet the DRV representatives in Paris, he could "warn them and tell them if there is an offensive there will be no telling what we will do."[18] The goal was to end the war before a major PAVN offensive began. He was also desperate to revive the talks so that he could have some control over the rate of the US withdrawal and military operations, even though Laird guarded these decisions closely. Kissinger constantly worried that Vietnamization was becoming too central in Nixon's overall scheme for the war, replacing negotiations as the central way that the United States would extricate itself from Vietnam.

The president's lack of faith in negotiations was apparent in his first major foreign policy report to Congress on February 18, 1970. It was a sober assessment of the administration's foreign policy and had first been proposed by Kissinger shortly after Nixon's election. Kissinger envisioned a document that would "serve as a conceptual outline of the President's foreign policy, as a status report, and as an agenda for action." He hoped that it would "simultaneously guide our bureaucracy and inform foreign governments about our thinking."[19] What he got from Nixon instead was a vague commitment to negotiations to end the war and open-ended promises about military victory. Nixon told Congress that "peace requires a willingness to negotiate," yet concluded, "As South Vietnam grows stronger, the other side will, we hope, soon realize that it becomes ever more in their interest to negotiate a just peace."[20] Even though Kissinger had penned many of these words, he was surely disappointed by Nixon's insistence that Hanoi would negotiate only when South Vietnam could stand on its own. Kissinger was forever skeptical that that day would ever come. He disingenuously continued to prosecute the war, even to expand it, in the belief that South Vietnam was no match for the Communists militarily.

Kissinger also feared that Nixon had entered into one of his many periods of depression in early 1970, and that the president was therefore incapable of focusing on the importance of diplomacy. In his *Diaries*, Nixon chief of staff H. R. Haldeman recorded the pattern to which the chief executive repeatedly fell victim. He often followed a public victory, in this case the November 1969 Silent Majority speech, with a severe "letdown."[21] For weeks after, Nixon was not able to grasp the complexities of his own grand strategy. He often isolated himself in the White House, ruminating about his failures and insecurities. Since time was of the essence, Kissinger spent weeks stroking Nixon's bruised ego so that the president would remember the grand chess game that both had created to bring Hanoi to the bargaining table. This was no time to lose nerve, Kissinger told his aides in private, no time for Nixon to hide inside a bottle.[22]

Kissinger was troubled by all the hand-holding he had to do for Nixon. He told his aides, "It would have been very different with Rockefeller."[23] The former New York governor would have been "so much more normal" and would have immediately grasped the genius of Kissinger's strategic moves against Hanoi.[24] Instead, Kissinger had to do his job and care for Nixon's fragile emotional state. When Nixon got in one of these moods, he recalled, the president "hated to put himself in a position where he might be rebuffed."[25] He was careful not to put too much faith or substance on the line in Paris. In every negotiation, Kissinger reported, "my instructions included some expression that Nixon did not really expect success."[26] This gave Nixon the cover that his fragile ego needed and, if things should go wrong in Paris, it gave him the opportunity to tell Kissinger, "I told you so." Eventually, he agreed to allow Kissinger to meet privately with his Vietnamese counterparts, if for no other reason than to establish a record of having done so. Kissinger was thrilled. He finally had complete control over all that was important on Vietnam, despite Laird's strong fingerprints on Vietnamization. He was aware, however, that he had to show progress in the secret talks or the president would shut him down. Nixon's views toward the Paris contact would play a dramatic role in how Kissinger approached negotiations for the remainder of the war. He understood that Nixon always kept his eye on the concept of "peace with honor" that he had announced at the beginning of his presidency, even if the details of the secret meetings in Paris escaped the president.

Kissinger was eager to go to Paris in early 1970 because Hanoi had sent Le Duc Tho, a high-ranking member of the Politburo, to assist Xuan Thuy. Kissinger and his Vietnamese counterparts met three times between February 21 and April 4, 1970. Their first meeting took place at 11, rue Darthe, Choisy-le-Roi, a working-class suburb of Paris, at the residence of the DRV delegation, in what Kissinger later described in his memoirs as the "small living room" of a house "that might have belonged to a foreman in one of the factories in the district."[27] Here, Kissinger met Le Duc Tho for the first time. For the next three years, these two men would be the principal negotiators in Paris charged with finding a solution to the Vietnam War. For their efforts, Kissinger and Tho would be awarded the Nobel Prize for Peace. After their initial meeting, Kissinger described Tho this way:

> Gray-haired, dignified, rather short, invariably wore a black or brown Mao suit. His large luminous eyes only rarely revealed the fanaticism that had induced him as a boy of sixteen to join the anti-French Communist guerrillas. He was always composed; his manners, except on one or two occasions, were impeccable. He knew what he was about and served his cause with dedication and skill. That cause was to break the will of the United States, to destroy the government in Saigon it was supporting, and to establish Hanoi's rule over a country our predecessors had pledged to defend.[28]

A Habit of Misrepresentation and Revisionism

Kissinger often called his Vietnamese counterparts in the party "fanatics." He usually attributed their dedication to the revolution to some childhood trauma spurred on by French imperial actions. This is an interesting construction given the lengths that Kissinger has gone to in his own life to discredit his horrific experiences in Nazi Germany with helping to formulate his worldview. He once told historian Jeremi Suri that his childhood in Furth, Germany, had very little to do with his subsequent political and emotional development. "The political persecutions of my childhood," Kissinger assures us, "are not what control my life."[29]

But Kissinger clearly overstates the case. His views on power and democracy were certainly shaped by his European experiences as a young man. He favored the United States in the world system because American democracy also allowed for the use of its preponderant power in a realistic way. He believed that European democracies were weak—especially the Weimar Republic—and this had allowed Hitler to come power and expand his terror. The United States, in contrast, was not afraid to wield its power and take the lead in international affairs when its interests were threatened. Kissinger thought that Americans enjoyed and supported decisive leaders who understood that the world was a dangerous place. They were not all that concerned with democracy as long as fearless leaders handled real threats, as Franklin Roosevelt had done during the Second World War. Kissinger wanted to temper the progressive impulse in America that had led liberal Democrats to support nation building and anticommunism in South Vietnam, however. He was constantly reminding his critics that he had "inherited this mess" in Vietnam and that only a statesman of his caliber could extricate the United States from Southeast Asia and, at the same time, tame America's ambitions.[30] He once stated, "I am impatient with people who thought all they needed to do was make a profound proclamation that made them feel good." "I mean," he added, "I had seen evil in the world, and I knew it was there, and I knew there were some things you had to fight for, and that you cannot insist that everything be to some ideal construction that you have made."[31] This was Kissinger's central belief and it came from his understanding of Europe in the 1930s. He wanted to apply this conviction to Vietnam, and Le Duc Tho would be his partner in this enterprise.

The first meeting in Paris showed how far apart Kissinger and the Vietnamese really were on many substantive issues. But it also showed the lengths to which Kissinger was willing to go, including purposefully deceiving the president, to keep the contact alive. He constantly misrepresented the DRV's position to Nixon and to America's allies in Saigon, whom he never consulted on substantive issues. Kissinger actually conceded a number of key points during the 1970 secret talks. He covered up his deception by carefully controlling the flow of information to the president and by constantly revising the narrative of his time in office. Few public figures have gone to greater lengths to control the historical record of their time in office than Kissinger.

Indeed, Kissinger has spent much of his time out of government revising his actions inside of government. In 1979, just four years after the end of the Vietnam War, he published the first of his massive, two-volume memoirs.[32] Each volume contains over 1,500 pages of published writing and notes. In addition, Kissinger selected the passages relating most directly to the Vietnam War and published them separately in 2003, under the title *Ending the Vietnam War*.[33] In each of these books, he presents himself as a clear-eyed realist who fixed the mess in Vietnam that he had inherited from liberals in the Kennedy and Johnson administrations. He is a compelling writer, and the sheer weight of his work makes challenging him on details a daunting task. Still, fierce critics lined up when they saw that Kissinger was clearly trying to manipulate the public record. The two most interesting challenges came from two of Kissinger's former Harvard colleagues, McGeorge Bundy and Stanley Hoffmann.

Bundy, who had served as Kennedy and Johnson's national security adviser, argued that Kissinger had often offered "doubtful interpretations" of the past. He was particularly concerned about the "gravity of distortions" in Kissinger's memoir, *White House Years*.[34] Specifically, Bundy criticized Kissinger for blaming Watergate, and not his own policies, for the Vietnam debacle. He thinks Kissinger purposefully garbles the public record about conversations the Nixon administration had with the Saigon government over the DRV's violations of the 1973 peace agreement so as to mask the administration's weak position. Kissinger claims that promises made to Nguyen Van Thieu that the United States would reenter the war if Hanoi violated the agreement were real. Shortly before the final peace agreement was signed in January 1973, Kissinger drafted a letter on Nixon's behalf to President Thieu, stating, "We will respond with full force should the settlement be violated by North Vietnam."[35] After the Fall of Saigon, Kissinger claimed, "It never occurred to me that we could lose fifty thousand men and then not insist on enforcing what they had achieved."[36] But no one else inside the government knew of the promises Nixon made to Thieu. "Not even the Joint Chiefs of Staff were informed that written commitments were made to Thieu," said Admiral Elmo Zumwalt, who was commander of US naval forces in Vietnam. Making Bundy's point even more bluntly, Zumwalt said, "There are at least two words no one can use to characterize the outcome of this two-faced policy. One is 'peace.' The other is 'honor.'"[37] Bundy argues that Kissinger was playing fast and loose with the facts to hide his own role in the Vietnam fiasco. Kissinger knew that the United States would never be able to return to Vietnam after signing the 1973 peace agreement, and to say otherwise was to "seek ignoble self-protection by cursing the darkness of Watergate."[38]

Hoffmann believes that posterity was so much on Kissinger's mind when he was writing his memoirs that we have to ask whether he was "entirely candid."[39] Hoffman is particularly critical of Kissinger's handling of the war in Vietnam. He claims that Kissinger tended "to interpret America's successive [peace] proposals in such a way as to put maximum emphasis on continuity, and to present the North Vietnamese as the ones who made the decisive concessions."[40] Hoffmann goes on to suggest that it was the United States that gave up on its demands that Hanoi withdraw its troops from South Vietnam before any agreement could be signed. Kissinger's treatment of the mutual troop withdrawal is indeed problematic.[41] He also steadfastly clings to his contention that Hanoi made concessions all along and especially after the 1972 Christmas bombings (which will be discussed in a later chapter). Finally, Hoffman concludes that the memoirs are tainted with Kissinger's overall desire to be "right," arguing that this need "merges with his other unattractive bias, vindictiveness."[42] Nothing highlights Kissinger's willingness to distort the record for his own ends, and his vindictiveness, more than the secret peace talks with Le Duc Tho and Xuan Thuy in 1970.

The February Meeting

Kissinger began the first secret meeting on February 21 on the offensive. He argued that the DRV wanted to place conditions on the negotiations that guaranteed "political predominance" for the Communists in South Vietnam and "then we [the US] will rely on your good faith and self-restraint for the future."[43] He suggested that Hanoi's allies in Moscow were growing tired of these conditions and that Hanoi should be careful or it would find "that the international situation has complications which may mean that Vietnam will not enjoy the undivided support of countries which now support it."[44] He also suggested that "Hanoi's position" in South Vietnam had not improved since their previous meeting in August 1969, and hinted that the trend would continue in this direction for the foreseeable future.[45] The balance of forces in South Vietnam, Kissinger argued, did not warrant Hanoi's insistence on political preconditions. He warned that President Nixon had used his Silent Majority speech to achieve public support for the war and that Vietnamization had actually made it possible for the United States to continue to support the South Vietnamese government indefinitely, something he told Le Duc Tho, even if he did not believe it himself.

Tho and Thuy noticed a subtle, but important, shift in the American position when Kissinger began talking about the need for a mutual troop withdrawal from South Vietnam. Kissinger acknowledged that there needed to be a mutual troop withdrawal, but he also stated that the Nixon administration would not insist that North Vietnamese troops be put on the same legal standing as American forces in South Vietnam. He claimed that the United States sought "a practical, not a theoretical, end to the war."[46] In other words, he was conceding the point that North Vietnamese troops were not foreigners in South Vietnam. This was the first of many steps that Kissinger would take in regard to the North Vietnamese in South Vietnam. (The last would come in January 1973 with a peace agreement that allowed ten North Vietnamese main force infantry divisions to remain in South Vietnam after the signing of the agreement and the final US troop withdrawal.) He also insisted that Hanoi did not have to publicly announce the North Vietnamese troop withdrawal, "so long as it in fact took place."[47] Finally, he hinted that the United States would drop its insistence that North Vietnam's withdrawal from South Vietnam had to happen before the United States completed its redeployment.

To the Vietnamese, these concessions were signs that Washington had begun to see the presence of North Vietnamese troops in South Vietnam differently. Although he made no mention of it to

Kissinger, Tho told his associates in Hanoi that he thought Washington would eventually be forced to concede on the mutual troop withdrawal to end the American war.[48] North Vietnamese troops would be allowed to stay in South Vietnam, he predicted, as a result of an agreement with the United States on all other matters.[49] Kissinger always couched these "concessions" with like sacrifices from North Vietnam when reporting to the president—he would explain to Nixon that the DRV was ready to discuss its own troop withdrawals from South Vietnam—as a way to gloss over the subtle changes in what he had already said to the Vietnamese negotiators.[50] Hanoi viewed Kissinger's remarks as a sign that America's will was beginning to wane even if its commitment to punishing North Vietnam militarily was not.[51]

Following the first secret meeting, Kissinger remarkably told Nixon, "This has been an important meeting, certainly the most important since the beginning of your administration and even since the beginning of the talks in 1968."[52] Kissinger insisted that Tho "gave the impression of being much more ready for business than before,"[53] and that he was ready "to accept some rather significant changes in their position." One indication of this change, according to Kissinger, was that the North Vietnamese negotiators "dropped their demand that the GVN [South Vietnam] be changed as a precondition to substantive talks, saying that this could be discussed later."[54] Another was that "they did not use the word 'unconditional' when speaking of US withdrawals, and they did not challenge me when I said we could discuss the withdrawal of all non–South Vietnamese forces."[55] Kissinger went on to claim that North Vietnamese negotiators "stated flatly that now is the time to negotiate" and that they appeared "worried about Vietnamization."[56] Unbelievably, he told Nixon that "there are faint suggestions that they may be ready to talk seriously about troop withdrawal on a reciprocal basis."[57]

It is really difficult to fathom Kissinger's overly optimistic reporting to the president following the February 21 meeting. Although Rogers and Laird had no idea that Kissinger was meeting in secret with Hanoi's representatives in Paris, Nixon was copied on the official summaries of the meetings and could clearly see that Kissinger was making false claims, plus a handful of Americans had been in the room with Kissinger.[58] Curiously, the morning session only included a summary of the conversation, but the afternoon discussions were transcribed word for word. Taken together, these two documents, now available at the Nixon Presidential Library and Museum in Yorba Linda, California, show us that Kissinger was deliberately misleading the president on the substance of the secret talks.[59] Neither Le Duc Tho nor Xuan Thuy had announced any changes in the DRV's position. In fact, during the morning meeting, Thuy reiterated the terms he presented during the August 1969 secret talks, claiming that North Vietnam demanded a timetable for the complete withdrawal of all US troops from South Vietnam, without saying a word about redeploying Hanoi's troops fighting in South Vietnam. Not a word.

Furthermore, Tho insisted that the very first issue for the secret talks with Kissinger was the American troop withdrawals, stating, "We feel that you have not [sic] good will and are not prepared to settle the matter." The North Vietnamese negotiators also demanded that political and military matters be taken together, something Kissinger had opposed from the start. In sharp contrast to Kissinger's summary to Nixon, Thuy again insisted that "the Thieu-Ky-Khiem" regime in Saigon had to be dissolved prior to any agreement and that only a new government "without Thieu-Ky-Khiem" could bring peace to South Vietnam.[60]

Contrary to Kissinger's claims, Tho sharply criticized Vietnamization. Vietnamese sources make it clear that he saw Vietnamization as a thinly veiled device to hide a unilateral and inevitable US withdrawal. In other words, party leaders in Hanoi shared Kissinger's view that Laird's policy was undermining the US position in Vietnam. As Kissinger rightly feared, the withdrawal of US troops convinced Hanoi to endure the bombings long enough for the Nixon administration to completely withdraw from Vietnam. Tho taunted Kissinger, claiming that "we have many hardships to go through. But we have won the war. You have failed."[61] When Kissinger balked at this suggestion, Tho explained, "Before, there were over a million US and puppet troops, and you failed. How can you succeed when you let the puppet troops do the fighting? Now, with only US support, how can you win?"[62] This was hardly the language of a man who was ready to concede on any major points, at least as Kissinger presented them. He must have understood this. Almost every one of his claims to Nixon about the progress in Paris proved false.

To make matters worse, Kissinger had not consulted with South Vietnamese president Nguyen Van Thieu or any political leader from Saigon. The State Department confirmed in late 1970 that "there has been no real consultation with the GVN on settlement issues since 1968; the only subjects discussed during 1969 and 1970 have been POWs and (at present) a ceasefire."[63] Kissinger was content to speak for the US allies in Saigon because he held them in such utter contempt. Kissinger often called Thieu "an insane son of a bitch" and the rest of South Vietnam's leaders "bastards."[64] All Vietnamese, above and below the seventeenth parallel, were just a "bunch of shits," according to Kissinger.[65]

It now seems incredible that Kissinger had asked so many ordinary Americans and Vietnamese to make huge sacrifices for a government he held in such disdain. Furthermore, when the South Vietnamese government refused to follow his lead on the negotiations, he often threatened that he would seek a bilateral peace agreement with Hanoi that left Saigon out in the cold.[66] It is curious that he would not budge on the removal of a government that he did not consult, did not respect, and was easily willing to abandon. Several other Saigon political scenarios surfaced before the 1971 South Vietnamese election, but Kissinger explored none of them, remaining content to defend Thieu in Paris while criticizing his capabilities in Washington.

For his part, Thieu did not trust Kissinger or Vietnamization. He had not been consulted when Nixon adopted Laird's policy, but he was later forced to accept it in public or risk losing US aid altogether. Had he known about Kissinger's deception in Paris, Thieu would have been livid and probably would have gone public with his complaints. Thieu constantly questioned Kissinger's loyalty and worried that the American might make a separate peace with Hanoi that left South Vietnam vulnerable.[67] Even though Thieu gained some benefit from the air war over Laos, Cambodia, and North Vietnam, he detested Kissinger's management of the war. There is some indication that Thieu tried to get word to Nixon that Kissinger was not to be trusted in Paris.[68]

That begs the question: Why would Kissinger construct such an elaborate fabrication to the president of the United States? Perhaps Kissinger wanted to ensure that the secret talks in Paris (which were actually secret talks inside the secret talks taking place at avenue Kléber in Paris) replaced Vietnamization in Nixon's mind as the way the Vietnam War ended. But to cement this thinking in the president's mind, Kissinger needed to show progress in Paris. This led him to make unsubstantiated claims about progress.

The March Meeting

On March 16, Kissinger again met with Xuan Thuy and Le Duc Tho at the DRV delegation's house in Choisy-le-Roi. He began the meeting by summarizing Tho's comments from the February 21 meeting as follows: "any effort by either side to bring military pressure in Vietnam or in one of the related countries would be inconsistent with our purpose here."[69] Tho immediately challenged this, claiming that "this is a misinterpretation of what I have said," and clarified that he was only talking about "pressure in negotiations" and that military pressure would continue until an agreement was signed. Furthermore, Tho claimed that the United States was "the side which is constantly making military pressure."[70] Kissinger's effort to get a nonescalation guarantee in Paris vanished quickly. In his memoirs he wrote that his proposal was "contemptuously rejected with a pedantic lecture that every war had its high points with which it was impossible to interfere."[71] This would not be his last frustration on that day.

Kissinger also failed to extract concessions from Hanoi on the prisoner-of-war issue. In the avenue Kléber meetings, the diplomats often spoke of the mutual release of prisoners after an agreement was signed, but those talks were short on specifics. During the March 16 meeting, however, the issue formed the backdrop of Kissinger's troop withdrawal strategy: he had come to view the prisoner-of-war issue as a clever negotiating tactic by which to bring up the issue of a mutual troop withdrawal from South Vietnam. If Hanoi acknowledged that it wanted to negotiate the release of North Vietnamese troops being held in South Vietnamese prisons, then by default it had to acknowledge that its troops were fighting in South Vietnam, something that it would not do in public. This approach, Kissinger suggested, "could give us a handle for pressing the point further, thereby helping to establish one of the basic points in the Administration's policies on Vietnam."[72] According to historian Jeffrey Kimball, Kissinger hoped that he could convince Hanoi to withdraw its troops from South Vietnam and to release US prisoners of war without a political settlement, whereby the Nixon administration could declare victory: the president could boast to the American public that he had brought US troops home, secured the safety of the prisoners of war, and ended the war honorably.[73] Postwar aid could keep the Saigon government in power indefinitely, Kissinger thought.

North Vietnam was not at all interested in his complicated schemes. Le Duc Tho and Xuan Thuy rejected his proposals outright. No amount of dire military threats or shrewd negotiating tactics were going to stop Hanoi's demands that the United States must unilaterally withdraw all of its troops from South Vietnam or that a political solution involving the southern Communists in the National Liberation Front (NLF) or Provisional Revolutionary Government (PRG) was a necessity. These points were precisely why Hanoi continued to prosecute the war.

Nixon and Kissinger were deceiving themselves by engaging in such far-fetched schemes, further complicated by the fact that they made these strategic decisions in isolation. Neither consulted Congress, and Kissinger especially cut out State and Defense. Walter Isaacson, an early Kissinger biographer, believes that Nixon and Kissinger would have done themselves a favor by making their own negotiating terms and actions public: "It would have made it more difficult for critics of the war to allege that Washington was the only stubborn party."[74] But it would also have subjected them to greater public scrutiny, including their manipulation of the prisoner-of-war issue. They may also have been criticized for so narrowly defining what was acceptable in the negotiations, including their limited view of South Vietnam's political future.

Perhaps most alarming to Kissinger, however, was the realization that Saigon would have to be brought in from the cold on the secret negotiations taking place in Paris. From the moment he entered the Nixon White House, he feared that US interests in Vietnam would one day be at odds with Saigon's needs and that this would expose serious tensions within the alliance. Kissinger warned Nixon of this reality in a private memo: "The lack of an agreed position with the Government of [South] Vietnam will require you to make decisions on our position which could, if later revealed, embroil us in difficulties with Saigon. This is risky, but I see no other way to proceed if we are to maintain momentum and secrecy."[75] In other words, Kissinger purposefully kept Saigon in the dark about the content of the secret meetings taking place with Thuy and Tho. Although he later claimed, "I cabled full reports of every session by back channel to Ambassador Ellsworth Bunker in Saigon to brief Thieu,"[76] a close examination of the record reveals that these reports were often sanitized or incomplete, with Kissinger "often personally going over the memo and excising paragraphs."[77]

Nixon worried that a public fight with Saigon would cause the American public to question the US mission in Vietnam. Sooner or later, he surmised, many Americans would ask whether Thieu was worth the continued sacrifice when so many of his policies ran counter to democratic traditions. It is doubtful that Kissinger concerned himself with this issue. Keeping the negotiations secret and out of view of many in the administration and in Saigon meant that he did not have to answer such troubling questions. As long as the president was willing to allow him to meet secretly in Paris, Kissinger could continue to construct elaborate and dubious negotiating schemes. In fact, he admired Nixon for allowing him to do so. Haldeman noted that Kissinger "is fascinated by the complexity of P's [the president's] mind and approach. K [Kissinger] loves this kind of maneuver as does P, and K is amazed by P's ability at it."[78]

Kissinger asked Nixon for approval of his spring 1970 negotiating posture in a series of memorandums he sent to the president just before the second meeting with Le Duc Tho in Paris. Kissinger explained that his negotiating strategy this way: There were two basic issues in Paris: (1) mutual withdrawal of non–South Vietnamese military forces, which the United States insisted upon; and (2) a political settlement in South Vietnam, which North Vietnam required. On the troop withdrawal, Kissinger wrote to Nixon stressing that "agreement...on a verifiable mutual withdrawal is in our and the GVN's [South Vietnam's] fundamental interests; even if there is no political settlement," adding, "the North Vietnamese will almost certainly not wish to withdraw their forces until they have a good idea of the shape of the political settlement." To get Hanoi to agree to the mutual withdrawal, Kissinger suggested that the United States "put forward a precise and fairly attractive proposal for a mutual withdrawal" requiring "absolute reciprocity."[79] The only issue that really mattered to the United States, he assured the president, "was reciprocity on troop withdrawals."[80] The attractive proposal was a mutual troop withdrawal from South Vietnam on separate but concurrent schedules. Kissinger then quickly informed Nixon of everything that would quickly follow in Paris once he got agreement on the mutual troop withdrawals.

The problem for Kissinger in 1970 and throughout the negotiations was that he had nothing to deal with to get the reciprocity he so desired. The only bargaining chips he ever used were North Vietnam's desire to speed up a unilateral US troop withdrawal and the coercive threat of increased military attacks against North Vietnam. Nixon approved his negotiating strategy, however, writing a handwritten note on one of the memos that reads: "We need a breakthrough on principle and substance. Tell them we want to go immediately to the core of the problem."[81]

But the core of the problem for the United States remained the North Vietnamese troops operating in South Vietnam. Hanoi never deviated—not once—from its insistence that North Vietnamese troops had a right to be in South Vietnam and that they would remain there following any agreement. Le Duc Tho made this perfectly clear to Kissinger in meeting after meeting, beginning with their discussions on March 16. After listening to Kissinger's elaborate scheme about the concurrent withdrawal, he flatly rejected any proposal that required the North Vietnamese troops to leave South Vietnam. "But when speaking about a schedule," he explained to Kissinger, "your program shows two concurrent programs for the withdrawal of yours and North Vietnamese troops, to be completed in the same period. Therefore your proposal amounts to a mutual withdrawal." Not only did Tho insist that North Vietnamese troops would not leave South Vietnam, he complained that the US withdrawal was "withdrawal by driblets."[82]

Still, Kissinger plugged away, trying to convince Tho that he had a meaningful withdrawal schedule for the United States that the DRV could match. He even declared that the United States was now prepared to offer a specific timetable for the US troop withdrawal. "I am today prepared to present such a schedule to you," Kissinger told his Vietnamese counterparts in Paris. All US and allied troops would be withdrawn from South Vietnam "over a sixteen month period from the date of an agreement."[83] He then gave the monthly withdrawal schedule based on the number of US troops in Vietnam as of April 15, 1970. That number was 422,000. Beginning with 5,000 troops withdrawn in the first month, the United States pledged to increase its monthly redeployments to 10,000, then 27,000, then 35,000, then 40,000, until all US troops were removed from Vietnam.[84] But he was not establishing an exact timetable for the American withdrawal. What Kissinger really was doing was tying that withdrawal date to the signing of an agreement, linking Hanoi's willingness to secure a deal with the ultimate US withdrawal. That process could be sped up if Hanoi cooperated—or it could be slowed down and supported by US air attacks against important North Vietnamese assets. As Kissinger was fond of telling Tho, it was Hanoi that controlled the pace of the US troop withdrawal. Tho and Thuy sat quietly, listening to this explanation of the US withdrawal.

Then, Kissinger immediately dove into the need for North Vietnamese troops to be withdrawn from South Vietnam, Laos, and Cambodia as well. "We reach here the heart of the problem," he told his fellow diplomats. "Both Minister Xuan Thuy and Mr. Le Duc Tho said at the last meeting that a settlement had to be on the basis of reality," he stated. "I said at our last meeting that reality requires some reciprocity. It is for this that we are at these negotiations."[85] Kissinger's insistence that the DRV withdraw its troops from South Vietnam as Vietnamization was in full swing speaks directly to the weakness of the US negotiating position: he and Nixon were convinced that Hanoi would one day agree to this condition to achieve an agreement. Part of their self-deception was to consider Hanoi's refusal to agree to a mutual withdrawal a technical, rather than political, problem.

Kissinger and Nixon concurred that North Vietnamese troop withdrawals presented Hanoi with several problems, but mistakenly believed these problems could be managed in negotiations. Kissinger suggested that the United States offer a specific timetable for its own withdrawal, but "without proposing a timetable for theirs."[86] He wanted to create "two concurrent schedules" for troop withdrawals and thought that this approach would help Hanoi if the major reason for rejecting such proposals in the past had been "merely one of image."[87] He and Nixon agreed that if Hanoi rejected this proposal, North Vietnam's position "will be clear."[88] Since Hanoi had not once accepted in theory or practice that its troops in South Vietnam operated under the same moral and legal conditions as US troops, it should have come as no surprise to Kissinger that Le Duc Tho once again rejected any mention of North Vietnamese troop withdrawals during the March 16 meeting. In fact, Hanoi's representatives in Paris made the most forceful statement against this idea to date, adding that "US troops should be withdrawn within six months" and that "military problems should be linked to political problems."[89] Furthermore, Tho refused to discuss any political solution that preserved any member of the South Vietnamese government. This was a position Hanoi would stick to until it forced concessions from the Nixon administration that guaranteed North Vietnam's troops would stay in South Vietnam.

The April Meeting

The April 4 meeting did not go much better for Kissinger. Le Duc Tho insisted that the troop withdrawal deadline was "wrong" because it was longer than six months and depended on the settlement of other issues. Hanoi's negotiators asserted, again, that a mutual withdrawal was unacceptable. In fact, the entire transcript of this meeting is filled with vehement resistance to any discussion of mutual troop withdrawals. Xuan Thuy spoke at length on this topic. He told Kissinger that "the US has brought US and other foreign troops allied to the US one-half the way around the world for aggression in Vietnam. Therefore, the US must completely withdraw all US and allied troops from Vietnam without imposing conditions on the Vietnamese people."[90] He emphatically declared that "as to the Vietnamese people who are fighting on their own soil, it is the legitimate self-defense right of any nation. Therefore, the question of mutual troop withdrawal does not arise."[91] Later in the meeting, Tho drove home the point that no settlement was possible without removing "Thieu-Ky-Khiem" and other leaders "opposed to peace, independence and neutrality."[92] He clearly stated that Hanoi simply could not "accept your military or political proposals."[93]

Remarkably, two days after the April 4 meeting in Paris, Kissinger again told Nixon that the negotiations had gone well. He claimed that Tho had "indicated a readiness to discuss the with-drawal of their forces linked to ours" and that North Vietnamese negotiators "went somewhat further than before in indicating their readiness to recognize the GVN [South Vietnam]," even if they still "asked for the removal of Thieu, Khiem, and Ky."[94] Kissinger called these "two significant concessions" and suggested that Hanoi was also willing to accept the US point "that a settlement had to express the balance of political forces."[95] He led Nixon to believe, falsely, that he had done as the president wished and demanded from Hanoi a time limit for reaching a comprehensive agreement. When Hanoi refused, Kissinger claims, he broke off the talks. The transcript of the April 4 meeting clearly reveals that Tho was willing to meet Kissinger again only if "you have new proposals."[96] The meeting ended with both sides agreeing to "stay in relations" but with no new negotiations scheduled.[97]

Kissinger later confessed that he had fallen victim to Nixon's skepticism. He wanted to keep the channel alive; he concluded therefore that truthful reporting of these meetings threatened that goal because the president was not fully committed to a negotiated settlement, even if he liked the secrecy and grand strategy behind it. "I fell into the trap of many negotiators of becoming an advocate of my own negotiation," Kissinger later wrote.[98] In retrospect, he also believed that the first round of secret negotiations with Le Duc Tho in 1970 collapsed because "diplomacy always reflects some balance of forces and Tho's assessment was not wrong."[99] In other words, Kissinger fully understood that Hanoi was not going to concede any of its main points because it thought that the United States was in an untenable position. If Washington could not inflict its will on Hanoi with over 500,000 US troops in South Vietnam, how was it going to succeed when it was forced to withdraw those troops because the American public demanded it? How could Washington ask Saigon to do alone what they could not do together? Kissinger shared these fears, and occasionally he shared them with the president.

After the collapse of the secret negotiations in early April 1970, then, Kissinger's goal was to try to change the balance of forces in South Vietnam to the advantage of the Saigon government while recognizing that the US would continue to withdraw its troops. He explored no other options because he was still committed to using US hard power assets to end the war through negotiations. Thus, he helped Nixon develop a new, two-part strategy to accomplish this task. The first part was to publicly claim support for in an in-place cease-fire that supported the territorial status quo. The second was to expand the war into Cambodia to cripple Hanoi's ability to infiltrate troops and supplies into South Vietnam, hoping that this would force the DRV to bend the knee. For the remainder of 1970 and 1971, Kissinger embraced this new strategy.

Target: Cambodia

On April 20, 1970, during one of his many public speeches on Vietnam, President Nixon told the American people that "no progress has taken place on the negotiating front."[100] He explained that Hanoi still insisted that the United States "unilaterally and unconditionally withdraw all American forces" and that "we overthrow the elected Government of South Vietnam," allowing the NLF to come to power in Saigon.[101] He then described what his administration had been doing to end the war, claiming that it had left no stone unturned. The United States, he said, had "stopped the bombing of North Vietnam," had withdrawn US forces from South Vietnam, had "dealt with the National Liberation Front as one of the parties to the negotiations," and agreed in principle to "removal of all of our forces from Vietnam."[102] And still, Nixon complained, "there is no progress at the negotiating table."[103] To get things moving in Paris (he meant the secret meetings between Kissinger and Tho), Nixon announced for the first time that the only way forward in Vietnam was "a fair political solution" that should "reflect the existing relationship of political forces within South Vietnam."[104] He surprised many in Congress by supporting "shaping machinery that would fairly apportion political power in South Vietnam."[105]

That machinery would be a standstill cease-fire that granted control over territory held without granting any seats in a coalition government in Saigon. In other words, the Nixon administration was willing to concede PRG/NLF control only over territories it already controlled in South Vietnam. The president was not at all interested, however, in giving the Communists uncontested seats in the Saigon government. His administration used this concession to quiet its domestic critics, especially in Congress, but few took the bait. Most understood that Nixon's plan would give the Saigon government preponderant power because it held the cities and the national government. The NLF's control of South Vietnam was at an all-time low, and the ARVN's pacification program had emptied the countryside. Under these conditions, Nixon was willing to concede territory under the NLF's control because that territory was limited and did not threaten Saigon. Nguyen Van Thieu quickly supported Nixon's plan, claiming that "sometimes you have to give up a leg to save the body."[106]

But Hanoi rejected Nixon's overture outright. Party leaders understood that the Communists had suffered a series of military setbacks caused in part by Saigon's deadly pacification program in the countryside, which was killing nearly twenty-five thousand NLF cadres per year. Communist losses translated into a rapid depopulation of the countryside. The intense use of firepower to achieve the pacification program's goals made village life untenable. Vietnamese peasants flooded the cities to find safety and security, leaving the countryside a depopulated area in Saigon's control. According to most reliable statistics, only 20 percent of the total population of South Vietnam lived in cities in 1960. That number swelled to 43 percent by 1971. Kissinger and Nixon's plan was to take advantage of this forced urbanization by calling for a standstill cease-fire and territorial control. It was a thinly veiled attempt to grant Saigon control over previously held NLF territory by taking a snapshot of a temporary reality. The Communists rejected the move. Kissinger therefore turned his attention to Cambodia.

On March 18, 1970, Colonels Lon Nol and Sirik Matak overthrew the long-standing leader of Cambodia, Prince Norodom Sihanouk. Since coming to power in 1954, Sihanouk had pledged Cambodian neutrality in the war in neighboring South Vietnam. Once Hanoi decided to try to oust Ngo Dinh Diem, Cambodia had been used as a staging and supply sanctuary for North Vietnamese troops, and even sometimes for southern Communist forces belonging to the PRG/NLF. Sihanouk had routinely claimed that Cambodia was a small country and was doing the best it could to remove foreign troops from its soil. Successive US administrations wondered just how devoted to neutrality Sihanouk actually was, often charging him with conspiracy.

Although there is no documentary evidence linking Nixon or Kissinger directly to Sihanouk's overthrow, both certainly welcomed the coup. Kissinger wrote Nixon that Lon Nol had sharp disagreements with Sihanouk over the presence of PAVN troops in Cambodia and that he would be a faithful ally. Lon Nol's staunch opposition to Hanoi "will create serious problems for the VC/NVA," Kissinger claimed, "which will have considerable reason to take a more hostile line toward Cambodia."[107] Nixon immediately approved substantial covert aid to the new Cambodian government to shore it up against an obvious hostile response to the coup from Hanoi. The White

House also continued Operation Menu air attacks, and the president ordered that US military leaders plan for joint US-Saigon attacks on PAVN sanctuaries. Much to Kissinger's delight, he also demanded that the administration "dust off the seven-day plan for attacks in North Vietnam."[108] Operation Duck Hook was back on the table as an escalation option.

For the next month, Kissinger carefully coordinated the military offensives in Cambodia. He managed the B-52 strikes and Lon Nol's attacks on the sanctuaries. He advised Nixon that the United States had to do more, however, if it was to save the Lon Nol government, fearing that Hanoi "cannot tolerate the loss of its Cambodian sanctuaries, and must do something to remove the Lon Nol government or force a change in Phnom Penh's policies."[109] He urged the president to move quickly. "The United States could not stand by and watch the Cambodian collapse and ultimately the collapse of the US effort in Vietnam."[110] Toward the end of April, Nixon received an intelligence report suggesting that Hanoi "was moving to isolate Phnom Penh," so as to "bring military pressure on it from all sides, and perhaps, ultimately, to bring Sihanouk back."[111] Kissinger backed up this reporting with some intelligence analysis of his own. If Cambodia fell to the Communists, he warned, it would lead to "a profound psychological shock in South Vietnam" and Hanoi's victory would make it impossible for Saigon to "preserve itself against pressures from all sides without a very large continuing presence of US forces." Most important, American credibility, something always at the top of the list of the national security adviser's concerns, would be shattered because "in the rest of Asia, there would be a feeling that Communism was on the march and we were powerless to stop it."[112]

Nixon shared Kissinger's concerns over Cambodia. "I think we need a bold move in Cambodia," he wrote Kissinger on April 22, "to show that we stand with Lon Nol."[113] General Abrams agreed.

For years, Abrams had been eager to attack North Vietnam's sanctuaries inside Cambodia, and now that Sihanouk was gone, there was little fear about violating Cambodian neutrality. Instead, attacks inside Cambodia could now be justified on the grounds that the United States was helping a new government and easing the military threat against South Vietnam. Hitting North Vietnamese troops inside Cambodia might also save American lives. Nixon therefore quickly endorsed a Defense Department proposal that South Vietnamese troops attack a North Vietnamese sanctuary inside the Parrot's Beak, a part of Cambodia that jutted out into South Vietnam only 30 miles from Saigon. The United States would provide cross-border artillery support and increased military aid to the Lon Nol government. The attacks would be swift, overwhelming, and were designed to end "the policy of minimalism and neutrality."[114] Laird supported the proposal because no American units or advisers would cross the border. If the operation demanded it, Laird could authorize US tactical air support, but only after consulting Abrams.

Without Laird's knowledge, however, Nixon revealed to Kissinger and General Wheeler that the attacks on the Parrot's Beak were only the first phase of allied cross-border operations in Cambodia he was planning. Two days later, on April 24, the president met in secret with Kissinger and a handful of military leaders to discuss a second phase that included a combined US and ARVN operation against base area 352/353 and an area known as the "Fishhook" because of its geographic footprint. The mission's purpose was to destroy Central Office South Vietnam (COSVN) headquarters and the complex of logistics facilities, ammunition depots, and POW camps in the area. Nixon was nearly obsessed with wiping out COSVN headquarters, which he often called the "Communists' Pentagon."[115] Kissinger later falsely reported that his commitment to the invasion of Cambodia came hesitantly and belatedly, and only after he was convinced that Hanoi wanted to march on Lon Nol's government. In fact, Kissinger was a key proponent of the Cambodian attacks. He played a far more active role in the decision to involve US troops than he allowed at the time or since. He told Nixon that he thought the attacks in the Fishhook should begin right after the ARVN launched its solo attack on the Parrot's Beak.[116] General Wheeler, chair of the Joint Chiefs of Staff, agreed. Wheeler had been in on the planning of the Cambodian invasion in private sessions with Nixon and Kissinger throughout April.

On the afternoon of April 26, Nixon finally called Rogers and Laird into a meeting at the White House to inform them of the invasion plan. That morning, Kissinger reminded the president that "care should be exercised at today's meeting not to surface the fact that General Wheeler has been conducting intensified planning to implement the attacks on base areas 352/353 without the full knowledge of the Secretary of Defense."[117] Rarely did Kissinger allow such a naked power grab to enter the public record, but there are few other ways to interpret his actions in the Cambodian planning than to conclude that he was still desperately trying to diminish Laird's influence in making Vietnam policy.[118] At the same time, Nixon and Kissinger believed that attacks inside Cambodia would convince Hanoi "that we are still serious about our commitment in Vietnam."[119] The Cambodian incursion, therefore, met two of Kissinger's policy criteria: it isolated Laird and conditioned the secret talks in Paris. That it did not lead to a better outcome in South Vietnam is a tragedy.

During the meeting, Laird and Rogers raised strong objections to the plan. Laird objected to the use of American troops inside Cambodia, and Rogers thought that the attacks would threaten the public support Nixon had built up for his Vietnam policies following the Silent Majority speech. They both warned that Congress would not sit still for an invasion of Cambodia. Nixon expected strong criticism from Congress, he told his two aides, but he believed he could quiet his critics on Capitol Hill if "he can get it [the Vietnam War] wound up this year." Nixon thought that such decisive action in Cambodia would allow him "to keep enough pressure on," and if the United States did not "crumble at home," the war could end on honorable terms.[120] His meaning here is hard to gauge. He periodically alternated between believing that the war would end through Kissinger's negotiations in Paris, or it would end in some decisive military action. His madman strategy reflected this duplicity. This vacillation no doubt added to Kissinger's problems. But on Cambodia they agreed. The United States could condition the negotiations in Paris, strike a military blow against Hanoi, support the South Vietnamese government, and maybe save some American lives, all by attacking North Vietnamese sanctuaries and COSVN headquarters inside Cambodia's border.

The next day, Nixon met with his top national security advisers again to go over the final plans for the Cambodian attacks. During this April 27 meeting, Laird told him that repeated attacks on Cambodia would stretch an already thin Defense budget to its breaking point. He also warned the president that public outcry could play into Hanoi's "waiting game."[121] If the American public reacted negatively to the Cambodian invasion, Laird said, Hanoi would simply wait until public opinion forced Nixon to speed up the US troop withdrawal. The entire plan was counter to US strategic goals, Laird concluded. (His fears proved prescient.) Nixon would have no part of Laird's pessimism. Not only did the president approve the two Cambodian attacks on April 28, he reserved the right to order new attacks on a case-by-case basis.

Kissinger's role in the planning of the two Cambodian invasions has long been in doubt because both he and Nixon went to great lengths to conceal their secret plans. Nixon in fact asked Kissinger to step out of the April 28 meeting so that it did not appear to Rogers and Laird that he was conspiring with his national security adviser over Cambodia. Nixon provided even more cover for his secret plotting with Kissinger when he told Laird and Rogers that he was moving forward with the Fishhook invasion plan even though "Dr. Kissinger was leaning against it."[122] But the record is clear; Kissinger supported the two-phased attacks on Cambodia from the very beginning.

For reasons only he could fathom, Nixon felt compelled to inform the American people of his plans for attacks on Cambodian soil. Against the advice of all of his advisers, he argued that such a bold and brazen act needed to be explained. Once again his political instincts betrayed him. He never anticipated the national outrage that his speech or actions would evoke. Nixon appeared on television on April 30, to explain that the United States would not act "like a pitiful, helpless giant" in the face of North Vietnamese efforts to undermine Lon Nol and use Cambodia as a staging area for further attacks against Americans in South Vietnam.[123] Appearing nervous and sweaty, the president pointed to a map of Cambodia and explained that the goal was to "attack the headquarters of the entire communist military operation in South Vietnam."[124] He then uttered a bold-faced lie: "For five years," he claimed, "neither the United States nor South Vietnam has moved against those enemy sanctuaries because we did not wish to violate the territory of a neutral nation."[125] He purposefully did not mention that Kissinger had been carefully planning and coordinating the secret Menu bombings of those sanctuaries for over a year. Kissinger did nothing to dissuade the public of this erroneous view. Indeed, he told the press the same lie later that evening.

The fallout from the Cambodian invasion was swift. As journalist Walter Isaacson astutely noted, "The domestic calm that had been purchased by troop withdrawals was quickly shattered."[126] On May 4, at Kent State University near Cleveland, Ohio, young National Guardsmen fired into an unarmed crowd of students who were protesting the Cambodian invasion, killing four and wounding several others. Ten days later, police fired upon students at Jackson State in Mississippi who were protesting the war and racial injustice. Two students died and several more were wounded. Massive protests erupted on hundreds of college campuses. At several major universities, research buildings and ROTC offices were attacked as symbols of complicity with the widening war. Over 100,000 protestors marched on the White House on May 8, forcing the police to build a bus barricade to keep the crowd away from the president. Journalist Tom Wicker spoke for many when he wrote that the invasion of Cambodia confirmed that Nixon "does not have and never has had a plan to end the war."[127]

The president did not handle the protests or criticism well. Telephone logs show that he spent much of his time phoning aides, especially Kissinger, whom he called eight times on the evening of May 8 alone. Transcripts from these calls reveal that Nixon was belligerent, defiant, and vengeful. He ordered Kissinger to fire "everyone of those son of bitches," referring to the foreign-service officers who had signed a letter of protest against the Cambodian invasion.[128] Nixon called the protestors "bums," claiming that they were fortunate to be in college. When nearly forty university presidents signed a letter calling for an American withdrawal from Vietnam, Kissinger told Nixon that they were "a disgrace."[129] Still, Kissinger spent much of May meeting with college students and administrators, trying to calm nerves. He had little success.

Kissinger's trouble stretched from college campuses into his own office. During the deliberations over Cambodia, he had asked his staff to develop plans for the invasion. William Watts, a Kissinger staffer, told his boss that he objected to the policy and could not work on it. Kissinger told Watts that he was not surprised, since his views had always represented "the cowardice of the Eastern establishment."[130] Watts resigned.

Despite the defections from his own staff, Kissinger's biggest concern was the congressional response to Cambodia. He had long feared that Congress would simply cut funding for Vietnam or pass legislation demanding an immediate US withdrawal. He always saw his secret negotiations in Paris as a race against time. Time seemed to be running out when on May 1, Senator Frank Church (D–ID) declared that it was now time for the Nixon administration to "acknowledge the futility of our continued military intervention in Vietnam," and admit "the impossibility of sustaining at any acceptable cost an anticommunist regime in Saigon, allied with, dependent on, and supported by the United States." Vietnam was, Church concluded, "a war without end." The time was right for "Congress to draw the line against an expanded American involvement in this widening war" and to begin "to put an end to it."[131] Senator John Sherman Cooper (R–KY) joined Church in introducing an amendment to demand the removal of all American troops from Cambodia by June 30 and requiring congressional approval before troops could be sent there again. The Cooper-Church Amendment was the first of many steps taken by Congress to claw foreign policy back from an imperious president. The next came from Senators George McGovern (D–SD) and Mark Hatfield (R–OR), who introduced their own amendment calling for the removal of all American troops from Vietnam by the end of 1970.

Kissinger saw both efforts as an "unnecessary restriction" to Nixon's role as commander in chief.[132] Kissinger prepared Nixon for a May 4 meeting with members of Congress (the same day as the Kent State attacks), writing that the incursion into Cambodia was not a new war; rather, a response to the needs of the current war in Vietnam. "The action in Cambodia should not be viewed as an independent use of the US armed forces involved in the general question of the president's responsibility to Congress under the power to declare war. It should be defended as a Presidential action under his Constitutional authority to take all reasonable action to protect our troops." Kissinger concluded that the Cooper-Church Amendment was unconstitutional because "only the President is constitutionally empowered to deploy American forces in the field."[133]

Kissinger spent much of May lobbying Congress. He claimed that passage of Cooper-Church would signal to America's allies that the United States could not be trusted to live up to its security guarantees. International credibility had always been important to him, but now it had taken on a sense of urgency. He told his aides that he feared Cooper-Church would pass and therefore undo all the progress that he had made in Paris.[134] This was hyperbole, of course, because there had been no progress in Paris. Eventually, Kissinger did convince some Democrats to vote against the amendment, but the Nixon White House still feared its passage. The Hatfield-McGovern Amendment simply did not have the votes. Boxed into a corner by a bipartisan amendment, the president felt he had no choice but to slowly withdraw American troops from Cambodia. He announced that all US forces would be out of Cambodia by June 30, but he put a Nixon-like spin on it. US troops would be withdrawn, he explained, because the Cambodian invasion was "the most successful operation of this long and difficult war." He explained that American and South Vietnamese forces had "captured and destroyed far more in war material than we anticipated; and American and allied casualties have been far lower than expected." The invasion had done its job, he concluded; it had "eliminated an immediate danger to the security of the remaining Americans in Vietnam" and it had won "some precious time for the South Vietnamese."[135] Nixon made no mention of the protests or congressional opposition.

Despite the announced withdrawal of American troops from Cambodia, the Senate still voted to support the Cooper-Church Amendment on June 30 by a vote of 58–37. The House rejected the amendment, however, allowing the Nixon administration to continue air operations in Cambodia (Menu) and send money and supplies to Lon Nol. It was the first time Congress had come close to restricting the president's hand during the war, but it would not be the last. Kissinger later defended the administration's decision to invade Cambodia this way: "What we faced was a painful, practical decision: whether the use of American troops to neutralize the sanctuaries for a period of eight weeks was the best way to maintain the established pace and security of our exit from Vietnam and prevent Hanoi from overrunning Indochina. Reasonable men might differ; instead, rational discussion ended."[136] In the final analysis, he found the "merits of the case" to invade Cambodia "overwhelming" because he thought it strengthened his hand in Paris.[137]

By the summer of 1970, it was clear that Kissinger's hopes for a quick settlement to the war had vanished. He was now forced to develop a plan that could pressure Hanoi into restarting negotiations in Paris. Military attacks could condition the talks, Kissinger thought, but they could not deliver the knock-out blow. He would have to negotiate a settlement to the war while US troops were leaving Vietnam by the tens of thousands. Vietnamization had placed serious hardships in Kissinger's path, and the Cambodian invasion had rekindled the antiwar movement and awakened the sleeping Congress. It would now be more difficult to negotiate an honorable peace with Hanoi than it was when Kissinger had first come to the White House. Still, the administration stuck to its clumsy formula about troop withdrawals, the Saigon government, and coercive threats.

CHAPTER FOUR

THE STANDSTILL CEASE-FIRE, 1970–1971

"THE DECISION TO PROPOSE a standstill cease-fire in 1970," Kissinger wrote in his postwar memoir, "thus implied the solution of 1972. That North Vietnamese forces would remain in the South was implicit in the standstill proposal; no negotiation would be able to remove them if we had not been able to expel them by force of arms."[1] A mutual troop withdrawal was one of the cornerstones of his war for peace, and he abandoned it rather casually in 1970 and without consulting Saigon. The end result was an unmitigated disaster for South Vietnam.

The idea of a standstill cease-fire had circulated in Washington since the Nixon administration took power in January 1969. Previously, Nixon and the South Vietnamese government had rejected such proposals, Nixon agreeing with his South Vietnamese allies that a standstill cease-fire placed Saigon at a distinct disadvantage militarily because it was impossible to monitor the PLAF's movements. Outside of South Vietnam, several high-ranking US military officials also doubted that the Army of the Republic of Vietnam (ARVN) could hold its own against superior North Vietnamese troops. But American troop with-drawals were forcing the US hand and Kissinger worried that "a strategy of relying on Vietnamization" would "not be compatible in-definitely with a strategy of negotiations."[2] He feared that the United States would lose its bargaining chip of troop withdrawals long before the negotiations needed to ensure Saigon's future would be complete. Time was always on his mind, and there simply was not enough of it.

In late May 1970, Kissinger's war research team, the Vietnam Spe-cial Studies Group (VSSG), produced a study exploring a variety of cease-fire options and the path of future negotiations in Paris. This study was kicked around the National Security Council for months until it was finally the subject of a meeting on July 21, 1970. Kissinger concluded from this meeting that the United States had three broad choices: "1) Concentrate on disengagement and leave the question of political settlement entirely to the North and South Vietnamese; 2) Make a major effort to seek a political settlement and hinge our withdrawals on this objective; and 3) Continue on a middle course, withdrawing while attempting to build South Vietnamese strength and meanwhile seeking a political resolution."[3] He told Nixon that a cease-fire was the "most important single proposal to move to-ward a settlement" and that it also had great "public relations effect here and throughout the world."[4] Yet, he ultimately recommended that Nixon "not make any decision on a cease-fire proposal" at this time.[5] Kissinger wanted the president to wait until the new ambas-sador at large for negotiations, David Bruce, was well established in Paris. Hanoi had long insisted that the Nixon administration was not serious about ending the war because it had not replaced Henry Cabot Lodge Jr. as chief negotiator for the US at the avenue Kléber secret peace talks. Appointing Bruce was an important move in the eyes of the North Vietnamese leadership, Kissinger had concluded, and he thought that it might even condition the secret talks in Choisy-le-Roi.

Bruce had had a distinguished career in the Foreign Service before Nixon named him to his new post. At the dawn of the Cold War, in 1948, President Harry S. Truman had sent Bruce to Paris as US ambassador. Truman's secretary of state Dean Acheson claimed that "it is no exaggeration to say that not since Benjamin Franklin had anyone been closer to or more understanding of the French situation."[6] President Eisenhower named Bruce US ambassador to West Germany in 1957 during a crucial moment in the Cold War. Bruce was not as well liked in Germany—many feared he was too much a Francophile—but he was effective. Eisenhower praised Bruce for his calmness in one of the most severe stress points of the confrontation with the Soviet Union. Bruce returned from Bonn in time for the 1960 presidential election. An early supporter of John F. Kennedy, Bruce was severely criticized by some in Washington for his large campaign donations to the Democratic Party. After his election victory, Kennedy briefly considered Bruce for the position of secretary of state. Many of Kennedy's closest advisers feared that Bruce, then aged sixty-three, was too old to keep up with the best and brightest Kennedy brought into the administration. Bruce instead was given the US ambassadorship to Great Britain in 1961, a position he held until Nixon's inauguration in January 1969. Bruce assumed his long tenure with the State Department was over until he got the call from Nixon to go again to Paris in the summer of 1970.

Bruce was an inspired choice to lead the negotiations at avenue Kléber. Kissinger was especially pleased by it. Bruce had written a book about the earliest US presidents, and Kissinger claimed that its author's admirers found in Bruce "many of the same sturdy qualities."[7] Most telling, however, was his description of Bruce: "Handsome, wealthy, emotionally secure, he was free of that insistence on seeing their views prevail through which lesser men occasionally turn public service into ego trips."[8] In other words, Bruce was going to be the perfect complement to Kissinger's secret negotiations, where the real work was done out of sight, in Choisy-le-Roi. Or at least that is what he believed at the time. Once established, Bruce reported that he supported Kissinger's standstill cease-fire.

September Meetings

Kissinger put forward the formal cease-fire proposal in Paris on September 7, in a meeting with Xuan Thuy. Le Duc Tho was not present for the discussions, making Kissinger all the more skeptical of good results. Kissinger doubted that Hanoi would accept the cease-fire, but he told Nixon it would test North Vietnam's willingness to "settle for anything less than total victory."[9] He told several journalists that Hanoi's "demands were absurd," but that the cease-fire proposal "might shut up some in this country."[10] After announcing his willingness to abide by a standstill cease-fire, Kissinger warned the North Vietnamese: "We are nearing the time when the chances for a negotiated settlement will pass. After a certain point you will have in effect committed yourself to a test of arms. I do not want to predict how this test against a strengthened South Vietnam, supported by us, will end nor how long it will last. But you must recognize that it will make any settlement with the United States increasingly difficult."[11] But Thuy countered with a telling statement of his own: "We are not afraid of threats. Prolongation of fighting doesn't frighten us. Prolongation of negotiations doesn't frighten us. We are afraid of nothing."[12]

Sensing that he was losing the moment, Kissinger then announced that the United States was ready to announce a twelve-month schedule of troop withdrawals and would make a promise to leave no residual American forces or bases in South Vietnam after the war. This was a major concession, according to Kissinger. "No other ally of the United States—not Europe, or Korea, or Japan—had been asked to defend themselves entirely by their own efforts," he later said of the total

US troop withdrawal. He also repeated the Nixon administration's desire to create an international conference that would oversee all-South Vietnamese elections. The United States would not, however, "agree to change leaders of SVN [South Vietnam] beforehand."[13] Kissinger then conceded that the National Liberation Front (NLF) was a reality and that "we should agree to recognizing that all political forces existing in SVN [South Vietnam] were realities."[14] Elections in South Vietnam following an agreement "would offer opportunities for each side to achieve whatever popular support it could muster," but there could be no political guarantees about the election outcome for any of the participants.[15] But a political guarantee had been precisely what Nixon and Kissinger had promised the South Vietnamese government. A political guarantee and a mutual troop withdrawal were the most important elements of Kissinger's war for peace, and now both were in jeopardy.

Yet Hanoi flatly rejected the standstill cease-fire proposal of September 7. The North Vietnamese leadership argued that the proposal would restrict People's Liberation Armed Forces (PLAF) troops to areas they presently controlled without assuring them any role in a political settlement, no matter what Kissinger said about the postwar government in Saigon. Since South Vietnam had gained the military advantage in 1970, a temporary condition according to party leaders, there could be no deal. Thuy also dismissed the significance of Bruce's appointment in Paris, stating that the new ambassador did not represent a significant policy change in Washington. He condemned the United States for using force in Cambodia to press Hanoi at the negotiating table. Finally, Thuy reiterated Hanoi's long-standing position that before it would sign any agreement, Nguyen Van Thieu and the rest of the South Vietnamese political leadership had to be replaced.[16] A frustrated Kissinger asked Thuy, "If Mr. Nixon asks me, and surely he will, what I have achieved coming here and whether the minister has said anything different from what was said at Kléber street, what answer should I give him?"[17] Thuy told Kissinger that Nixon had nothing new to say, particularly in connection with political issues, and therefore "minister Xuan Thuy did not say anything new either."[18] Kissinger concluded that for Hanoi, even a unilateral US withdrawal was not enough. Party leaders demanded that the United States also engineer a "political turnover before we left."[19]

Hanoi's hardline position during the September 7 meeting was no doubt designed to force more Kissinger concessions. If he was already waffling on a mutual troop withdrawal and he was willing to recognize the political legitimacy of the NLF/PRG (Provisional Revolutionary Government), perhaps the North Vietnamese could also get the United States to give up on the Saigon government altogether to achieve a timely end to the war. Hanoi's leadership also wanted to press Kissinger on the neutrality of Cambodia and Laos and force the erasure of the Demilitarized Zone (DMZ) as an international border. All these goals could be accomplished, Hanoi concluded, if North Vietnam could simply outlast the US military assaults and allow domestic US political pressure to mount, forcing more compromises in Paris.

Shortly after the September 7 meeting, Nguyen Thi Binh, the PRG's foreign minister and delegate in Paris, announced a new, eight-point peace program designed to push Kissinger even further in this direction. Kissinger claims that Thuy had not mentioned the PRG's peace proposal during their September 7 meeting, proving that Hanoi was "more interested in propaganda than in negotiations."[20] The record seems to support this claim, though Binh's announcement had been planned for months and was part of a much larger diplomatic offensive. At the core of the PRG's proposal was the promise that Communist forces would refrain from attacking departing US troops and that Hanoi would begin immediate negotiations on the release of American POWs in exchange for the withdrawal of all US troops and allied forces by June 30, 1971. Of all of Hanoi's first principles in the negotiations, getting a fixed date on the final US withdrawal was the most important—naturally because an announced fixed date of withdrawal would have given Hanoi everything it needed to take Saigon by force. It would have been impossible for the Nixon administration to go back on a publicly announced withdrawal date, and so Kissinger purposefully never gave one. Still, this new timetable brought the PRG's public demands for a complete withdrawal more in line with what Hanoi's negotiators had been insisting upon in Paris for months.

Most important to Kissinger, the PRG statement still demanded the ouster of Thieu, Ky, and Khiem, something that the US simply could not support. Binh's announcement also reinforced several long-standing party principles, including "free" elections in South Vietnam supervised by an interim coalition government (the PRG, neutralists "standing for peace, independence, neutrality and democracy," and members of the Saigon government other than almost anyone currently holding political power), and the gradual reunification of Vietnam through negotiations between the Vietnamese themselves without American interference. Binh's Eight Points moved Hanoi's hardline position on the composition of the coalition government just enough to tantalize Kissinger, but the party remained committed to its conviction that domestic pressures would eventually force an American withdrawal.

Kissinger was apoplectic when he heard the new PRG proposal. On the surface, the nine-month timetable appeared to be a Hanoi concession, since Xuan Thuy and Le Duc Tho had previously demanded a six-month timetable, but the clock started immediately on the nine-month proposal and not when an agreement was signed. He was also leery of the PRG's makeup of the coalition government. He bitterly complained that this coalition government would have been hand-picked by Hanoi and was to be provisional. Its final job was to negotiate a settlement with the PRG. "After we had overthrown our own allies," Kissinger wrote in his memoirs, "a

Communist-dominated government was to negotiate with the Communists to decide South Vietnam's future."[21] He rejected Hanoi's "version of a fair negotiated outcome," hoping to place the blame for the lack of progress in the peace talks squarely on the Communists.[22]

Following the September 7 meeting with Thuy, Kissinger remarkably reported to the president once again that he was optimistic about the progress of negotiations in Paris and that he saw signs of flexibility in the PRG's new peace program. Again it appears that Kissinger put the best face on the substance of his secret negotiations so as to keep Nixon committed to the process. He worried that continued bad news and a lack of progress might convince the president to scrap the secret talks altogether. Therefore, in a private memorandum to Nixon dated September 17, Kissinger suggested that there were indeed "two new elements" in the PRG's proposal that showed promise. The first was "the suggestion that they will talk to us about POWs"; and the second, the "lengthening of the schedule for our withdrawal to nine months." Kissinger was not forthcoming about the start date of the timetable. He concluded that the PRG's proposal was probably "intended to generate maximum impact in the U.S.," but that it should still be explored to "see how much flexibility is behind their schedule and the degree to which we can separate their hard demands for our unilateral withdrawal from our desire to pursue other subjects."[23] He followed this hopeful report with an even more positive analysis of the PRG proposal to Nixon on September 22, in which he claimed that the new PRG proposal was "less assertive" than earlier Communist proposals. Specifically, the PRG peace plan implied that the United States "can quickly and painlessly extricate ourselves from Vietnam if we will only...set a withdrawal date." Kissinger also claimed that there was no "assertion that we must 'renounce' Thieu-Ky-Khiem, as the Communists had frequently demanded."[24]

Despite Kissinger's enthusiasm, Nixon harbored grave doubts about the secret peace contacts. The president had always been pessimistic about Hanoi's motivation for meeting Kissinger secretly. He also had deep reservations about the standstill cease-fire. He recognized its tremendous propaganda value, but was unsure whether Kissinger was the right messenger. To truly gain the public relations value of the cease-fire proposal, Nixon thought that he might have to use the bully pulpit of the presidency to publicly announce his new concession. Kissinger worried that Nixon might use the proposal as a measure to keep the antiwar movement and Congress off his back and nothing more. Following the Cambodian invasion, Nixon had retreated inside the White House, a move that worried Kissinger greatly. "Within the iron gates of the White House, quite unknowingly, a siege mentality was setting in," Charles Colson, Nixon's special counsel, later explained. "It was now 'us' against 'them.' Gradually, as we drew the circle closer around us, the ranks of 'them' began to swell."[25] Kissinger worked very hard to be in the "us" group, even though he often felt slighted by the president.

Kissinger, of course, saw this development firsthand and was convinced once again that Nixon's dark moods might threaten the peace talks. He knew that the president was prone to view life as a series of disappointments punctuated by minor successes—it was in his nature to "brood alone" and to believe that "every success brings a terrific letdown."[26] He captured Nixon in this period in his memoir, writing that "Nixon would be sitting solitary and withdrawn, deep in his brown stuffed chair with his legs on a hassock in front of him, a small reading light breaking the darkness, and a wood fire throwing shadows on the wall of the room. The loudspeakers would be playing romantic classical music, probably Tchaikovsky."[27] The loneliness and despair of Richard Nixon would play a role in the secret talks, and Kissinger believed that he needed to manage the president carefully.

But Nixon did not always want to be managed. He sensed that Kissinger did not always see the big picture clearly. With the 1970 midterm elections approaching, the first referendum on the Nixon presidency, the message on Vietnam had to be clear and consistent. Nixon confided in his chief of staff, H. R. Haldeman, that he often caught Kissinger bluffing.[28] Nixon was also worried that Kissinger's rivalry with Rogers was having a negative impact on the administration, largely because Kissinger was so "jealous of any idea not his own."[29] Nixon wondered out loud whether Kissinger had "reached the end of his usefulness."[30] Haldeman responded that Kissinger was indeed "obsessed with these weird personal delusions" and that he did not think this was "curable."[31] Nixon suggested that Kissinger's secret talks in Paris might have to come to an end because it was getting increasingly difficult to keep them from Rogers. Then again, Nixon could always replace Rogers as secretary of state, as he often threatened to do.

Kissinger hoped that a second meeting in Paris would brighten Nixon's mood and restore the president's faith in his national security adviser and the peace process. As Kissinger left for Paris for a September 27 meeting with Le Duc Tho and Xuan Thuy, he had no way of knowing that Democratic Republic of Vietnam (DRV) premier Pham Van Dong had met secretly with Chinese premier Zhou Enlai. Dong told his benefactor that Hanoi held no illusions about the secret talks with Kissinger in Paris. He believed that the United States still held out hope for a military victory and was not yet ready to concede defeat. He believed that Nixon was using the peace talks at avenue Kléber and his public pronouncements on the diplomatic effort to end the war "to deceive the world."[32] Still, Dong reported, Hanoi saw "some advantages of the diplomatic struggle."[33] The goal was to win support among moderates in South Vietnam and influence "the antiwar public opinion in the US."[34] Zhou promised China's continued support in Vietnam's revolutionary war against the Americans.

Dong spent the week in Beijing, eventually meeting with Chairman Mao Zedong on September 23. Mao ridiculed the Nixon administration's effort to negotiate a secret peace deal with Hanoi. He was especially critical of Kissinger, whom he called a "stinking scholar, a university professor who does not know anything about diplomacy."[35] Mao declared that troubles between China and the DRV in the past had been the fault of "mandarin ambassadors" representing China in Hanoi and that the future looked bright between these two fraternal allies.[36] He was especially pleased to learn that Hanoi had not abandoned its commitment to "the unconditional withdrawal of American troops" from Vietnam and that it still insisted upon the removal of the Saigon government before it would sign any peace agreement. Mao, of course, saw both of these requirements as good for China and therefore good for Vietnam. At the end of his meeting with Pham Van Dong, Mao uttered the words Hanoi's leaders had longed to hear: "I see that you can conduct diplomatic struggle and you do it well. Negotiations have been going on for two years. At first we were a little worried that you were trapped. We are no longer worried."[37]

What the North Vietnamese leadership did not realize, however, was that Mao was also exploring the possibility of rapprochement with the United States. He had concluded that the United States might be a useful partner in containing the Soviet Union in Asia. Likewise, Nixon believed that China could help with its allies in Hanoi and be a crucial part of a new world order following the American withdrawal from Vietnam. Both superpowers wanted to use a new relationship to reorient their own power and international perceptions of that power. When a back channel through Pakistan confirmed Mao's interest in meeting with Nixon, the president assured China's leader that he was willing to consider a change in US policy toward Taiwan and all US military matters in East Asia.

The US/ARVN invasion of Cambodia had made it impossible for Mao to capitalize on the secret contacts taking place in Poland between Chinese and US diplomats because it would have been seen as abandoning the revolutionary war in Cambodia, but by the end of September 1970, conditions were once again ripe to explore a new relationship. The president wasted no time letting Mao know that if invited to China, the president of the United States would surely make the trip.

At the same time, Kissinger reported to Nixon that no progress had been made in Paris. He complained that the meeting was "unproductive" and that no new talks were scheduled.[38] Hanoi had categorically rejected the new timetable for the US troop withdrawal and had not even acknowledged the standstill cease-fire proposal. Kissinger later claimed that Hanoi missed a golden opportunity to embrace the cease-fire, because "so many in our government had invested so many hopes in it that the administration was governed by a rare unanimity as planning proceeded."[39]

Nixon took Hanoi's rejection as a signal that North Vietnam was using the negotiations with Kissinger as a diplomatic ploy and nothing else. With US midterm elections less than a month away, the president could not afford to have Vietnam cast a shadow over American politics. Nixon told his top national security advisers that he planned to put Hanoi on the defensive by going public with the latest US peace proposal. Kissinger understood that you did not disagree with the president when it came to elections, so he supported Nixon making a public speech outlining the standstill cease-fire sometime before the US election. He realized that Hanoi had already rejected this proposal, but he told the president a public offer might "give us some temporary relief from public pressures," something Nixon had believed all along.[40]

An October Surprise

Nixon proposed the already rejected standstill cease-fire in a televised speech from the Oval Office at the White House on October 7, 1970. He told those watching that he was announcing a "major new initiative for peace." The new proposal was made possible, he claimed, "because of the remarkable success of the Vietnamization program over the past 18 months." He then outlined the cease-fire, claiming that the goal was to put an end to the killing. The cease-fire was to cover "a full range of actions," including bombing and acts of terror. Cambodia and Laos would also commit to the cease-fire, he claimed, because conflict there was closely related to the ongoing war in Vietnam. Nixon then proposed an international conference, along the lines of the 1954 Geneva conference, to "deal with the conflicts in all three states of Indochina." The president pledged that "we are ready now to negotiate an agreed timetable for complete withdrawals as part of an overall settlement." It is unclear whether Nixon's use of the plural "withdrawals" was meant to underscore the idea that he still expected a mutual troop withdrawal, but no one in the press highlighted this interesting word choice at the time. After making some vague references to the need for a political settlement in South Vietnam, he ended his speech by proposing the "immediate and unconditional release of all prisoners of war held by both sides."[41]

The press response to Nixon's speech was overwhelmingly positive. The *New York Times* noted with approval that the president had not mentioned mutual troop withdrawals.[42] The *Wall Street Journal* said: "However Hanoi finally responds, in fact, the President has put forth an American position so appealing and so sane that only the most unreasonable critics would object to it."[43] One conservative Arizona newspaper, the *Daily Citizen*, claimed that Nixon's overture was a major breakthrough in the negotiations: "Perhaps no leader of any nation has made such a far-reaching proposal from a position of strength, he has established an acid test for Hanoi's peace intention."[44] Perhaps the most interesting sign of support for Nixon's peace proposal came from the An Quang Buddhist faction in Saigon. Thich Huyen Quang, a spokesperson for the group that was fiercely opposed to the Saigon government, welcomed the idea of standstill cease-fire, maintaining that it held promising possibilities.[45] Key members of Congress also praised Nixon for announcing the new proposal, though many Senate Democrats asked, "What took so long?"[46]

For his part, Kissinger praised the speech, claiming that it was a watershed moment in the war and that Nixon had "presented a comprehensive program that could well have served as the basis for negotiation except with an opponent bent on total victory."[47] He called the president shortly after the speech to congratulate him. Nixon replied, "As you know, I don't think this cease-fire is worth a damn, but now that we have done it we are looking down their throats."[48] Still, Kissinger told him, there was some value in making these proposals, even if they went nowhere.

The euphoria over Nixon's speech was short-lived. Journalists soon noticed that he had not mentioned mutual troop withdrawals. Reporters peppered the administration with questions for two days until a White House spokesperson finally had to admit that there had been "an oversight," and that the president still "insisted on matching troop reductions by the other side."[49] Rather than deflect interest in the story, the White House remarks sparked a heated controversy. Nixon eventually tried to set the record straight, stating that what he was offering was a "total withdrawal of all of our forces, something we have never offered before," but then he added the important clause: "if we had a mutual withdrawal on the other side."[50] A follow-up briefing with the White House confirmed that the Nixon administration's position had not fundamentally changed. The White House insisted that "we would expect that all outside forces would return to the borders of their countries."[51] In the negotiations and in public, the administration considered the PAVN an "outside force." But despite the administration's attempts to gain public relations value by announcing the new standstill cease-fire, Nixon essentially had not altered the US position. Washington was still calling for a mutual troop withdrawal, coupled with a political settlement that kept Thieu in power. The standstill cease-fire Nixon proposed was only temporary and still built on the back of an expected mutual troop withdrawal.

It did not take Hanoi long to respond to the speech. The party's official newspaper, *Nhan Dan*, criticized the speech in several articles. Nguyen Thi Binh told reporters in Paris that Nixon's speech was a clever "maneuver to deceive world opinion." Xuan Thuy added, "What can I say of the five points put forward last night by President Nixon? Only a gift certificate for the votes of the American electorate and a cover-up for misleading world public opinion."[52] Hanoi reiterated its position that it held fast to its demands for a complete and unconditional US troop withdrawal and the "overthrow of the puppet leaders in Saigon."[53] Implicit in these statements was the requirement that North Vietnamese troops be allowed to stay in South Vietnam following any agreement. Hanoi's leaders decided that Kissinger's private proposal made public by Nixon during the October 7 speech was, like its predecessors, carefully conceived to yield nothing of substance. The Nixon White House did seem to recognize that any political settlement in South Vietnam had to include the PRG, Le Duc Tho concluded, but it also clung stubbornly to the idea of a mutual troop withdrawal.

But Hanoi's leaders also understood that Kissinger could be pushed on this issue in Paris. His September 7 cease-fire proposal was the first recognition that the United States was going to find it difficult to get a timely peace and force North Vietnamese troops from South Vietnam. It would only be a matter of time, Hanoi's

Politburo believed, before the cease-fire would move from a diplomatic ploy used by Nixon and his national security adviser to the cornerstone of the final agreement. Time was on Hanoi's side and Kissinger's strategy and tactics were helping to speed up the clock.

Pivoting to Laos

Nixon's October surprise played well in the US for a few days, but the midterm elections yielded a net loss for Republicans in Congress. Within a few short weeks of the speech, Congress also made significant cuts to the overall Defense budget. Kissinger complained that the "Defense budget is below the tolerable level," but Laird understood the political pressure to rein in spending, and the surest way to do this was to continue the withdrawal of American troops from Vietnam.[54] When Hanoi did not take the bait on the standstill cease-fire proposal and Congress cut Defense spending, Kissinger understood that the Nixon administration had one more chance to inflict military harm on North Vietnamese troops before Hanoi launched a major offensive against South Vietnam. With the debate over the new cease-fire proposal circulating in Washington, Kissinger met secretly with Nixon to explore a plan for a massive ARVN attack into Laos.

Nixon was favoring the idea of a total troop withdrawal in 1971, coupled with increased air attacks against North Vietnam and the quarantine of Haiphong harbor. He sensed that he had to do something drastic before the 1972 US election to make it appear that peace was imminent in Vietnam. Kissinger rejected this plan. Through Haldeman, he warned the president that "if we pull them out by the end of '71, trouble can start mounting in '72 that we won't be able to deal with and which we'll have to answer for at the elections."[55] He feared that a sudden US withdrawal would convey "such a sense of impatience to Hanoi that it would simply buckle down and endure the bombing,

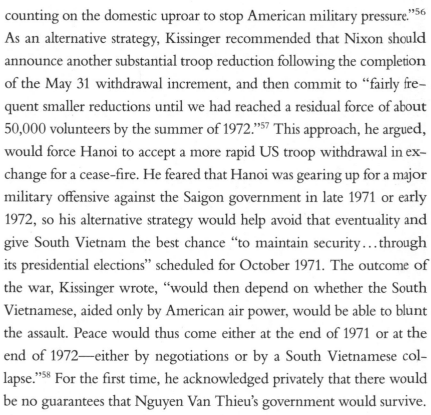

counting on the domestic uproar to stop American military pressure."[56] As an alternative strategy, Kissinger recommended that Nixon should announce another substantial troop reduction following the completion of the May 31 withdrawal increment, and then commit to "fairly frequent smaller reductions until we had reached a residual force of about 50,000 volunteers by the summer of 1972."[57] This approach, he argued, would force Hanoi to accept a more rapid US troop withdrawal in exchange for a cease-fire. He feared that Hanoi was gearing up for a major military offensive against the Saigon government in late 1971 or early 1972, so his alternative strategy would help avoid that eventuality and give South Vietnam the best chance "to maintain security...through its presidential elections" scheduled for October 1971. The outcome of the war, Kissinger wrote, "would then depend on whether the South Vietnamese, aided only by American air power, would be able to blunt the assault. Peace would thus come either at the end of 1971 or at the end of 1972—either by negotiations or by a South Vietnamese collapse."[58] For the first time, he acknowledged privately that there would be no guarantees that Nguyen Van Thieu's government would survive.

Still, Kissinger was optimistic that he could enhance Saigon's political and military position in South Vietnam before the American withdrawal was complete. On November 18, 1970, Congress had approved $1 billion in supplemental appropriations for the war, so there was no current worry about it pulling the plug on US efforts in Vietnam, even though the overall Defense budget saw huge reductions. In proposing his alternative strategy to Nixon, Kissinger suggested a combination of superpower diplomacy with the Soviet Union and China in order to leverage Hanoi's concessions and quick military strikes. The cornerstone of his plan was armed attacks against North Vietnamese troops now using Laos as a sanctuary. He claimed that the 1970 attacks inside Cambodia had "delayed Hanoi's logistics buildup for at least fifteen months," and now the time had come to attack the North Vietnamese troops operating freely inside Laos to buy time for Saigon and weaken the DRV. With just the right amount of military force, Kissinger insisted, he could negotiate the best chance for South Vietnam's survival. Nixon liked the plan. He, too, believed that the Cambodian invasion had "gravely undermined Hanoi's capacity to conduct offensive operations," thus buying much-needed time for Saigon.[59]

The plan to strike North Vietnamese forces inside Laos had been workshopped in Kissinger's office for months. His deputy, General Alexander Haig (who had been promoted recently), held regular meetings on the subject in the basement of the White House, and in December 1970, Haig traveled to Saigon to meet personally with Military Assistance Command, Vietnam (MACV) commander General Creighton Abrams and to discuss the plan with Thieu.[60] US intelligence reports indicated that Hanoi had two primary goals approaching the 1971 dry season. The first was to resupply and reinforce North Vietnamese troops in southern Laos. The second was to launch large-scale military operations in the spring and summer against Quang Tri and Thua Thien provinces in the lowlands of Military Region I, the northernmost regions of South Vietnam.[61] Nearly six thousand PAVN troops per month marched along the Ho Chi Minh Trail into southern Laos in preparation for the offensives.[62] This region had great strategic value since the east-west Route 9 was the only passable road from Tchepone in southern Laos all the way to Dong Ha along the Cau Viet River near South Vietnam's coast. Whoever controlled Route 9 could control military traffic along the DMZ, a vital strategic and tactical asset for all sides in the war. Accordingly, Abrams determined that the time had come to attack the PAVN in Laos to stop it from marching on Quang Tri, the northernmost province in South Vietnam. Haig and he agreed that South Vietnamese troops, backed by US air power, could strike a blow against North Vietnamese troops in southern Laos. Abrams was "extremely enthusiastic about this operation" because of

his "growing faith in the capabilities" of the ARVN.[63] He carefully planned an ARVN attack on the major North Vietnamese logistic corridor at Tchepone in Laos. He suggested that the South Vietnamese troops would seize the town and then secure the airfield for a sufficient amount of time for combat engineers to enlarge the runway for aerial resupply. If Saigon's army could hold out long enough, special operations forces could then take over the operation.

An excited Haig returned to Washington to discuss the Laos plan with Kissinger, claiming, "We are within an eyelash of victory in Vietnam."[64] Kissinger, too, was incredibly enthusiastic about the prospects in Laos, telling Nixon, "I've looked at this concept and it really looks good."[65] Of course, he warned Nixon not to let Laird in on the plan or "he'll try to kill it."[66] Once again, Kissinger purposely kept the secretary of defense out of the planning stages of a military operation, by implying that only he and Nixon understood the full importance of military operations in Laos, so it was best to close the circle tight in the White House.[67] Throughout his tenure as national security adviser, Kissinger would repeatedly propose policies that he knew Laird and Rogers would reject, so as to win favor with the president. Sometimes, these policies were of dubious strategic value. The Laos attacks, however, satisfied his personal desire to control all aspects of Vietnam decision making as well as important strategic imperatives.

Nixon agreed. He told Kissinger "it was about time to rip them up, finish them off."[68] At a December 23 meeting at the White House, where Nixon finally informed Laird of the plan to invade Laos, the president blamed the Johnson administration for not taking this "bold action three years ago."[69] Laird was incensed that Kissinger had once again tried to cut him out of military planning in Vietnam, and would visit Kissinger at the White House on February 18, a week into the operation in Laos, to complain about his treatment. Recalling the visit in a phone conversation with Nixon later that day, Kissinger relayed that "Laird is a little bit jumpy," but that he would be all right. "He's calmed down a little?" Nixon asked. "Yes," Kissinger assured the president, adding that Laird "is a funny guy" who "maneuvers like a maniac." Nixon concluded that Laird was a "rascal," but "by golly he's our rascal."[70] Eventually, Laird supported the invasion plan, telling Nixon, "Let's take a crack at it."[71]

Despite the Kissinger-Laird feud, planning for the Laos attack moved forward in January 1971. For the next month, Abrams provided the administration with the details of the complex operation. The administration hit a sticking point in deliberations in early February 1971, when Kissinger and Laird disagreed again, this time over the length of the operation. Laird suggested that the administration stick to the six- to eight-week time frame that had been planned all along, but Kissinger now insisted that there should be no fixed termination date: if all went well, he argued, the ARVN could stay in Laos indefinitely. Eventually, Laird relented. He understood that the president was committed to the attack plan as Kissinger presented it, and that there was little he could do to alter its time frame. He told Nixon, however, that if Hanoi reinforced its troops in Laos, the United States should remain flexible and maybe consider shortening the operation.[72] His comments were prescient.

For its part, the Saigon government was supportive of the Laos operation as well. General Coa Van Vien, chairman of the South Vietnamese Joint General Staff (JGS), had been proposing a similar plan since 1965, and Thieu himself initially backed the idea enthusiastically. When General Abrams presented the plan to Thieu and his top generals, they were optimistic, arguing that if the ARVN offensive did not take place in early 1971, it would be too late and it might not take place at all.[73] Thieu told Abrams that "military movement into the Laos panhandle would shorten the war" and prove that Saigon could launch offensive military operations.[74] South Vietnam's ambassador to the United States, Bui Diem, later recalled that Thieu and his generals were fully supportive of the invasion, saying that "their enthusiasm came as no surprise," since the ARVN had made strong military gains in 1970 and were full of confidence following the 1970 raids on Cambodia.[75] Because of the Cooper-Church Amendment, recently modified and passed by both houses of Congress in January 1971, the United States would be able to offer only tactical air support. This would be the first major test of Vietnamization, requiring South Vietnamese troops alone to conduct primary operations as boots on the ground. To further incentivize the ARVN, all combat troops were given 100 South Vietnamese dong extra pay for each day they fought in Laos. Extra food allowances were also given to the families of all South Vietnamese troops engaged in the offensive, now called Operation Lam Son 719, named after the birthplace of Emperor Le Loi, who had defeated an invading Chinese army in the fifteenth century.[76]

It is surprising that Kissinger pushed so hard to attack Laos when he knew it rested on the back of the ARVN. He had repeatedly stated that he was skeptical of the ARVN's military capabilities and had complained relentlessly that Vietnamization had weakened the American position in Vietnam. He also had recent intelligence estimates suggesting Hanoi's strength in the area was nearly twenty-five thousand troops and that two more North Vietnamese divisions were likely to arrive soon. Hanoi ordered that southern Laos be held at all costs, and the buildup there was evident to the NSC. There was also significant reason to believe that Hanoi could reinforce its divisions rapidly. Still, Kissinger pushed on, supporting the Laos invasion in key meetings with the president and NSC. Rogers was openly hostile to the plan, and Laird was cautiously optimistic at best. This meant that Kissinger was alone among Nixon's civilian national security advisers in fully supporting the Lam Son operation. He even overrode the objections of several senior US military leaders in Washington, including army chief of staff General William Westmoreland, who had served as MACV commander for years. Westmoreland told Kissinger that the operation was too complex, required too much close air coordination and communication, for the ARVN to be successful.[77]

But Kissinger found others who shared his enthusiasm for the Laos attacks, even if they were somewhat skeptical that the ARVN could handle the complex operations. He partnered with Admiral Thomas Moorer, the chairman of the Joint Chiefs of Staff, General Abrams, and General Haig, all enthusiastically backing Lam Son 719, though the military men always concluded that success rested upon "all-out US military support of ARVN."[78] Even at this late stage of Vietnamization, the top American military leaders worried about the military effectiveness of the armed forces of South Vietnam.

Eager to show that the ARVN was indeed ready to engage in offensive military operations against the North Vietnamese, Thieu announced to the press on February 8, 1971, that the ARVN had launched an attack inside Laos. Within a few days, however, the operation stalled. ARVN units found it difficult to move along Route 9, a road not designed for heavy armed personnel carriers and tanks. Abrams's plan had called for the swift movement of ARVN troops toward Tchepone, but Thieu ordered his commander, General Hoang Xuan Lam, to stop his forces at the town of Ban Dong, barely 11 miles inside Laos. The ARVN First Armored Division failed to advance, even though paratroopers and South Vietnamese marines had landed north of Ban Dong to secure the ARVN flank in its attack on Tchepone. Thieu also ordered General Lam to cancel the operation altogether if he incurred three thousand casualties.[79] There is some speculation that Thieu, who flew to Laos to inspect the problem personally, was apparently worried that high ARVN casualty figures in Laos would have a negative impact on the upcoming South Vietnamese elections, scheduled for that fall.[80] Thieu, like his predecessor in the presidential palace in Saigon, also used the Airborne Division as coup protection, and therefore did not want it to fully engage in the operation against the North Vietnamese in Laos. Such was the intrigue in Saigon.

By February 22, it was clear that something had gone terribly wrong. The PAVN had attacked key South Vietnamese positions along its northern flank, and virtually every South Vietnamese unit was engaged in heavy fighting against the enemy. Poor weather conditions and skilled PAVN antihelicopter artillery made a bad situation worse. Dozens of helicopters were lost and hundreds were hit with artillery fire. The American media reported that the operation had bogged down and that the ARVN were severely outnumbered. Laird held a press conference on February 24, assuring the press and the public that Lam Son 719 was not focused on any specific piece of ground or territory but, rather, was intended to "slow up, to disrupt, the logistics supplies, to cut off and to downgrade the capability of the North Vietnamese to wage any type of warfare in South Vietnam."[81]

Kissinger was conspicuously silent. Eventually, he sent a report to Speaker of the House Carl Albert (D-OK), claiming that the Laos attacks had been a success because Hanoi would now have fewer options against South Vietnam. Kissinger wrote, "The combination of enemy manpower and logistics setbacks resulting from the Lam Son operation make it unlikely that the enemy will mount major offensive activities in South Vietnam or Cambodia, despite evidence that the enemy planned to mount such offensives."[82] Behind the scenes, however, he worried that the ARVN was now in static defensive military positions and would not be able to take Tchepone, a goal that he had set as imperative to success. He confronted Moorer, who assured him that once the ARVN secured its bases, he would see swift action. Kissinger warned the admiral that the ARVN had better turn the battle around, because "if we get our pants beaten off here I tell you we have had it in Vietnam for psychological reasons."[83]

Sensing that he was not getting a straight story from Moorer, Kissinger asked Westmoreland to assess the Laos operation. The general's response: that Tchepone was too "ambitious a goal for the number of ARVN soldiers committed to the operation" and that many of the South Vietnamese commanders were "no fighters."[84] On February 26, Kissinger briefed Nixon on Laos, writing, "The North Vietnamese not only have moved substantial forces into the area, but they also seem to have [s]helved the cautious, economical style of fighting that has been the hallmark of Communist forces for most of the past two years."[85]

When Laird found out that his nemesis had once again gone behind his back and over Abrams's head, he was furious. He reportedly claimed that Kissinger was as "jumpy as a cat" about the course of operations in Laos.[86] Nixon was once again dragged into the dispute between his top national security officials just as the Lam Son operation was at its lowest point. He complained that all the infighting in Washington and Saigon was not helping the ARVN: "If the South Vietnamese could just win one cheap one, take a stinking hill…bring back a prisoner or two," he grumbled.[87] Kissinger blamed MACV for not pushing the ARVN hard enough. He instructed Ambassador Bunker to tell Thieu that he had to keep up the fighting in Laos until the end of April, or risk that Lam Son 719 would be the "last chance that the ARVN will have to receive any substantial US support on the scale now provided."[88]

Eventually, the ARVN did enter Tchepone, but only stayed long enough, in the words of President Thieu, "to take a piss."[89] With the help of massive US air strikes, the ARVN inflicted heavy losses on North Vietnamese troops, causing nearly thirteen thousand causalities. But the ARVN lost momentum and withdrew under heavy PAVN pressure. Later North Vietnamese claims to have killed more than 20,000 RVNAF troops were grossly exaggerated, but the truth was still hard to bear for Kissinger.[90] Westmoreland confirmed that the United States lost about 150 helicopters and nearly 100 tanks and armed personnel carriers.[91] Other sources suggested that South Vietnamese losses were much higher than reported, possibly as many as 7,500 casualties in the ARVN First Corps alone.[92] "Our materiel losses are shocking," Westmoreland warned Kissinger.[93] When press crews captured photographs of the hasty ARVN retreat, giving lasting evidence of problems with Vietnamization, Nixon and Kissinger complained bitterly about the media coverage, agreeing that it was turning an ARVN military victory into a psychological defeat.[94] Even though the ARVN incursion had accomplished some of its goals, and South Vietnamese forces had fared well against enormous odds, there was still a great deal of dissatisfaction in Washington.

Nixon, however, was quick to declare a victory for the Laos operation. On April 7, he gave a television address to the nation, announcing, "Tonight I can report that Vietnamization has succeeded." He continued, "Because of the increased strength of the South Vietnamese . . . and because of the achievements of the South Vietnamese operations in Laos I am announcing an increase in the rate of the American withdrawals."[95] He oversold the Laos operation because that is what he needed to do to sustain Vietnamization.

The Finger-Pointing Begins

Behind the scenes, however, the president and Kissinger blamed Abrams for overselling the ARVN's capabilities and for the failures in Laos. The postmortem on Lam Son 719 suggested that General Lam only used about half of the combat troops available to him in the operation. Indeed, Nixon blamed Abrams for the entire debacle. He told Haldeman that he wanted to fire Abrams, but would not because it did not matter who the MACV commander was, in the face of US troop withdrawals.[96] There are reports that Nixon even sent General

Haig to Saigon to replace Abrams as head of MACV, but that the president changed his mind a few days later and Haig returned home.[97] For Kissinger's part, he declared that he "wouldn't believe a word Abrams says anymore."[98] He also blamed the South Vietnamese armed forces for what he considered a debacle in Laos. In his memoirs, Kissinger writes, "It was a splendid project on paper," but that it eventually failed because "South Vietnamese divisions had never conducted major offensive operations against a determined enemy outside Vietnam and only rarely inside."[99] Furthermore, in an effort to absolve himself of any responsibility for the problems in Laos, he argues that the Cooper-Church Amendment hindered the advisory role of the United States precisely when South Vietnam needed it most.

Finally, Kissinger blames Nixon. He suggests that the president's "reluctance to give orders to his subordinates" meant that he had forced Laird into accepting the invasion plan and supporting it in various NSC meetings. In that environment, Kissinger complains, no one was willing to stand up and question the efficacy of the Laos invasion.[100] His penchant for reworking history is on full view with his rendition of Lam Son 719. Few supported the attacks with as much vigor as he did, but when things went wrong he cast blame far and wide. The record is clear, however, as General Bruce Palmer has explained, "The more immediate origins of the March 1971 incursion into Laos, namely the White House, illustrate how closely President Nixon and his NSC staff dominated the overall control and conduct of both the war and the closely interrelated negotiations to end the war."[101] Kissinger was at the center of Lam Son 719, and its limited successes meant that he now had to rely more heavily upon negotiations to secure a safe US withdrawal and Saigon's future.

But what Kissinger never fully appreciated, and what Laird had tried to impress upon him repeatedly, was that in a democracy military actions always have political consequences. He had hoped to slow the clock for Saigon by attacking Laos, but public pressure to end the war actually intensified as a result of the invasion. The same thing had happened following the Cambodian attacks the previous year. Each new military escalation brought a sharp public rebuke, and Kissinger never quite learned how to manage this reality. He had supported the tremendous gamble in Laos and now he had to rethink his strategy. His only recourse was to ask Hanoi for another meeting in Paris.

Sensing that time was running out on the usefulness of such negotiations, Kissinger approached Nixon with a radical idea: that it was doubtful if the administration could keep up the pace in Vietnam without Congress "giving the farm away."[102] With each passing week, he told the president, Congress grew closer to passing an amendment to force the administration to bring the troops home all at once or to stop funding the Saigon government. (He had no idea, of course, that he played a major role in this scenario.) With one eye on Nixon's desire for a supportive public, Kissinger proposed that the US should approach Hanoi once more with the most comprehensive peace offer yet. If Hanoi wanted to negotiate, the war could be over by Election Day. If Hanoi refused, there would be another military test in 1972 and the United States could launch air attacks against North Vietnam and PAVN sanctuaries to force Hanoi to bend the knee. Kissinger concluded that at the very least a new proposal would strengthen Nixon's hand the year before the US presidential election at home and around the world.[103]

On March 26, as events in Laos were coming into sharp focus, Nixon accepted Kissinger's recommendation "to press for a settlement during the next secret meeting" in Paris.[104] He understood that this might be his last, best chance for peace before the 1972 election, and he wanted no mistakes. He was also growing increasingly interested in the prospects of détente, the easing of strained Cold War relations with the USSR and China. He thought that his high-level trips to the Soviet Union and China would not only get the Vietnam

War off the front pages of the newspapers, but might also lead to some diplomatic pressure on Hanoi from its powerful Communist allies. Kissinger and Nixon thought that Hanoi "must be concerned about any relaxation of tensions between the United States and its Communist allies," thus making the spring proposal all that more attractive to the DRV.[105] The president was squarely focused on his 1972 reelection campaign, and every decision on Vietnam mattered.

Again, to Paris

With Nixon's full approval, Kissinger left for Paris on May 31, carrying with him a new seven-point program that was "the most sweeping plan we had yet offered."[106] In exchange for the release of American POWs, Kissinger pledged to withdraw all US troops from South Vietnam. Although no specific deadline for their removal was included in his plan, he assured Hanoi that "when the Minister [Xuan Thuy] says that this fundamental proposal is acceptable...I will tell you the deadline for the troop withdrawal."[107] The other important aspects of the proposal included a cease-fire, international supervision of the agreement, and respect for the Geneva Accords of 1954 and 1962. Kissinger told Nixon that this seven-point plan would "clearly establish" whether Hanoi had "any interest at all in negotiations" or whether it would continue "to insist upon the overthrow of the Saigon government."[108]

But the most important aspect of the proposal was Kissinger's offer to allow North Vietnamese troops to stay in South Vietnam following a cease-fire if Hanoi promised no more infiltration into South Vietnam, Laos, and Cambodia.[109] This was a major departure from the standstill cease-fire Kissinger offered privately in Paris on September 7, 1970, because there would be no formal mechanisms in place for monitoring troop movements once the United States withdrew. It was a smokescreen for a unilateral US troop withdrawal with no reciprocity from Hanoi. Kissinger thought that this was what Hanoi had been waiting for all along.

But why did he concede on the mutual troop withdrawal, something that he had stubbornly clung to in negotiations since his first meetings with Hanoi's negotiators in Paris? It now seems clear that Kissinger's willingness to yield on this important issue was directly tied to his belief that the Laos attacks had been a failure and that, as a result, public pressure was mounting to end the war sooner than he or Nixon wanted to. Publicly he had praised the Lam Son operation, but privately he admitted that Laos "comes out clearly as not a success."[110] Nixon called the ARVN a "poor excuse" for a military and believed that there was "goddamn poor execution" on Abrams's part.[111] The marches and protests in Washington by the Vietnam Veterans Against the War (VVAW) during the Laos attacks also unnerved the Nixon administration, so there was plenty of pressure on the negotiations to bear fruit. As the Laos operation unraveled, Kissinger began to explore with Nixon the idea of allowing North Vietnamese troops to stay in South Vietnam in exchange for a well-timed final agreement. During several lengthy phone conversations with Nixon in April and May, Kissinger had raised the possibility of dropping the mutual troop withdrawal request. He told the president, "We can either not have mutual withdrawal, but just negotiate a cease-fire for our withdrawal and the prisoners, which would give everybody another year to gear themselves up without Communist attacks."[112] The implication was clear: if Nixon wanted a settlement just after the 1972 US presidential election, Kissinger had to make some compromises in Paris.

Kissinger understood that the troop withdrawal issue was important, but he shared the president's belief that punishing Hanoi militarily "with a high level of air sorties at least through the US elections" was equally so.[113] He agreed with Nixon that Saigon should be given "everything it needs in the way of helicopters, planes, artillery, and

supplies," but eventually the South Vietnamese would have "to protect themselves."[114] In other words, going into the May 31 meeting,
Kissinger was committed to allowing Saigon to face Hanoi alone and
with North Vietnamese troops already inside South Vietnam as part
of the peace agreement. US air power would provide cover for the
ARVN, but eventually Saigon would have to win the war on its own.

Many scholars have called this Kissinger approach "a decent interval." They claim that he was merely trying to buy Saigon enough
time to decouple in the minds of most Americans the timing of the
US troop withdrawal and the inevitable PAVN military victory over
South Vietnam.[115] They argue that Kissinger negotiated an agreement
that amounted to a suicide pact for Saigon but was a face-saving defeat
for the United States. This interpretation has gained currency among
scholars because of Kissinger's subsequent discussions with the Chinese prime minister, Zhou Enlai, in the summer of 1971, when he
told Zhou that the United States required "a transition period between
the military withdrawal and the political evolution...If after complete
American withdrawal, the Indochinese people change their government, the US will not interfere."[116] In Paris, Kissinger suggested that
the United States could not leave behind a unified Vietnam under the
Communist banner, but once American troops were withdrawn, they
would not return and the United States would not intervene in any
political settlement that would follow. Kissinger also implied that there
had to be a cease-fire of about eighteen months to uncouple, in the
minds of most Americans, the US withdrawal from what would in-
evitably follow in Vietnam: the collapse of South Vietnam.[117] Nixon
agreed with these sentiments, commenting that "simply ending the
war in the right way" might not save South Vietnam.[118]

Although there is ample evidence that Kissinger explored the decent interval with Zhou in July 1971, he remained committed, at least
in principle, to the idea that he could coordinate punishing military

strikes against North Vietnam with diplomacy in Paris on May 31 to get a favorable outcome for Nixon just before the election. South Vietnam was not primary in his mind; getting Nixon reelected was—and this meant dealing with Hanoi, not Saigon. Kissinger shared the view with the president that the United States could always use its "hole card," the massive bombing and mining of Hanoi and Haiphong in North Vietnam to force Hanoi to make concessions in Paris following the Laos debacle.[119] He also believed that diplomatic breakthroughs with the Soviet Union and China offered a ray of hope in Vietnam. Like Nixon, Kissinger thought that "the Chinese might put...some pressure on Hanoi," and that détente threatened to undermine the DRV's entire position.[120] Diplomatic success in Moscow and Beijing also could have a positive impact on the domestic political climate; something Nixon was always sensitive to. Kissinger told the president that he would also warn Moscow to "tell their little yellow friends to stop these games. We are not going down quietly."[121] Nixon agreed, telling his closest aides that he was not going to "go out of Vietnam whimpering."[122]

Kissinger and his associate Winston Lord worked out the details of the proposal well in advance of the May 31 meeting in Paris. Lord sent him a memo on April 12, outlining where the negotiations stood at that point and summarizing for Kissinger what would be gained with the new approach of not insisting on a North Vietnamese withdrawal from South Vietnam.[123] The key for both seemed to be that the North Vietnamese would not be allowed to have a "net increase" of forces inside South Vietnam. Rotating troops would be permitted under the cease-fire, but the number of troops would be constant. Furthermore, the proposal banned infiltration into Laos and Cambodia, making it possible for South Vietnam to concentrate on the forces already in the country. Kissinger reasoned that Hanoi might be interested in this new proposal, even if it did not topple the Saigon government, one of the DRV's top demands. Instead, it called for political negotiations between the PRG/NLF, Hanoi, and Saigon, concluding that "political matters should be settled among the Vietnamese themselves."[124] Kissinger decided not to tell Thieu all the details of his latest proposal, fearing that it might create panic in Saigon. Instead, he flew to Paris somewhat confident that Hanoi would see the dramatic change in the US position and agree to a quick settlement.

What is truly interesting is just how unsure Kissinger was about the technical aspects of his own negotiating position this time around. Astonishingly, during one lengthy meeting with his senior review group prior to the Paris meeting, the national security adviser asked, "Let's assume we negotiate a ceasefire in place. Has anyone ever studied what either side will do the month before the ceasefire takes effect to achieve the best position?"[125] Perhaps Kissinger knew all along that Hanoi would reject his latest offer, so the details of what would happen to North Vietnamese troops inside South Vietnam did not seem all that important at the time. What the PAVN was allowed to do was certainly important to Thieu and the Saigon government, who must have shared a sigh of relief when Hanoi rejected Kissinger's May 31 proposal outright.

Despite rebuffing Kissinger's latest offer, Hanoi had noticed that he was slowly meeting some of its demands. It was delighted to see that the United States no longer insisted on a mutual withdrawal from South Vietnam, and Hanoi's leaders clearly understood that the lack of any enforcement mechanism on infiltration played in their favor. The main sticking point, however, was that Kissinger still insisted that Thieu remain in power. Hanoi also strenuously objected to Kissinger's unwillingness to set a date for the US troop withdrawal. Despite their reservations, Hanoi's representatives agreed to meet again at the end of June.

When the parties met again on June 26, Kissinger noticed that the usually "dingy" North Vietnamese delegation apartment now had a formal negotiating table instead of easy chairs. He took this as a sign that Hanoi was finally serious about negotiations.[126] After the usual pleasantries, Xuan Thuy asked him to clarify an important point for Hanoi: "The last time Mr. Special Adviser [Kissinger] said the US would fix a date for troop withdrawal, when it knew about the release of the POWs, but would not fix a date if it is not clear about the prisoners." Thuy asked whether it was correct that Kissinger was still unwilling to give a date for the total US withdrawal, but still wanted the POWs returned?[127] Kissinger responded that the seven points were a package, that if Hanoi accepted all of the "essential principles"—the cease-fire, neutrality for South Vietnam, and the release of the POWs—then the United States would certainly set a date for the total US withdrawal.[128] Thuy looked encouraged. After a short tea break, he emerged from an upstairs room holding a paper that contained the official North Vietnamese response to Kissinger's seven points.

Presenting Hanoi's new nine-point plan, Thuy joked that Hanoi's proposal was "more earnest than yours to end the war" because it contained two more points.[129] The only new provision in Hanoi's nine points was that the United States would now be liable for postwar reparations. Thuy offered a somewhat modified condition on the South Vietnamese government. The United States no longer had to overturn the Thieu government, as previously required; now it merely had to "stop supporting the Saigon government."[130] Kissinger rejected the call for reparations outright, but in reporting to Nixon, he once again chose to accentuate the positive. He claimed that for the first time in two years of solid negotiations, Hanoi had made a "concrete rejoinder" to a US proposal. Instead of offering a list of demands, he reported that Hanoi's nine points were presented as a "negotiating document" and that compromise seemed possible.[131] He told Nixon that Thuy and Tho were willing now, for the first time, to bargain. He was especially encouraged that Hanoi was willing to accept the entire US seven points as a basis for negotiation.

The sticking point for Kissinger remained, however, what Hanoi expected the United States to do with the Saigon government. The North Vietnamese had not called for a US-supported coup against Thieu as it previously required, nor had it insisted on the formation of a coalition government as a condition of the agreement. Instead, Hanoi seemed to be asking the United States to be neutral in the upcoming South Vietnamese presidential elections, now scheduled for October 1971. If the United States did not openly support Thieu, then it might be able to support another candidate, one more to Hanoi's liking. There had long been speculation in South Vietnam that the Communists and some third-wave leaders were supporting the candidacy of General Duong Van Minh (Big Minh). Minh had carried a serious grudge against Thieu ever since 1964, when Thieu had provided the military support to oust Minh in a bloodless coup.

Minh had come to power following the assassination of South Vietnamese president Ngo Dinh Diem in November 1963, but he had angered the Americans in Saigon by steering an increasingly independent course. On January 30, 1964, forces under the control of General Nguyen Khanh arrested Minh and stripped him of power. After his incarceration, Minh returned to Saigon and was active in several pro-democracy groups. As the former chief of state of South Vietnam, Minh was an attractive candidate for a formal alliance with the PRG/NLF. US intelligence reported that Minh had maintained a degree of respectability among Saigon's elite, even as it appeared that he had made contact with the Communists. Minh had enough popular support to cause Thieu political headaches, and his appeal for a negotiated settlement with the PRG/NLF was an appealing option for many South Vietnamese. The PRG eventually launched a full-scale diplomatic offensive to have Minh put on the ballot. In early June 1971, he announced his candidacy, but Thieu pushed through a new law in the National Assembly that required all presidential candidates to obtain the signatures of 40 percent of its membership. When Minh easily met this challenge, Thieu called upon the US embassy to pressure Minh to withdraw his candidacy. Eventually, Minh relented. There has always been some speculation that Minh was put forward by his friends in the PRG and then told to resign when it would create the most embarrassing situation for the United States.[132]

Kissinger wrote at the time, "For all his faults, Thieu has been a loyal ally. Moreover... American complicity in the coup against Diem would make our involvement in Thieu's removal even more unpalatable."[133] His unwavering support for Thieu is somewhat ironic, given that he never consulted with the South Vietnamese president when he was making important decisions about Saigon's future during the negotiations. Yet Thieu's removal was the key sticking point in these negotiations, and Kissinger consistently defended the legitimacy of a man that he clearly did not trust or choose to rely upon in any way. What the possibilities were in Saigon went unexplored during the 1971 elections because no one in the Nixon administration wanted to take a closer look at South Vietnamese politics. The South Vietnamese were cast by the Nixon administration as passive actors in their own history, one of the greatest tragedies of the Vietnam War.

Still, Kissinger continued to believe that there was room for negotiation in Paris. He met twice in July 1971 with Xuan Thuy and Le Duc Tho, and in both meetings he reported to Nixon that Hanoi had conceded on some points. One of the major areas of change was Hanoi's willingness to call war reparations "US contributions to heal the destruction of war."[134] This removed the guilt clause from the notion of reparations. Kissinger vaguely suggested postwar loans and grants could help rebuild all three war-torn nations, but he never explored this option fully in Paris. This was a major point that could have been explored more fully, but it was never given any serious thought. Another opportunity for leverage in the negotiations left unexplored. He also stated for the first time that the administration was prepared to set a US troop withdrawal date of nine months after an agreement was reached. Hanoi wanted a fixed deadline—something he refused to provide—but eventually agreed that the POW releases and the US troop withdrawal could be linked. Kissinger reported to Nixon that real progress was being made in Paris, but that the big breakthrough they had hoped for would not happen before the South Vietnamese elections.[135] Still, he argued that Hanoi was serious about negotiations and that "the shape of a deal" was now emerging in Paris.[136] This was more wishful thinking on Kissinger's part. Hanoi's consistent demands never wavered until it felt that favorable balance of forces in South Vietnam allowed it to delay some of its objectives until after an agreement.

Two more meetings in Paris in the early fall of 1971 moved the United States and Hanoi even closer together on military matters, but the major political issues still kept them apart. Kissinger proposed a new timetable for US troop withdrawals, August 1, 1972, as long as a final agreement was signed by November 1, 1972, thus assuring Nixon of a peace dividend at the polls. He told his North Vietnamese counterparts that even this date could be adjusted because it was not a matter of principle but merely a technicality. On principle, Kissinger insisted, Hanoi and Washington were not far apart. Thuy agreed, claiming that "the political problem is still unsettled and . . . our withdrawal deadlines are far apart," but the other issues "can be resolved."[137] All the United States had to do to get an immediate settlement, Thuy implied, was to exclude Thieu from the upcoming elections. In Hanoi, party leaders thought this proposal gave the United States a face-saving way out of Vietnam. If the United States simply removed Thieu from the possible presidential candidates in South Vietnam, it could withdraw with its POWs released and a public pledge that the people of South Vietnam would settle the political issues themselves. But Kissinger later declared that he was not prepared to "toss Thieu to the wolves."[138]

Despite Kissinger's claims of great progress in Paris, Nixon was losing patience with the negotiations and with his national security adviser. He thought Kissinger did not understand how Communists negotiated. Their method, the president claimed, was "to keep talking and to screw you behind your back while they are doing it. To them, this is a tactic to win, not to work out an agreement."[139] In Hanoi, they called this *vua danh, vua dam*, "fighting while talking." Nixon was particularly agitated because antiwar protests had picked up in 1971 and because Congress was still bent on forcing an American withdrawal from Vietnam. On June 22, the US Senate passed the Mansfield Amendment, calling for a mandatory withdrawal of all US forces from Vietnam nine months after passage of the bill and an end to all American military operations following the release of US prisoners of war. Kissinger, according to Haldeman's notes, "got very cranked up about" the amendment because it dealt a blow "for his negotiations in Paris."[140] Kissinger called the amendment "the most irresponsible performance I have ever seen for public short-term political gains."[141]

Even more disturbing to Nixon was the publication of what became known as the Pentagon Papers. Initiated by former secretary of defense Robert S. McNamara, who had served under presidents Kennedy and Johnson, the analysts who put the material together hoped to provide a history of decision making in Vietnam based on secret Defense Department documents. One of the analysts, Daniel Ellsberg, who had helped Kissinger prepare NSSM-1 and who had years of experience in Vietnam, had grown so disenchanted with the war that he approached a reporter at the *New York Times*, Neil Sheehan, with copies of the report. The papers confirmed what critics of the war had long been arguing, the US government had been lying to the American public about the conduct of the war for years.

Although the report stopped before Nixon's tenure as president, he was still unsettled by the leak. He saw its publication as an affront to the presidency. Following publication of the first report in the *Times* in June 1971, the president asked the US federal courts to enjoin the *New York Times* from publishing any further reports, which it did immediately. The government's injunction against the *Times* went before a Nixon-appointed judge, who questioned the paper's patriotism. He granted the injunction, pending an evidentiary hearing. This order was the first time a federal court had stopped a press from reporting based on an issue of national security.[142] The *Washington Post* also gained a copy of the top-secret report, forcing the Nixon administration to seek another injunction, this time in the nation's capital. Eventually, the cases were combined and made their way to the US Supreme Court, where the justices—in a vote of six to three—denied the government the injunction, and the papers continued their publication of the Pentagon's clandestine analysis.

Nixon's disappointment over the Court's ruling was matched only by his displeasure with the lack of progress in the secret negotiations. He had hoped that the surprise announcement that summer that he would be traveling to China would have had a dramatic impact on Hanoi's stance, as Zhou Enlai had promised Kissinger that it would. Kissinger told the president that China's leaders would talk to Hanoi and that they "may exert some influence."[143] Kissinger had no way of knowing that Mao and Zhou had already decided to reject his request to pressure Hanoi to change its negotiating position.[144] After the October 3 elections in South Vietnam, in which Nguyen Van Thieu was the only presidential candidate and won reelection with 94.3 percent of the vote, the Paris talks stalled.

Kissinger asked to meet with Thuy and Tho in Paris in early October, but Hanoi refused, stating that its diplomats would not meet with him again unless he had something new to say. Kissinger claimed he did, and so sent a revised proposal to the US military attaché at the American embassy in Paris, General Vernon Walters, who met with DRV delegate Vo Van Sung on October 11.[145] Kissinger's revised eight points offered two new terms: He shortened the duration of the complete US troop withdrawal from August 1 to July 1, 1972. Furthermore, he promised that Thieu, having just been reelected, would resign one month before a new election in South Vietnam, which would include the PRG/NLF, took place.[146] This was the only time Kissinger explored an alternative to Thieu, and it was merely a diplomatic ploy. Thieu agreed to this proposal only because Nixon gave him a guarantee that Hanoi would not accept this new offer.[147] Nixon was right. Hanoi once again rejected Kissinger's proposals outright. There were no further meetings between Kissinger and his Vietnamese counterparts in Paris for the remainder of 1971.

At the beginning of 1971, Kissinger had believed that he could persuade Hanoi into meaningful negotiations to end the war ahead of the 1972 US presidential election. He thought he could entice Hanoi to agree to a timely end to the war and the return of American prisoners in exchange for allowing North Vietnamese troops to remain in South Vietnam and by granting political legitimacy to the southern Communists. But Hanoi wanted more, and its leaders thought that they could force further Kissinger concessions because of US domestic political pressure to end the war and loss of life. It was clear to North Vietnamese negotiators that the US national security adviser's position on Thieu was also collapsing in 1971. He no longer insisted on political guarantees for the South Vietnamese government, only that the United States not be the ones to replace Saigon. Hanoi had to do that on its own and after the eventual US withdrawal, Kissinger insisted. But Hanoi smelled growing weakness in his negotiating position in 1971. His strategic blunder of supporting the invasion of Laos, thus exposing Vietnamization's weaknesses, further convinced the North Vietnamese that Kissinger's time to shape an agreement to his liking was running short. Time favored Hanoi as the United States faced another presidential election year in 1972 and the political pressures that went with it.

CHAPTER FIVE

A WAR FOR PEACE,
JANUARY 1–AUGUST 31, 1972

HENRY KISSINGER HAD a very tough month in January 1972. He began the New Year with a call to Nixon's chief of staff, H. R. Haldeman, in which he shared his suspicion that "someone had been getting to the P [Nixon] on Vietnam." He feared that the chief executive was under "terrible pressure" and that Nixon might "bug out" of Vietnam. The president, he predicted, was going to go public with his secret negotiations, threatening everything that had been accomplished. Kissinger's instincts told him that this was the "totally wrong" approach and that it was dangerous to "show any nervousness." As he had so many times before, he ended the phone call with a declaration that Hanoi was "ready to give," ready to make serious compromises in the secret meetings in Paris.[1]

Kissinger had every reason to worry. Nixon was convinced that the war was eating away at his 1972 reelection chances. A Harris Survey taken in March 1971 revealed that Senator Edmund Muskie (D-ME) had a five-point lead on Nixon.[2] Recent polling data suggested that

Muskie was also ahead of Senator George McGovern (D-SD), for the Democratic nomination. Like McGovern, Muskie was a sharp critic of the Nixon administration's policies on Vietnam, but he had a stronger following within the party and across the nation because he had captured the public's imagination as a candidate who possessed unusual candor and directness. His campaign slogan reflected this feeling: *Believe Muskie*. Muskie formally announced his candidacy on January 4, 1972, but in the weeks leading up to his declaration he was already campaigning heavily and with good results. He told a large audience in Manchester, New Hampshire, home to the first primary of the 1972 presidential election, that "he had been wrong in supporting American involvement in the Vietnam war and that the United States must now withdraw totally whatever the consequences."[3] Muskie was a formidable candidate, his incumbent opponent fretted, and his antiwar message was loud and clear.

Kissinger's anxiety over a potential Nixon change of heart in Vietnam was, therefore, well placed. Adding to his concerns, however, was the unsettling feeling he had that Nixon had lost faith in his abilities as national security adviser. Nixon was not returning Kissinger's phone calls and he had not consulted him about Vietnam in weeks. Several incidents had shattered the president's confidence in Kissinger. He had backed Pakistan, at Kissinger's constant urging, during its brief and wholly unsuccessful war with India and East Pakistan (now Bangladesh), much to the public's dismay. Although the public outcry was not nearly as virulent as for Nixon's actions in Cambodia, Laos, or Vietnam, he and Kissinger were severely criticized for supporting genocide by the Pakistani military. Pakistan had invaded East Pakistan in March 1971, following election results that brought 160 of the 162 parliamentary seats in East Pakistan to the opposition party, the Awami League. General Yahya Khan, Pakistan's military ruler, quashed the election results abruptly. Protests broke out all over East Pakistan, and calls for independence from Pakistan were universal. Khan quickly approved military strikes to put down the unrest. Hundreds of thousands of Bengalis were killed and another 10 million sought refuge in neighboring India. To stem the tide of refugees and bring stability on its eastern frontier, India launched counterattacks against the Pakistani army operating inside of East Pakistan, forcing a Pakistani retreat and leading to the formation of an independent Bangladesh. The Nixon administration had been secretly sending military supplies to General Khan and supported his invasion plans.

According to Gary Bass, a Princeton University scholar who has written extensively on the slaughter in East Pakistan, Kissinger's obsession with this issue forced Nixon to consider firing him. The national security adviser "ranted and raved" about India's role in the war with Pakistan, the president told one of Kissinger's associates, Alexander Haig. "He's personalizing this India thing," Nixon complained, and he was concerned that Kissinger was about to "crack up."[4] Haig told Haldeman that Kissinger "had a sense of failure about South Asia and seemed to be physically exhausted."[5] Nixon assumed that Kissinger's ongoing feud with Secretary of State William Rogers was to blame, since the State Department had been openly critical of Pakistan.

The flap over India and Pakistan only grew worse when Jack Anderson of the *Washington Post* ran a front-page story on the Nixon administration's "tilt" toward Pakistan. Anderson's reporting contradicted everything that the president had said in public about the crisis. The story even suggested that the national security adviser had approved sending Jordanian F-104s to Pakistan. Anderson wrote that Kissinger "assured reporters that the US wasn't anti-India at the same time he was instructing government policy makers to take steps against India."[6] But the sentence that made Nixon cringe was: "It was precisely this sort of secret maneuvering that got the US deeply embroiled in the Vietnam war before the American people realized it [was] in the public interest, therefore, to publish excerpts from the secret documents"—a not-so-thinly veiled reference to the publication of the Pentagon Papers.[7]

Nixon was furious over Anderson's piece and he thought that someone in Kissinger's office must have leaked material to the *Post*. A full White House investigation revealed that the president's fears were well grounded. Charles Radford, a yeoman in the US Navy serving as a liaison between the Joint Chiefs of Staff (JCS) and the National Security Council (NSC), had passed top-secret documents to Anderson. Radford had served in the US embassy in India and was rightfully offended by Kissinger and Nixon's distortions about the administration's neutrality in the conflict. Furthermore, the JCS had correctly feared that Nixon and Kissinger were not completely forth-coming in their own deliberations on the conflict. That is why the JCS had ordered Radford to gather information. Radford had access to the Nixon and Kissinger deliberations in planning meetings and he had opportunity because the NSC was a bit sloppy with its burn bags.

Nixon blamed Kissinger for the leak to the *Post*. "The real culprit is Henry," an enraged president told Haldeman.[8] He also informed his close staff that Kissinger never accepted responsibility for problems in-side his own office. "He doesn't want to admit to himself that this could be" his own fault, he complained.[9] "Henry is like a child," he contin-ued; "I won't have Henry have one of his childish tantrums. I will not discuss it with him."[10] Nixon pushed Kissinger aside for the remainder of December, which led to the national security adviser's call to Halde-man on New Year's Day. "I am out of favor," Kissinger told one of his friends in the press. Kissinger blamed Rogers and everyone at the State Department for undermining his credibility with the president just when the negotiations over Vietnam were at the most crucial stage. Kissinger worried that he might not get another chance to go to Paris.[11]

Nixon did not let him off the hook easily. He told Halde-man to inform Kissinger that he was planning to make another announcement on Vietnam troop withdrawals before the Congress returned in January and that he might use that occasion to reveal the secret meetings in Paris. Nixon thought that he needed to appeal to moderate voters in the upcoming presidential election, so disclosing Kissinger's meetings took away from the argument of many that the chief executive of the United States was not serious about peace. By exposing the talks, Nixon could make it appear that the only obstacle to peace was Hanoi. He also planned to speed up the American troop withdrawal, announcing the redeployment of another 70,000, leaving a residual US force of only 69,000 in South Vietnam. He could announce that Vietnamization had been such a success that a quicker US withdrawal was possible. He could then outline a program of support for South Vietnam that did not sound like a full-scale retreat. US aid to Saigon would continue, and the United States would intensify its bombing raids in the Democratic Republic of Vietnam (DRV) north of the twentieth parallel and increase mining operations near the major North Vietnamese ports. All of this Nixon threatened to do without any input from Kissinger.

The crisis inside the White House eventually blew over because Nixon needed Kissinger again. With the summit meetings in Moscow and Beijing in the near future, the president wanted to make sure that Kissinger was feeling secure and that he would be useful. It would have been impossible to usher in a new national security adviser right before such a momentous foreign policy move. Still, he kept Kissinger at arm's length about the content of his Vietnam speech right up until January 12, when he asked for Kissinger's advice in advance of his troop withdrawal announcement now scheduled for January 13. Nixon understood that to keep Kissinger contributing to the administration, he needed to stroke his bruised ego. He realized that once he announced that Kissinger had been meeting with Le Duc Tho, his national security adviser would be at the center of a media frenzy, something Kissinger relished almost as much as his exclusive proximity to the president. Eventually, both *Time* and *Newsweek* featured Kissinger on their cover, billing him as "Nixon's Secret Agent."[12] Kissinger called Hugh Sidey at *Life*, who was also planning to put him on the cover, suggesting that running a picture of him without the president was a problem. "Why don't you have a picture of Nixon striding over my prostrate body," Kissinger joked. Or of "me kissing the ring?" Sidey explained that the "cover story is on the Nixon speech, but you are the face on the cover."[13]

Nixon had decided to split the Vietnam talk in two to gain the most public relations value. The first, on January 13, would cover the troop withdrawal announcement, and the second would outline the administration's current policy and explain to the world that Kissinger had been meeting secretly with the Vietnamese in Paris. Nixon knew that the public and press would want answers to some complicated questions on the nature of the secret talks, so he asked Kissinger to rehearse a few with him, asking him, "Why at this point did we decide we are going to break with the secrecy veil and put out this information?" Kissinger assured him that the administration's critics, especially the Democrats in Congress, would understand that there was a gap between the public and private peace talks that was "so enormous that we can no longer" keep the private channel secret.[14] Years later, Kissinger explained the decision to go public this way: "It became imperative to enable the American public to understand that we had made every effort to negotiate an end to the war."[15] He was back in the inner circle.

Nixon went on the air January 25 as planned, announcing the outline of the eight points that Kissinger had presented to Le Duc Tho in October 1971. He told the viewing public that there were two paths to peace: negotiations, which "is the path we prefer," and Vietnamization. He stated that Vietnamization had been so successful that "almost one-half million Americans will have been brought home from Vietnam over the past three years" and that US combat losses have been reduced "by over 95 percent." But the "path of Vietnamization has been the long voyage home," he explained. "It has strained the patience of and tested the perseverance of the American people." Then, Nixon asked, "what of the shortcut, the shortcut we prefer, the path of negotiation?"

He then dropped his election-year bombshell: that he had sent Kissinger to Paris "as my personal representative on August 4, 1969, 30 months ago, to begin these secret negotiations" with the North Vietnamese.[16] Nixon ended his speech by telling the American public that he had instructed Ambassador Porter "to present our plan publicly at this Thursday's session of the Paris [avenue Kléber] peace talks, along with alternatives to make it even more flexible."[17] One of those alternatives was Nixon's surprise announcement that President Nguyen Van Thieu and Vice President Huong "would be happy to resign one month before the new election." The president wanted to be clear: that his offer "will show unmistakably that Hanoi not Washington or Saigon—has made the war go on."[18]

As Nixon had predicted, Kissinger was now in the spotlight. The national security adviser now fielded interview requests on the details of the secret talks for weeks and even made a trip to Congress to testify in hearings on the war. In a lengthy press conference with reporters on January 27, he asked the American public for understanding and to support the administration's peace initiatives in Vietnam. He told reporters that both sides remained far apart in Paris, largely because of Hanoi's refusal to make concessions in return for an American withdrawal. He also insisted that North Vietnam's demand that the United States remove Thieu from power before the implementation phase of any agreement was a nonstarter. Asked by reporters why Hanoi insisted on linking military and political issues in any settlement, Kissinger replied that Hanoi apparently "had little confidence in its ability to win a political struggle in the South if the United States continued its economic support after withdrawing its forces."[19] If one did not look too closely at the details, Kissinger's charm and wit covered all the loopholes in the Nixon proposals nicely.

Still, the reaction in Congress was mixed. Nixon supporters claimed that the president's offer was "fair and just" and that his speech showed that he had "repeatedly done all that he could reasonably and honorably do" as the commander in chief. Three leaders of the Democratic Party in the Senate were more critical. Senator J. William Fulbright, chair of the Foreign Relations Committee, worried that "what looks generous to us may not look generous to North Vietnam. We may have to do more," he explained. Muskie had major doubts about the specifics of Nixon's offer, but he applauded the president for committing to a full US troop withdrawal once an agreement was signed. The most severe criticism of Nixon's speech came from presidential hopeful Senator George McGovern, who observed that "at the same time Mr. Nixon was bitterly opposed to the McGovern-Hatfield proposal to end the war, he was at the very same time offering it to the other side."[20]

Lost in this whirlwind of activity was the fact that the Nixon administration had offered Hanoi no new proposals. The president's speech outlined offers that had already been put forward by Kissinger in the secret meetings and soundly rejected by Le Duc Tho and Xuan Thuy. Of course, the speech was not intended to move the negotiations forward; it was designed instead to show Nixon as a reasonable leader who had made every effort for peace. This fact was not lost on members of Congress who now claimed that Nixon had not gone far enough in his previous attempts to end the war and that Hanoi was sure to reject all schemes until its conditions were met. He took this criticism—just before he left for China—hard. He was even more irate when the *Washington Post* called his speech "The Same Old Shell Game."[21] He complained to Haldeman that the *Post* had "deliberately screwed us, and we're going to have to get back at them."[22] Nixon ordered his press secretary, Ron Ziegler, to hold back on press credentials for *Post* reporters asking to cover the China trip.

Kissinger did not understand Nixon's obsession with negative press over his speech, so he focused instead on getting the president and Hanoi to agree on yet another secret meeting in Paris: to occur just after he and the president had returned from their February 21 trip to China. He thought that the idea of the first US president in history to visit Communist China would move Hanoi to make some concessions in Paris. Several weeks after this invitation, Hanoi accepted, suggesting a meeting for mid-March. Kissinger agreed, but then received a series of postponements from Hanoi. When North Vietnam finally did accept a date, it was only after the Politburo and Central Committee had already committed the Vietnamese Communist Party (VCP) to launch a major military attack against South Vietnam, now known as the Easter Offensive of 1972.

Kissinger understood that Hanoi had been marshaling its resources in order to launch an offensive since Operation Lam Son 719 ended. He also understood that a major attack during a US election year served several of Hanoi's main goals. It would nullify the election results in South Vietnam, take the sting out of Nixon's trips to China and the Soviet Union, and highlight the weaknesses of Vietnamization once again. Hanoi also understood that it would be difficult for Nixon to reverse the American troop withdrawals in an election year, so in the summer and early fall of 1971 it made plans for the offensive. Historian Lien-Hang Nguyen argues convincingly that Le Duan and Le Duc Tho were the thought leaders behind Hanoi's offensive strategy.[23] She suggests that the two party officials triumphed over more cautionary People's Army of Vietnam (PAVN) generals by advocating an all-out military offensive designed to "thwart big power collusion to force Hanoi's hand."[24] At the party's Twelfth Plenum, held in late

January and early February 1972, Hanoi's leadership therefore decided to abandon its strategy of stockpiling forces and saving its resources for an offensive designed to topple the Saigon government. Le Duc Tho carefully orchestrated the diplomatic cables from Kissinger while he and Le Duan planned the military offensive that both thought would force the Americans to sign a favorable agreement. Like Kissinger, Tho held military and diplomatic matters in the palm of his hand. And like Kissinger, he thought military escalation was the best way to force concessions in the secret talks in Paris.

The North Vietnamese offensive began midday on March 30 as several PAVN divisions opened fire from positions near the Demili-tarized Zone (DMZ) and from just inside Military Region I, the five most northern provinces of South Vietnam. Utilizing newly acquired Soviet machinery, especially T-54 tanks and 130-mm howitzers, the North Vietnamese launched an impressive artillery attack against the Third ARVN Division, positioned along the DMZ. No one in the United States or Army of the Republic of Vietnam (ARVN) command had prepared for the North Vietnamese to cross the DMZ because it was thought Hanoi's army was simply not up to the task.[25] There had also been a de facto agreement dating back to the Johnson years that neither side would breach the DMZ. When the offensive began, there were relatively few US combat troops in Vietnam, and many ARVN units were without their American advisers. When Nixon heard that eight ARVN firebases had come under extreme attack, he ordered Kissinger to prepare a plan for bombing missions. Kissinger, however, was unusually reluctant to respond to the North Vietnamese attacks. He saw no need for panic and no need for a massive response. Kissinger even called the offensive a "major enemy probe," dismissing its significance and importance.[26] In retrospect, it appears that his reaction was in part fueled by the "soothing" ac-counts coming from the Pentagon. Defense Secretary Melvin Laird and his associates did not endorse immediate retaliatory action. Laird was always worried about Nixon's desire to launch reprisals, but he was especially worried in an election year.[27] He thought that any major American military action threatened the president's chances with the moderates and those were the votes that were going to swing this election. The result was rather anemic reporting from the Pentagon.

General Creighton Abrams, however, was extremely concerned over the North Vietnamese offensive, telling an anxious Nixon that the situation was "very serious."[28] Over the next several days, thirty thousand PAVN troops connected with the 304th and 308th PAVN divisions and regular infantry regiments from the B-5 Front drove south toward the Cua Viet River, capturing Camp Carroll on Route 9. The same ARVN general, Hoang Xuan Lam, who had been in charge of Military Region I during Operation Lam Som 719 remained in charge of South Vietnamese forces during Hanoi's offensive. General Lam ignored intelligence warnings about the North Vietnamese pending attacks and he had engaged in some rather dubious practices that left the ARVN unprepared. On April 2, Ambassador Ellsworth Bunker cabled Nixon and Kissinger that the ARVN was in dire straits and that the entire Military Region I might collapse.[29] Almost overnight, Kissinger went from mildly interested in the North Vietnamese offensive to deeply concerned that it might spell the end of South Vietnam. He urged the president to respond with the toughest measures possible. It was clear to Kissinger that Moscow was behind the offensive. Indeed, the Soviets supplied the bulk of the PAVN's heavy artillery and tanks. If the United States did not respond to Soviet-inspired aggression in Vietnam, he warned, American credibility around the globe would be "irreparably" damaged.[30] He urged Nixon to take the toughest possible stance against Hanoi's offensive. "If we were run out of Vietnam," Kissinger later said, "our entire foreign policy would be in jeopardy."[31]

Nixon agreed. He was in no mood for Laird's caution, and he did not trust his field commander, General Abrams, who he thought had stale ideas and was unimaginative. He warned Republican congressional leaders: "If this offensive succeeds...you will have a more dangerous world.... If the United States fails at this...no President can go to Moscow, except crawling. If we fail, we won't have a credible foreign policy."[32] Kissinger counseled Nixon to "blast the living bejeezus out of North Vietnam."[33] The president took the offensive personally, as a direct attack on his reelection chances and as Soviet provocation so near his trip to Moscow. He blamed Hanoi, however, for moving forward with this rash mission. "We are not going to let this country be defeated by this little shit-ass country," he yelled at Kissinger.[34]

In early April, Kissinger and Nixon concluded that they had to "carry the war to North Vietnam."[35] The only viable military option, they agreed, was direct US air attacks against North Vietnam. State and Defense both objected to the president's plans to lift the 1968 bombing restrictions against attacks inside North Vietnam. Nixon refused to listen and instead ordered one of his air force generals to recklessly "use whatever air you need to turn this thing around."[36] He told one of his aides that "the bastards have never been bombed like they're going to be bombed this time."[37]

But Nixon had problems in his command. Laird remained cautious, telling him that he should not be using air power against the DRV but should be protecting ARVN forces in Military Region I instead.[38] The Defense secretary also worried that renewed air attacks against North Vietnam would undo the domestic political advantage the president had created with his January 25 speech. The bombing raids might also create a negative international reaction. Nixon thought Laird was too cautious, but he was almost apoplectic when the air attacks were continually delayed. Admiral Moorer, chairman of the Joint Chiefs of Staff (JCS), blamed the weather, but Nixon insisted that the weather "isn't bad" and that "the Air Force isn't worth a—I mean they won't fly."[39] Kissinger, too, was pushing Laird to get the air attacks going. During a phone conversation on April 3 with Laird, he complained that "they only flew 132 sorties."[40] Laird responded that the "weather report… was not good," annoying Kissinger even further.[41]

Kissinger had always thought Laird was too cautious, but the Pentagon's response to the Easter Offensive was more than he could stand. He told friends that what the United States needed most was "a new Secretary of Defense" and a reorganization of "our military establishment." He believed that the Pentagon's lack of response to the crisis in Vietnam was a disgrace. He could counter their pitiful performance, however, by insisting that they act now against Hanoi or face the president's wrath. Kissinger often invoked Nixon's temper when he wanted to get things done at the Pentagon. Kissinger did not limit his sharp remarks to Laird. He sarcastically told his old friend Nelson Rockefeller that the United States possessed "a great Air Force. They can only fly over a desert in July."[42]

As the North Vietnamese offensive continued, Nixon kept pressuring Kissinger to push Laird and the JCS to do something. He complained to Kissinger that the military "has been screaming that they have been hamstrung for a number of years." Now was their chance to hit Hanoi without restraint and they were nowhere to be found. The president was especially irritated with Abrams, who was fond of saying that he was the field commander and knew what would work best militarily in Vietnam. Kissinger screamed at Laird that "somebody better get it into Abrams' head" that the president wanted swift retaliatory attacks against the PAVN "or he may not be Field Commander much longer."[43] Laird pushed back, claiming that Nixon's bombing plans might produce "massive casualties," and this fact created some unease in the command.[44] Kissinger wanted the air assaults to begin immediately, but he also assured Laird that the president would not tolerate "civilian casualties."[45] Such was the dilemma in Vietnam.

Kissinger also called Moorer during the first days of the PAVN offensive, complaining that not enough was being done to punish North Vietnam. Incredulous that General Abrams was in Bangkok during the Communist attacks, he asked Moorer to make sure the general got back to Saigon quickly. He wanted Moorer to understand that he did not think Abrams was taking enough direct action and responsibility to stop the North Vietnamese offensive. "He is not going to run this with a computer," Kissinger warned. He explained to Moorer that Nixon wanted him to know that "we are not going to lose this no matter what this costs...We want every commander to give us the maximum they can do without restraint." He included the mining of all North Vietnamese ports in the plan.[46] But again Kissinger chastised the military command: "For years they have been screaming about lack of restraint. Now we take the reins off and to get them to fly up north is like pulling teeth."[47] Now, he griped, the JCS could not seem to develop a target list that did not include massive civilian casualties.[48] Kissinger thought it was a way for the military command not to take the action the president had ordered. "They have lost us the war," he said of Abrams and Admiral John S. McCain, the commander of the US Pacific Command.[49] He was so angry with Abrams for dragging his feet on the air attacks that he told Laird, "I want two names to replace Abrams—who should replace Abrams?"[50]

Another of Kissinger's major concerns was that the Communists would launch a peace offensive before the United States could launch its military counteroffensive. "If they come in now with a peace offer before we hit them we'll look awful," he told Moorer, explaining, "We have to give the North Vietnamese a big clout" before there could be any agreement.[51] Kissinger wanted the military attacks against North Vietnam to condition the peace negotiations. He confided in Laird, one of the few times he did, that if South Vietnam did not collapse within thirty days, Hanoi "will be negotiating with us." It was imperative, therefore, that Laird pour steel on Hanoi to force its hand. "I don't know who is going to give up," Kissinger told him, "but it will not be the White House."[52] Stressing again how important it was for Laird to get the military moving, Kissinger added that Hanoi was not going to talk "until we get the back of this attack broken."[53]

On April 10, the military finally started that process. US aircraft began to bomb North Vietnam above the nineteenth parallel for the first time since the October–November 1968 bombing halt. American B-52 bombers hit North Vietnam for the first time since November 1967, targeting well-entrenched SAM-2 missile sites and other strategic assets. Within days, the US air attacks also included flying support and direct attacks against North Vietnamese troops inside South Vietnam, especially near An Loc. On April 16, eighteen B-52s and nearly one hundred fighter-bombers hit military supply dumps near Haiphong along the North Vietnamese coast. Nixon told several reporters that the United States would continue its attacks against military targets in North Vietnam until the offensive in South Vietnam stopped. Hanoi countered with a press conference of its own, claiming that over fifty civilians had been killed in the bombings.[54] Massive protests broke out in most major US cities and on college campuses across the country following press reports of the renewed bombing of North Vietnam.

But Kissinger justified the air attacks in bold terms. "We are trying to compress the amount of time the North Vietnamese have to decide whether the offensive is worth continuing and whether they have the means to continue it."[55] Like the old formulation of Johnson's limited war theory in action, he explained, Hanoi controlled the rate and force of the American response and it could end the air attacks at any time by halting its offensive. Furthermore, the White

House was not trying to force Hanoi to capitulate, he said; it was merely asking North Vietnam to stop its attacks on South Vietnam so that the United States could finish its timely withdrawal and then Hanoi would have to take its chances in a political struggle with Saigon. At least this is the rationale Kissinger frequently used when explaining why the United States resumed its air war over North Vietnam.

The bombing of North Vietnam was not without its political dimensions. Kissinger warned William F. Buckley, a longtime conservative who was often critical of détente and Nixon's efforts in Vietnam, that if fellow conservatives did not back the president and begin to sharpen their attacks against those who "are 100 percent off" they would surely get a McGovern presidency. "The more support we get," Kissinger pleaded with him, "the more violent we can be." By launching a fierce air war over North Vietnam, the national security adviser insisted, "We are saving American honor."[56] Kissinger asked Buckley to make sure that other conservatives knew just what was at stake in Vietnam and that the president had to reach out to Moscow and Beijing to achieve his foreign policy agenda.

Meeting with Brezhnev

With North Vietnamese forces continuing to march southward, Kissinger went to Moscow in mid-April for a pre–May summit meeting with Leonid Brezhnev, secretary-general of the Soviet Communist Party. Just before he left for Moscow, however, the national security adviser asked his aides to get as many military supplies into South Vietnam as possible.[57] Perhaps a confident Kissinger thought that he would make progress in his talks with Brezhnev? During their meetings, he made clear to Brezhnev that the United States was not pleased with Hanoi's provocative action and that Moscow stood to lose much that it had hoped to gain by supporting North

Vietnam. Brezhnev hinted that he had little control over events in Vietnam, but Kissinger had already heard from Soviet ambassador Anatoly Dobrynin that Moscow would try to get Hanoi more interested in negotiations. During the April meeting, Kissinger warned Brezhnev that Hanoi would face the "most serious consequences" if it continued with the offensive. Kissinger later told reporters that "I do not believe that there could have been any doubt in the minds of the Soviet leaders of the gravity with which we would view an unchecked continuation of a major North Vietnamese offensive and of attempts by the North Vietnamese to put everything on the military scales."[58] He had also threatened that if no progress was made on Vietnam, Nixon would be forced to cancel his May summit meeting with Brezhnev. This was an idle threat. The president needed to visit Moscow to make progress on his larger foreign policy goals, and the Soviets were well aware of this. They refused to take Kissinger's bait.

Brezhnev did, however, offer a new standstill cease-fire proposal for Vietnam and suggested that he could get Hanoi's assurances to support this new move. Kissinger flatly rejected Brezhnev's plan because it would give North Vietnam control over territory in Military Region I that the PAVN now occupied because of the Easter Offensive. Nixon was also in no mood to compromise. He had ordered Kissinger to talk about nothing else in Moscow "but progress on Vietnam." He needed Soviet help in pushing Hanoi toward negotiations and was convinced that Moscow backed the North Vietnamese push south. Kissinger reported back that he had made clear to Brezhnev that the United States would continue its punishing military operations against North Vietnam until Hanoi stopped its military offensive and withdrew its troops from South Vietnam. Nixon had suspended the bombing during Kissinger's trip to Moscow as a sign of his seriousness to improve relations with the Soviets, but also to signal his belief that the USSR had considerable sway over its allies in Hanoi. He was not pleased when Kissinger extended his stay in Moscow and spoke with Brezhnev about non-Vietnam topics, such as the upcoming summit and arms control. Nixon thought that his security adviser was playing into Moscow's hands, giving the Kremlin everything it wanted while the United States got no progress on Vietnam, and he angrily told Kissinger that he was about to renew the bombing to teach Hanoi a lesson. Kissinger begged Secretary of State Alexander Haig to help keep everyone "calm" until he returned because he believed that the Kremlin was doing everything it could to help Nixon in Vietnam.[59] Meanwhile, Nixon told Haig that Kissinger was "breastfeeding" the Soviets.[60] The president always worried that Kissinger overestimated his importance in negotiations. The trip to Moscow was a prime example of Kissinger's ability to put his own negotiations ahead of Nixon's office.

Still, Kissinger cabled Haig shortly before leaving Moscow with a rather rosy summary of his meetings. "It is my firm conviction that without my trip to Moscow the Summit would have collapsed and the delicate balance of our Vietnam policy would have disintegrated beyond repair."[61] Hanoi did not help Kissinger, however, when it announced that it was going to cancel his April 24 meeting in Paris with Le Duc Tho. It is probably just as well, because the president was in no mood to have Kissinger return from Moscow only to fly to Paris to meet secretly with Hanoi's negotiating team when North Vietnamese troops were still on the offensive.

Nixon was in a difficult spot. If the North Vietnamese offensive led to the collapse of South Vietnam, he feared he would pay for it dearly at the ballot box. Conservatives were already upset that Nixon had gone to China, and now Kissinger was in Moscow, helping to plan for the May summit, precisely when North Vietnam was trying to take South Vietnam by force with an offensive launched through the DMZ with Soviet-built tanks. If the president went through with the May summit, he would be toasting Moscow's leaders when their tanks were helping kill American and ARVN troops in South Vietnam. The optics in April just did not play to his favor.

While Kissinger was in Moscow, Abrams sent a gloomy report to Nixon predicting that the PAVN has "neither lost his resolve nor changed his aims."[62] Despite the heavy air assaults against North Vietnam, wrote Abrams, the North Vietnamese effort had successfully reversed ARVN military gains in each of the four military regions in South Vietnam, and the "total infiltration of personnel and units for 1972...already exceeds that for the same period in 1968." He warned that the North Vietnamese were "committed to and capable of" launching further military attacks through the summer of 1972. Accordingly, he asked the president whether there could be no further US troop deployments out of Vietnam until June 1972, something he must have realized went against Nixon's plans. He argued that any force level under sixty-nine thousand American troops and advisers "will magnify the existing turbulence...to an unacceptable level." Abrams cautioned that the ARVN was not likely to win the battle against North Vietnam without "substantial US material and moral support."[63] Few things annoyed Richard Nixon more than pessimistic field reports from Vietnam.

When Kissinger returned to Washington from Moscow, he immediately went to Camp David for a meeting with the president. He was expecting a "tense" meeting and he was "very distressed."[64] He felt that Nixon had not supported his negotiating position in Moscow; and cables demanding that he get progress on Vietnam, or else, hardly steadied his nerves. But Nixon was always averse to direct confrontation, so his Camp David meeting with Kissinger ended with both agreeing that Nixon should go public about the North Vietnamese offensive, his security adviser's trip to Moscow, and a new troop withdrawal announcement. What would not be mentioned in the speech, however, was that Hanoi had finally agreed that Tho and Kissinger would meet again in Paris on May 2.

May

The day before he left for Paris, Kissinger had one of his regular long and meandering phone conversations with the president. Nixon wanted to make sure that Kissinger understood that "the bargaining position we have isn't very strong right at this moment." He urged Kissinger not to worry too much about South Vietnam, but to "just remember they [Hanoi] are in for a hell of a shock if they turn us down." Nixon was referring to his April 25 speech, when he reiterated his Eight Points fully articulated during his previous January address to the nation. He was offering no new proposals; he wanted Kissinger to understand that clearly. His major incentive to offer Hanoi was "the fear they have for what we can do to them." Nixon promised if Hanoi did not accept his peace offer soon, "we will demolish them." Kissinger agreed, and then turned to his usual habit of fawning over the president, "Our biggest strength right now is your unpredictability and your toughness."[65]

Despite the tough talk, Kissinger was worried. North Vietnamese forces had just taken Quang Tri City, the first provincial capital captured during the offensive. It appeared that nothing was going to stop their march south, and soon Hue would be the target. The symbolism of the old imperial capital falling to North Vietnamese forces was almost too much to bear. The PAVN were taking on enormous casualties, but nothing was slowing them down. Nixon hated the idea that Hanoi was "kicking us" and that the United States was not "kicking them." Of course, he complained, "I am not sure the goddamned Air Force ever hits anything."[66] That had always been one of Laird's main concerns. He never thought the air attacks against North Vietnam were going to stop the Easter Offensive or win the war. "You can't win the damn thing just with air power...you gotta win this damn thing on the ground," he told Kissinger in early May.[67] The problem on the ground, Laird added, was not training, was not materiel (with the possible exception of the M41 Walker Bulldog, a light tank that was no match for the Soviet-built T-54), and was not mission; it was leadership. What the ARVN needed was to change "a few commanders right now" and a good "kick in the ass."[68]

But Kissinger did not see the problem in South Vietnam exclusively as a problem with the ARVN. He blamed Laird and Abrams for lying to the president about the ARVN's strengths and capabilities and the military command for its reluctance to mount a major offensive against Hanoi's key assets. If they had been telling the president the truth all along, Kissinger reasoned, Nixon could go to Moscow in May "very cool" and say, "All right, we are licking you sons-of-bitches." Nixon agreed, stating that now there were no good choices left in South Vietnam, but that he would still make them. "The only one who would consider doing nothing," the president told Kissinger, "would be Laird."[69] Although he relished Nixon's attacks on Laird, Kissinger had real problems facing him in Paris. How could he convince Hanoi that to continue the offensive would come at too high a price? How could he relay to Tho and the rest of the North Vietnamese leadership that Nixon meant it when he said that he was prepared to unleash hell on Hanoi?

When the meeting started, Tho noticed that Kissinger's personal demeanor had changed. The national security adviser "no longer had the appearance of a university professor making long speeches and continually joking," but was now instead "embarrassed and thoughtful."[70] But remarkably, Kissinger told Tho that he had nothing new to say. He reminded his Vietnamese counterparts that Nixon's proposals from last year had been effectively unanswered. He also suggested that the United States was serious about a settlement to the war, but that the "US will not negotiate at gunpoint. There is no reason to discuss a future agreement if the North Vietnamese invading forces are encroaching on our side."[71] Tho was disheartened but not surprised by Kissinger's comments. "After 7–8 months without meeting each other, I expected you to tackle the question of solution immediately," he told Kissinger.[72]

But, Tho's role in the planning of the Easter Offensive was proof enough that he had no intention of agreeing to any of Kissinger's proposals, nor did he think Kissinger was empowered to offer anything new. The entire Politburo thought that Nixon was unlikely to make any meaningful concessions in 1972, and this is what had led them to support the Easter Offensive. Tho and Le Duan made a strategic error, however, in thinking that the offensive would lead to a political uprising all over South Vietnam and that it would happen quickly. During the May 3 meeting in Paris, it was too soon to tell that Hanoi's offensive would not end the war militarily and that the ARVN would actually halt the attacks. Those realities were still weeks, if not months, away, and Kissinger left Paris empty-handed.

In his war memoir, Kissinger writes that the May 2 meeting was the culmination of his effort to secure peace and that he was disheartened that Hanoi wanted to continue its martial endgame instead, even though "there was no question that the back of the North Vietnamese offensive had to be broken militarily."[73] He was clearly engaging in wishful thinking, even though the North Vietnamese offensive eventually stalled. Preparing to go up the rungs of the ladder of escalation, Nixon wrote to Brezhnev the following day, complaining that the May 2 meeting in Paris was "deeply disappointing," especially since Kissinger had received assurances in Moscow that future talks with Hanoi would be productive. The president warned that he was prepared to take "the next steps" and that he was particularly disturbed that Moscow did not exert much influence over Hanoi since "Soviet military supplies provide the means for the DRV's actions." Finally, he asked the Soviet leader for his "assessment of the situation."[74] Nixon was not bluffing about the attacks, he told Kissinger. He shared that he had won $10,000 playing poker during World War II in the South Pacific because he would bluff, "but no one can remember an occasion when he [Nixon] was called that he didn't have the cards."[75] He thought he had all the cards in the spring of 1972, but he was clearly mistaken.

After sending the letter to Moscow, Nixon made plans to escalate the attacks against Hanoi. On May 8, he gave the order to launch massive air attacks near Hanoi and Haiphong. The military gave the bombings the code name Linebacker, because of the president's love of football. "We've crossed the Rubicon," Nixon told his national security staff.[76] Kissinger was delighted. After weeks of debate, the chief executive had decided to take stronger measures against North Vietnam, something that Kissinger had been urging all along. Kissinger knew that Nixon was quite angry that Laird and Rogers did not back him in his hour of greatest need, and he was equally angry with the JCS and Military Assistance Command, Vietnam (MACV). Once again, he alone supported the president's desire to retaliate with massive force to a provocation by Hanoi. Again, Kissinger saw strategic and personal benefit by backing the president's most audacious military plans. Nixon asked Kissinger, "Why in the world is Laird unable to see the critical situation in the South?" The national security adviser told the president that the only thing Laird cared about was Vietnamization.[77] Kissinger called the May 8 decision to escalate the air war over North Vietnam one of "the finest hours of Nixon's Presidency."[78]

Nixon announced the new raids in an address to the nation that same evening. He claimed that the North Vietnamese, supported by massive offensive weapons "supplied to Hanoi by the Soviet Union and other Communist nations," had killed over twenty thousand civilians in their brutal attacks on South Vietnamese cities in "wanton disregard of human life." He then reminded the American people that he had already offered Hanoi, through Kissinger's secret negotiations and his own public announcements, "the maximum of what any President of the United States could offer." Nixon then outlined the three options facing the United States in Vietnam: (1) the immediate withdrawal of all American forces, (2) continued attempts at a negotiated settlement, or (3) decisive military action to end the war. He stated: "There is only one way to stop the killing. That is to keep the weapons of war out of the hands of the international outlaws of North Vietnam." He then dropped a bombshell: the United States was going to mine the entrance to all North Vietnamese ports and intensify air attacks.[79]

The press and congressional reaction to Nixon's announcement was universally critical. The *New York Times* denounced the president's decision as a "desperate gamble" and "a threat to world peace."[80] The *Times* urged Congress to cut off all funds for the war to "save the President from himself and the nation from disaster."[81] The *Washington Post* declared that Nixon "has lost touch with the real world...the Moscow summit is in the balance, if it has not yet toppled over... The only relief in this grim scene is that Mr. Nixon is coming to the end of a term and the American people will shortly have the opportunity to render a direct judgment on his policy."[82] Senator Muskie, who had withdrawn from the presidential race on April 25, said that Nixon "was jeopardizing the major security interests of the United States."[83] George McGovern, the new Democratic front-runner for president, warned Congress that Nixon "must not have a free hand in Indochina any longer."[84] But two public opinion polls found that the president enjoyed tremendous public support for his actions against North Vietnam.[85] Still, over 1,800 people were arrested for protesting Nixon's decision. Police used wooden bullets and tear gas against protestors in Berkeley, and 715 National Guardsmen were called out to handle the protests in Minneapolis.

Over the next three days, a total of eleven thousand mines were laid in North Vietnamese coastal waters and ports as part of Operation Pocket Money. The intensified air attacks on key military and transportation systems (Linebacker) began that evening. For the next four months, US planes hit roads, bridges, rail lines, supply depots, and troop bases, dropping more than 150,000 tons of ordnance on North Vietnam.[86] Less than three weeks after the air attacks began, Kissinger and Nixon were on their way to Moscow for the summit meeting with the top Soviet officials. The USSR's relative silence on the new air attacks proved to Kissinger that the Soviets wanted the meeting with Nixon more than they wanted to help their friends in Hanoi.

When Nixon and Kissinger met with the Soviet leadership in Moscow in May, they were greeted by a firm lecture from Brezhnev: "You overestimate the possibility in the present situation of resolving problems in Vietnam from a position of strength."[87] But Kissinger noticed that the Soviets were most concerned with the ships and sailors they had lost during the Linebacker attacks, and actually had very little to say about any immediate Soviet response. They were "bellicose" and "rough," he later recalled, but their attack on the United States was for the record, to calm Hanoi's nerves, nothing else.[88] He had met with Dobrynin before the summit and had learned as much when one of the Soviet aides translated Brezhnev's response to Nixon's May 8 letter asking the general secretary for his assessment of the Vietnam situation. Brezhnev condemned US actions because he had to. He declared that the Soviet Union would not sit by and watch the United States bully an ally; there would be consequences for American actions. But when Kissinger asked for clarification, Dobrynin offered that the Soviet threat was only meant for "additional measures to those announced on May 8." For Kissinger, this meant that the international crisis over Linebacker and the mining of Haiphong "was over."[89]

Kissinger has suggested that when North Vietnam's leadership saw Moscow back away from the Linebacker crisis (and China was soon to follow with the obligatory condemnation but no action), it felt isolated and was therefore convinced that it had to return to the bargaining table in Paris. "Clearly someone had blinked," he later reported. "Less than a week after the resumption of full-scale bombing and the blockade of North Vietnam, efforts were being made to resume negotiations 'without preconditions'—a far cry from Hanoi's previous insistence on the 'correctness' of its terms."[90] A message from Le Duc Tho was delivered to Kissinger on May 12, confirming a readiness to resume talks. Kissinger believed that his critics thought that Hanoi would "be conciliatory only when we showed goodwill," and that Linebacker proved the opposite to be true.[91] Hanoi was now willing to meet because the United States had pressed it militarily, he claimed.

In Hanoi, the decision to reopen the secret Paris talks with Kissinger was a bit more complex. The US air attacks and mining in May had been quite devastating. There had been a steady stream of war materiel and supplies arriving in North Vietnam as seaborne imports before the mining, but by mid-May it had dropped to nothing. The Linebacker bombings had cut off the main North Vietnamese fuel lines to the south and destroyed most rail bridges and transportation depots in the north. As a work-around, thousands of tons of supplies were off-loaded in China for land transport to North Vietnam. By July 1972, over 60,000 tons of supplies had made it to North Vietnam through China.[92] According to some reports, almost 2,000 tons of military supplies crossed the northern border from China into North Vietnam every day.[93] Some US pilots reported seeing "bumper-to-bumper" truck traffic on major routes into North Vietnam.[94] By the end of May, even the CIA doubted that the bombing campaign could stop "increased levels of resupply" in the months ahead.[95] Despite this impressive movement of war materiel under intense bombing and mining conditions, Hanoi had difficulty moving supplies to multiple PAVN divisions engaged in conventional combat in South Vietnam. Even though Hanoi sent more than 600,000 tons of supplies to the PAVN in 1972, it was not enough to sustain the offensive. Hanoi also found it difficult in this environment to stockpile supplies.[96] In other words, it was impossible for Hanoi to sustain a conventional offensive because of logistical problems. In addition, North Vietnamese troop losses continued to pile up under American bombs and an ARVN counteroffensive. Some estimates suggest that North Vietnam lost nearly 100,000 troops during the entire Easter Offensive. Hanoi could replace PAVN losses without drying up its strategic reserve, but these fatalities put severe stress on North Vietnam.

Adding to that stress was the ARVN performance as it launched a counteroffensive to retake Quang Tri City and the entire province. Throughout the summer, the ARVN fought effectively against the North Vietnamese, taking full advantage of US air power. Few had expected the ARVN to prevail, but by mid-September, they had cleared the PAVN out of the provincial capital. These military factors certainly played a significant role in Hanoi's decision to meet with Kissinger again. It is more difficult to tell from the available documentation whether the Soviet and Chinese positions had much of an impact on Hanoi's decision to back off from its military goals and accept a meeting with Kissinger, but clearly Moscow and Beijing had little impact on what was said in Paris.

The VCP considered its options in May, and finally decided that it could no longer take South Vietnam by force. On June 1, the Politburo passed Resolution 220, ending its commitment to the military goals of the Easter Offensive. Hanoi could not deliver the knockout blow that Le Duan and Le Duc Tho had predicted, but the PAVN had caused considerable pain and consternation in South Vietnam.

President Thieu was forced to declare martial law and lower the ARVN draft age to seventeen. Over forty thousand ARVN troops that were released from service were called back to active duty. But Thieu remained in power despite these difficulties. Hanoi's decision to meet with Kissinger, therefore, was based partly on the pain that the US bombing and mining had caused, partly on the ARVN's military performance, and partly on the inability of the PAVN to take South Vietnam by force. And yet party leaders firmly believed that the offensive had paved the way for a new phase in the war, one that would require a smaller military footprint and increased diplomacy in Paris.

Opposition from Congress

Hanoi reasoned that the Nixon response to the Easter Offensive had created conditions that made a swift military victory over South Vietnam impossible, but the attacks had opened the door on diplomacy and the political struggle. The Linebacker bombings had revitalized the antiwar movement in the United States, but more important, they had moved Congress to take its most aggressive steps against Nixon and the war to date. There were several attempts to cut off all funds for the war. Senators Frank Church (D–ID) and Clifford Case (R–NJ) proposed an amendment to the foreign aid bill that would end funding for all US military operations in Southeast Asia except for the withdrawal of American troops (subject to the release of all prisoners of war). If the Senate passed the amendment, it would have marked the first time that either chamber had passed a provision establishing a cutoff of funds for continuing the war. The amendment was defeated in August by a vote of 48–42, but paved the way for a host of other congressional amendments to end funding for the war.

Laird spent much of June testifying before Congress on the war's ever-rising costs. Nixon had ordered Laird to send additional military equipment to Saigon as part of his Enhance Program, but Laird complained that these new expenditures were unfunded in the next two fiscal budgets.[97] These were not the kinds of debates Nixon wanted to have with Congress during an election year. Kissinger often complained that Congress was the enemy in Vietnam. "The most amazing thing," he told journalist Joe Alsop, "is that nobody— not Brezhnev or any communist [sic]—is as hard on us on Vietnam as our own people. No communist [sic] has dared to make the demands that the democrats [sic] are making."[98] It now seems clear that Hanoi understood that it might be impossible for Nixon to see the last stages of Vietnamization through because of a recalcitrant Congress. It was unlikely that Linebacker and the mining of Haiphong made it any easier for him to get congressional funding to keep the military pressure on Hanoi. This was not a new problem, as many congressional critics have claimed.[99] During the president's first term, there were eighty roll-call votes on Vietnam in Congress, almost all of them aimed at restricting funds or troops. Laird understood how Congress worked in this environment better than Kissinger or Nixon, and he was pushed aside during the summer of 1972 because he told them both what they did not want to hear.

With Laird on the sidelines, Kissinger did his best to help Nixon with the Congress. He called Mike Mansfield (D–MT) and asked whether the senator would be willing to do the president a favor. "All these various end the war amendments that are up ... I was wondering whether there was a possibility from your point of view of not to bring them up to a vote this week and wait until Congress reconvenes."[100] Kissinger assured the senator that the reason to delay the vote was that Hanoi was ready to bend the knee. "By the middle of July," he told Mansfield, "I think we'll see more clearly where we stand in negotiations."[101] He was quite confident that Hanoi was ready to negotiate and that the war would soon be over. US intelligence reports had suggested that Hanoi had ordered cadres in South Vietnam to begin preparing for both for a standstill cease-fire and for competing politically with the Thieu government.[102]

What Kissinger did not know at the time, of course, was that Richard Nixon's political problems were not confined to Congress. On June 19, 1972, two young *Washington Post* reporters, Bob Woodward and Carl Bernstein, published a story claiming that a former CIA officer, James McCord, who was now a salaried security coordinator for the Committee to Re-Elect the President (CREEP), was one of five men caught breaking into Democratic National Committee Headquarters at the Watergate Hotel in Washington on June 17. McCord had made several trips to Miami, according to Woodward and Bernstein, to meet with the other burglars. Former attorney general John Mitchell, who was heading up the Nixon reelection campaign, said he was "surprised and dismayed" over the allegations and that CREEP had no knowledge of the break-in or of McCord's relationship to the other men arrested at the Watergate.[103] The *Post* would continue to unravel this story until events at the Watergate and their cover-up eventually led Nixon to resign the presidency in August 1974. Against this backdrop of domestic turmoil and upheaval, Kissinger and Le Duc Tho met throughout the summer of 1972, looking for a way out of the Vietnam conundrum.

Summer Meetings

The big breakthrough came on July 19 when the two convened again in Paris. In their longest meeting to date, Kissinger and Tho were unusually cordial toward each other. Kissinger noted that Tho was "positive" and his nonpolemical approach meant that he was certainly serious about negotiations. Kissinger hinted to Nixon in a postmeeting memorandum that he saw some movement toward the president's January 25 proposal. If Hanoi wanted to accept the cease-fire proposal, it could then negotiate the political issues. Kissinger saw no harm "in following this string out." He told the president, "The minimum we achieve is building a reasonable negotiating record. The maximum we could gain is either a fair settlement or a temporary cease-fire." He noted that these goals were still distant, but "we are in a good position to explore the chances."[104]

What made the July 19 meeting so important, however, was that Kissinger did actually have something new to offer. He proposed a cease-fire of four months' duration, "during which period both sides would stop their military activity and negotiate the details of a settlement."[105] At the end of four months, the US would complete its troop withdrawal and then the POWs would be released. This was a very different proposal than the president had made on May 8 and Kissinger had outlined in the May 2 meeting in Paris. Previously, Nixon had demanded that the POWs be released before he would start the final phases of a US troop withdrawal. Kissinger had insisted throughout the spring that any standstill cease-fire would require the redeployment of North Vietnamese troops who had crossed the DMZ during the Easter Offensive. He now told Tho that they could stay in South Vietnam as part of the standstill cease-fire. When pressed for clarification, Kissinger agreed that this was a modified position from the president's May 8 speech. "When I met with you on May 2 we were discussing the withdrawal of all your forces to the positions of March 29, prior to the offensive." He now concluded that North Vietnamese troops could stay in "positions they now occupy."[106] This was an important concession for Hanoi. It also cleared the confusion caused by Kissinger's many previous formulations on the cease-fire. In the July 19 meeting, he had given the definitive US position as one of allowing North Vietnamese troops to stay in South Vietnam, thus forever forcing Saigon's hand.

This was good news for Hanoi. The PAVN's 325th and 312th Divisions, roughly twenty thousand troops, had been sent into Quang Tri Province to combat the ARVN's effort to retake the province. Despite suffering heavy losses, these divisions would now be allowed to stay in South Vietnam and be replaced and resupplied as the result of any agreement worked out between Kissinger and Tho. This was the news that Hanoi had been desperate to hear, since it was now convinced that the Nixon administration was not going to agree to overthrow Thieu before an agreement was signed. If Tho could get the Americans to agree to a complete troop withdrawal, a cease-fire, reconstruction aid, and the release of all political prisoners in exchange for a total cessation on bombing and mining, it might be worth the gamble. In other words, Hanoi's leadership saw an opportunity to settle the pressing military matters and force the United States to modify its commitment to Thieu. Hanoi was now willing to compete with the Saigon government for political control in South Vietnam because it believed that the United States would leave North Vietnamese troops in an advantageous military position inside South Vietnam. Hanoi's leaders sensed that Nixon was willing to give up on Thieu to settle the war. Kissinger had already suggested as much in the secret talks in Paris.

Kissinger did go further down the political road than he had ever gone before at the July 19 meeting. For the first time, he suggested that the United States was "seeking to separate our direct involvement from the political outcome, so that what happens later is the result of Vietnamese conditions, not American actions."[107] He told Tho that he understood Hanoi's political objectives in South Vietnam, implying that it was up to Hanoi to achieve them, however. "We do not want to accomplish" the overthrow of the Thieu government for you, Kissinger informed his Vietnamese counterparts.[108] He did say, however, that the United States would "remain neutral" in any election that might take place in Saigon. To Hanoi, this must have seemed as if Kissinger was resigned to the fact that South Vietnam was going to have to win the political struggle on its own against Hanoi. But North Vietnamese leaders also understood that any political struggle would ultimately depend on the balance of forces inside South Vietnam and the negotiations in Paris were giving Hanoi what it wanted in this regard. Playing for time allowed Hanoi to improve its military posture inside South Vietnam as well as build up its logistics and supply lines. Eventually, the Politburo concluded that Hanoi's diplomats could negotiate an end to the air war over North Vietnam in exchange for a face-saving peace for Nixon in an election year.

When it was Tho's turn to speak, he told Kissinger that the time had come to settle the war through negotiations. He suggested that the national security adviser, too, needed a quick settlement because the Nixon administration was facing public outcry from its actions in North Vietnam. Kissinger corrected Tho, arguing that "the popularity of the president has increased enormously after the decisions of May." He insisted that antiwar activist "Jane Fonda does not represent America." Some polls did show support for Nixon's military strikes, but the majority of Americans still wanted to see the war come to an end. Kissinger also agreed with Tho that the "original reasons which led to our involvement [in Vietnam] are no longer valid," so it was indeed time to reach a negotiated settlement. Tho was disappointed that Kissinger had not come with more specific proposals, namely an immediate US troop withdrawal and a cease-fire, but he reported to his colleagues in Hanoi that the "US showed it wanted a solution," even if Kissinger presented "nothing new."[109] But the July 19 meeting did set the precedent for how the secret talks would shape the final agreement.

Kissinger and Tho met again on August 1, for eight hours. Kissinger reported to Nixon that this was the "most interesting session we have ever had."[110] Notes from Hanoi confirm that its negotiators sensed movement in Paris. They reported that Kissinger was eager to get something done before the US presidential election, and therefore, seemed open to compromise on the political arrangements in South Vietnam. To explore this opening, the Politburo instructed Tho to "discuss the major principles based on our *maximum requirements* [italics in original] so that we might sound the US intention and force a comprehensive settlement."[111] Hanoi's negotiators in Paris were to employ this tactic "until the convention of the Republican Party," which in 1972 was held the third week in August in Miami Beach, Florida.[112] The negotiators were then to gradually steer Kissinger "towards our position of settlement."[113] At the August 1 meeting, Tho outlined what that might look like from Hanoi's perspective: the US should stop all military activities in Vietnam, withdraw all of its troops within two months, grant reconstruction aid, and support the creation of a coalition government.[114] For the first time, however, Hanoi did not insist that Thieu be removed from power before the signing of an agreement. This was indeed a major concession.

But it was a concession based on Hanoi's calculations that South Vietnam was not going to become another South Korea. Throughout the negotiations, Hanoi's diplomats argued that Kissinger wanted to have a military cease-fire but still an armed camp in South Vietnam with the Saigon government in power, just like what the United States had created in Seoul following the Korean War armistice in 1953. Truong Chinh, former secretary-general of the party and leader of North Vietnam's national assembly, warned that Vietnamization was just an American return to the Korean playbook. He argued that the United States had no intention of ever leaving South Vietnam and that instead it wanted to "leave behind a residual force for a long-term occupation of a number of military bases to be used as bridgeheads for helping the Saigon puppet army to continue its criminal persecution and massacre of our people and turn South Vietnam into a US neo-colony and military base."[115] But Tho had backed away from these dogmatic statements while in Paris and now conceded that Thieu did not have to be removed from power before an agreement.

Kissinger noticed the change right away. He later reported that Tho "had a whole new set of North Vietnamese proposals" at the August 1 meeting. Along with allowing Thieu to remain in power until a coalition government could form in Saigon, Kissinger argued that the North Vietnamese diplomats also gave up on their demand that the US unconditionally withdraw all of its troops before an agreement and on a fixed schedule. He declared that for all intents and purposes, the demand for an unconditional deadline for an American withdrawal "was dead."[116] Of course, this was a rather moot point, given that most US troops had already been withdrawn. However, the national security adviser still claimed it as a victory in the negotiations. He also told Nixon that Hanoi no longer saw the coalition government as provisional and that Thieu would have a veto power over some of its composition. The remaining issues— the cease-fire, POWs, and the cessation of American bombing and mining—were all technical issues that could be worked out in future meetings.

Clearly, the record shows that Kissinger once again overstated Hanoi's concessions. Tho still insisted on linking military and political issues and still required the United States to terminate all military aid and support to South Vietnam. Hanoi's diplomats also continued to support its condition that the cease-fire be confined only to Vietnam, allowing them freedom of action inside Laos and Cambodia. Hanoi did agree, for the first time, to announce the names of all prisoners held in Vietnam, but again it would not release any of the POWs until the shelling and mining stopped and the final peace agreement was at hand. Finally, Tho never agreed that the coalition government was going to be permanent, as Kissinger claimed.[117] The record is very clear that Tho still called the new coalition government "provisional." His official statement to Kissinger read, "A three-segment provisional government of national concord will be set up in South Viet Nam to carry out the tasks of the period from the restoration of peace to the general elections...in South Viet Nam."[118] And, Tho still insisted that "immediately after the signing of the overall agreement, Nguyen Van Thieu will resign."[119]

On August 14, Kissinger and Tho met again to go over the new positions. Before the meeting, Kissinger "thought Tho's proposals sufficiently serious to send the whole voluminous text to Bunker and Thieu."[120] He also sent a copy to Nixon, suggesting that he saw movement in Hanoi. Although nothing much came out of this meeting, Kissinger told the president that during the last three meetings in the summer of 1972, "we have gotten closer to a negotiated settlement than ever before; our negotiating record is becoming impeccable; and we still have a chance to make an honorable peace."[121] Nixon was not convinced. He told Haig that it was "obvious that no progress was made and that none can be expected."[122] He concluded that Kissinger needed to be discouraged from talking about progress in Paris, at least until the election was over. Nixon feared that his security adviser's enemies, of which there were many, would use the talks to harm the administration politically. He was especially critical of Kissinger's planned trip to Saigon to meet with Thieu shortly after his August 14 meeting in Paris with Tho. He thought any problems in Saigon would play badly in the United States just before the Republican National Convention, scheduled for the third week in August.

ROBERT K. BRIGHAM

Nixon had reason to be concerned. Kissinger ostensibly went to Saigon to inform Thieu of the progress in Paris. However, rumors circulated all over South Vietnam that he was coming to impose a settlement. Since he had rarely consulted with Thieu about anything, Kissinger's trip only added to Saigon's anxiety. Adding to Thieu's worries was the fact that the once-secret meetings in Paris were now front-page news. No substance was ever leaked to the press, but the time and place of the Kissinger-Tho meetings were now announced in real time. Kissinger claims that Thieu was more confident then than he had been in the past—but how would he know; he rarely met the man.

During their first meeting, Kissinger gave Thieu the working paper he was using to prepare for his next meeting with Tho. It was the first time that Saigon had seen specifics on the talks in Paris. The paper outlined the key US responses to the summer meetings, suggesting that the two sides were close on an agreement in principle. He told Thieu that they should know if a breakthrough were possible in two more meetings. The conditions of that agreement would remain consistent with long-held US first negotiating principles. Specifically, Kissinger reported that the United States would "not change its military position" except to move the troop withdrawal deadline from four to three months. Likewise, on the political front, Washington would reject a coalition government and instead support the creation of an electoral commission that would oversee free, open, and democratic elections among the South Vietnamese. The commission, now named the Committee of National Reconciliation, would consist of representatives from the PRG and the Saigon government and each would have veto power. Furthermore, all decisions made by the new commission would have to be unanimous. The only purpose of the commission was to supervise the elections. One important caveat that Thieu warmly received was Kissinger's insistence that the national election in South Vietnam form a government consistent with the polling. In other words, Kissinger thought that the majority of the South Vietnamese population would not vote Communists into office. He predicted that the Provisional Revolutionary Government (PRG) might gain "two out of twenty" governmental seats.[123] Kissinger had a special message for Thieu about the elections: "In our country, political opponents are taken into the cabinet not to be given influence but to be deprived of it."[124] It all sounded so good on paper.

Kissinger suggested that Hanoi might want to move more quickly than either Saigon or Washington did because its military situation was "bad and getting worse." He and Ambassador Bunker, who also attended the meeting, told Thieu that there would be no agreement of any kind before the US presidential elections and that this would add a certain amount of pressure to Hanoi's situation since the bombing and mining would continue. Furthermore, Kissinger stressed that the Nixon administration would never consider ending its military aid to Saigon before a final agreement was signed. He thought Tho was an imbecile for thinking he would. "I have to confess," Kissinger told Thieu, "that I have overestimated Le Duc Tho's intelligence." Finally, Kissinger suggested that Hanoi might make more concessions at the September 15 meeting because recent polls showed that President Nixon was going to win the national election in a landslide. After the election, if Hanoi had not agreed to a settlement, the US would "step up our air campaign and force a resolution that way." Accordingly, he suggested that Thieu's only public response to their meetings should be negative. "The only thing I ask you," Kissinger requested on the first day of his meetings with Thieu, "is not to say that you are satisfied with our discussions."[125]

Kissinger did not have to worry. Over the next two days, Thieu presented a long list of complaints, modifications, and additions to the Kissinger paper. He rejected the idea of a coalition government, the supervisory commission, national elections with the PRG participation, the end of US aid to South Vietnam, and the standstill cease-fire. He insisted that South Vietnam's current constitution be enforced throughout the cease-fire and that the National Assembly remain in power. He also suggested that any cease-fire had to involve Laos and Cambodia. Kissinger reminded Thieu that if Hanoi accepted a standstill cease-fire and a return of American POWs, Nixon would have to agree, that it was not wise for the Americans to dismiss all of Hanoi's proposals. He also hinted that Nixon might even be forced to accept a bilateral exchange that linked an end to the US bombing and mining in exchange for the American POWs. At every turn, Kissinger tried to make Thieu see that an agreement was near, but that there was more to gain by postponing its inevitability. What he did not want was for Thieu to accept Tho's August 15 proposals, or reject outright his own working paper for the September 15 meetings in Paris. But Thieu did reject Kissinger's working paper and Hanoi's proposals, making life pure hell for the Nixon administration.

Thieu's instincts told him that Kissinger was closer to a deal with Hanoi than he had acknowledged. He distrusted Kissinger, and with good reason. Thieu feared that Kissinger might sacrifice South Vietnam for Nixon's reelection. He believed that the security adviser so wanted to advance his career, to become secretary of state, that he might just "throw South Vietnam under the bus" to get Nixon what he wanted most; a second term.[126] He also feared that the United States would settle the remaining military issues, including a cessation of the bombing and mining, without consulting the Saigon government. If the Nixon administration withdrew its troops and made a bilateral agreement with Hanoi to end the bombing in exchange for the release of the POWs, it would leave Saigon in an extremely vulnerable situation. Thieu understood that a standstill cease-fire would also allow several main force North Vietnamese infantry divisions to remain in South Vietnam. All of this was simply unacceptable. He was even more upset when he received a letter from Nixon confirming what Kissinger had told him and suggesting that the time had come to get a settlement. Thieu believed, as did his staff, that Kissinger and Nixon were ready to settle political matters in exchange for the POWs. He told Kissinger as much during their last meeting on August 17.[127]

Kissinger left Saigon dejected. He always believed that Washington's negotiation position might one day put it at odds with Saigon's needs. It was just like Kissinger, though, to think that he could cut Thieu out of the Paris discussions for years and then simply fly to Saigon to commandeer South Vietnam's support. The irony here is rich. In Paris, he refused to overthrow the Saigon government for Hanoi, but in Saigon he refused to take Thieu's very real concerns seriously. When he claimed that he and Tho never discussed political issues at all in Paris, Thieu knew he was bluffing. The gambit lay bare the problems with Kissinger's overall negotiating strategy. He wanted to appear consistent and conciliatory at the same time in order to make progress and keep the secret talks alive. This meant that he had, by design, not fully shared the subtleties and nuances of the talks with Thieu until he was sitting in front of him in the Presidential Palace in Saigon. This strategy may have seemed prudent at the time, but it would explode during Kissinger's secret talks in September and October with Le Duc Tho, leading to one of the war's most controversial and deadly chapters and sealing Saigon's fate.

CHAPTER SIX

PEACE IS AT HAND,
SEPTEMBER 1972–JANUARY 1973

"WE WANT TO END this war rapidly," Kissinger told Le Duc Tho during their seventeenth private meeting in Paris, on September 15, 1972. "Not only to stop the suffering, but to provide justice to both sides. Not only to cease hostilities, but to turn energies to the tasks of peace and reconciliation. Clearly our two countries and our two peoples share an overriding interest in a peace that comes soon and a peace that will last."[1] Kissinger had come to Paris convinced that the "time was ripe for an overall solution."[2] Tho agreed. He wondered, though, whether the US national security adviser was using the negotiations as an election-year ploy. When pressed, Kissinger told Tho, "I think it is better that we settle before the election but not for the election."[3] Kissinger correctly understood that the Nixon administration had already garnered enough support among blue-collar Democrats and conservatives to secure the election. Settling the Vietnam War was not going to help or hurt the thirty-seventh US president in the upcoming election, but it was going to help Kissinger secure his place in the second Nixon administration. A deal on Vietnam would also allow him to focus his efforts on diplomatic openings with the Soviet Union and China, the heart of his foreign policy goals.

Nixon agreed that the war had to end so that he could make good on his promise of détente and the peace dividend that would come with it. After seven years of heavy combat losses and swollen defense budgets, he and the American people needed a respite from war. "This war has got to stop," he explained to Kissinger, "We cannot go along with this sort of dreary business of hanging on for another four years."[4]

Kissinger thought he could end the war in Paris in the fall of 1972 by tightly controlling the message so that there could only be muted objections to the specifics. He did not share his Paris talking points with the State or Defense Department and he bragged about it to Hanoi's diplomats, declaring that he did not want anyone else involved in the negotiations, especially "within our own government."[5] Only the president and Ambassador Ellsworth Bunker knew the specifics, along with Kissinger's closest staff at the National Security Council (NSC)—Alexander Haig, Winston Lord, John Negroponte, and Peter Rodman. Furthermore, Kissinger told Tho that the Saigon government had not been consulted on the particulars of the new proposals because they presented "great difficulties for our friends" in South Vietnam.[6] He would get Saigon's approval after the fact, he assured Tho. Kissinger held his new proposals closely because he knew that the compromises he was about to make in Paris would raise serious objections in Washington and Saigon. He was planning to concede on almost every important military and political point.

The new plan included a unilateral US troop withdrawal from South Vietnam in exchange for return of all prisoners of war. It also allowed all North Vietnamese main force infantry divisions in South Vietnam to remain in South Vietnam, even though there were still some questions about resupply and replacement. Kissinger never pressed

Hanoi on this issue. He continued to make vague references to Nixon about the need for the withdrawal of "some" of the People's Army of Vietnam (PAVN) troops from South Vietnam, but in Paris he never made it a condition of the agreement. Kissinger never challenged Tho when the Vietnamese Communist Party (VCP) leader remarkably declared that all regular PAVN infantry troops "were in North Vietnam" to stand without objection. Kissinger also pledged that once the United States left South Vietnam, it would not delay North Vietnam's plans. He understood that his meetings with Tho were cementing a process, which "as a result of local forces," might lead to significant changes in South Vietnam. The United States had "no intention to interfere in South Vietnam," Kissinger assured Tho, nor did it "insist on a pro-American government in Saigon." He then spoke the words that Tho most certainly thought he would never hear in Paris: "We will not oppose the unification of Vietnam and that after it is unified, we will respect its unity."[7] Just what was it that the United States and South Vietnam had been fighting for all those years if it was not the political future of South Vietnam? Kissinger was resigned to the fact that he could not give South Vietnam "a guarantee that they would prevail," so he hoped to pry some concessions from Hanoi as part of an overall compromise solution that gave South Vietnam a reasonable chance to survive on its own.[8] His calculations were hopelessly wrong.

One of Kissinger's most important concessions during the September 15 meeting was the timing of the cease-fire. During all previous negotiation sessions, he had argued that the cease-fire had to come at the beginning of any settlement. At this meeting, however, he agreed to Hanoi's condition that it come after the signing of the agreement. This concession was a great boon for North Vietnamese troops inside South Vietnam, who could now rebound from their tremendous losses suffered during the Easter Offensive. The delay in the cease-fire also allowed Hanoi to try to gobble up as much territory in South Vietnam as it could before the truce went into effect. Kissinger wanted to extend the cease-fire to Laos and Cambodia as well, but Tho would never agree to limit North Vietnam's infiltration routes. Without a region-wide cease-fire, Hanoi could also continue its support of the Communist forces working against the governments in Phnom Penh and Vientiane.

Kissinger thought that the cease-fire concession actually played to his advantage because the United States could keep the Linebacker attacks going right up until it signed the peace agreement. He understood from Tho's comments in Paris just how devastating the attacks had been. This was the last bit of leverage the Nixon administration had over Hanoi, since most of the US troops had now been withdrawn, so Kissinger did not object to the delay. The remaining US troops, Tho insisted, had to be withdrawn within forty-five days of the signing of the agreement. Kissinger implied that the United States preferred three months, but that this was not a deal breaker.[9]

Hanoi did make one important concession. In previous discussions, Tho had insisted that the Provisional Revolutionary Government (PRG) and the Saigon government dissolve and that a new coalition commission—the three-party Provisional Government of National Concord (GNC)—be formed to oversee all political matters. Now, he agreed to allow the Saigon government and the PRG to exist beyond the signing of the agreement.[10] Both would then be permitted to temporarily administer areas under their control. Slowly and deliberately, a new provisional commission would oversee the election of a constituent assembly that would then pick an executive. Kissinger argued for the direct election of the president by the entire enfranchised South Vietnamese population and proportional representation in parliament. This difference remained an important obstacle to peace following Kissinger's other concessions. But it also surfaced the idea that South Vietnam's president Nguyen

Van Thieu did not have to resign before Hanoi would sign on to a peace agreement. Kissinger saw this as a monumental victory, one that would indeed allow peace with honor.[11]

Hanoi and Saigon understood that this appearance of protection for Thieu meant nothing if there was no check on North Vietnamese forces operating in South Vietnam. What Kissinger agreed to as a safeguard against Communist aggression was meaningless if no enforcement mechanisms were attached. No penalty or reprisal was built into the agreement should Hanoi violate the terms proposed on September 15, only promises made to Thieu outside the agreement.

Kissinger probably knew at the time that these promises would be difficult to keep, given the mood of the US Congress and the American people. The Senate was home to most antiwar resolutions and amendments. Election projections for the 1972 Congress suggested that even more Democrats would occupy US Senate seats, and they indeed picked up two additional seats in the 1972 elections and held on to their majority in the House.[12] However, national election statistics suggest that Nixon's 1972 landslide win that November was a referendum on McGovern, not on the antiwar sentiments of most Americans. Public opinion polls still showed that nearly 60 percent of Americans characterized US involvement in Vietnam as "immoral," and 60 percent agreed that the war was a "mistake" and favored a complete US withdrawal.[13] Americans were exhausted from the war, and many of Kissinger's policies—especially escalation of the war into Laos and Cambodia and the renewed air attacks against North Vietnam—had pushed them to the limit. To his detriment, Kissinger never really understood how his provocative military tactics influenced US public opinion against the war.

Kissinger insisted that getting Hanoi to allow Thieu to stay in power following an agreement was a major North Vietnamese concession. No Vietnamese—north or south of the seventeenth parallel—saw it that way. Kissinger took great delight in showing a consistent record in Paris on the need to keep Thieu in office following an agreement. He boasted to Nixon that he was not going to do Hanoi's work for it by overthrowing Thieu as part of the peace agreement and that he had won a major victory with the September 15 concession. The electoral commission Kissinger agreed to meant that the Communists still had to deal with Thieu, and Kissinger saw this as a major improvement. But Tho still wanted more guarantees about Hanoi's freedom of action following an American withdrawal. The Politburo believed that the United States could easily use its air power to prop up the Saigon government indefinitely. Tho wanted to avoid a perpetual war at all costs, but told Kissinger that North Vietnam was not afraid: "If need be we will continue fighting" until the end of Nixon's second term, "we will do that."[14] Kissinger never doubted Tho's sincerity on this topic.

Hanoi's strategy to remove the United States from Vietnam permanently rested on trying to get an agreement before the US election or using public pressure in the United States to make sure that the US air war could not continue. North Vietnam's strategists assumed this meant an agreement could come as early as October 1972, but no later than January 1973, when the new US Congress was sworn into office. Tho pressed Kissinger on a date to finish an agreement in Paris even before the details were finalized. Even though Nixon favored waiting until after the US presidential election, scheduled for November 7, 1972, his national security adviser assured Tho that if they could agree on the general framework, then an agreement could be in place by October 15.[15] Kissinger confided in the president that it was impossible to work out all of the details by then, but there was some value in fixing the schedule.[16] He also told him that the September 15 meeting "was by far the most interesting session he had held," and that there was significant momentum toward an agreement. He was particularly pleased to report that Hanoi had made a major concession on the "coalition-type electoral commission," confirming that Hanoi had dropped its demand that Thieu had to resign before any agreement.[17]

This was good news for Nixon, who had rejected any type of coalition government with the Communists. In a lengthy meeting with Haig just before Kissinger left for his September 15 meeting in Paris, the president produced a recent poll, which confirmed "the fact that the American people are two to one against any kind of coalition with the communists [sic]."[18] But Haig tried to convince Nixon that the new commission was just "a fig leaf" that Kissinger had to agree to so as to move the process along. Without supporting this new commission, Haig confessed that "our proposal would have absolutely nothing new in either a public or private sense."[19] The president still balked. He claimed that Kissinger's NSC did not seem to understand that "the American people are no longer interested in a solution based on compromise." Instead, the public favored "continued bombing" and still wanted to see "the United States prevail after all these years."[20] Eventually, Nixon asked Haig to tell Kissinger to take a tough line in Paris or else he would end the negotiations. Kissinger was ordered to take a stance that "would appeal to the Hawk and not the Dove."[21]

Nixon pollsters did not share the complete domestic picture with the president. The data proved that 45 percent of Americans polled in April 1972 favored stepping up the bombing and the same number opposed it. Once the bombing started, there was a significant shift in support for the bombing of North Vietnam, but most Americans still favored a complete US withdrawal from Vietnam. The polls do not make sense without the context. Nixon's pollsters confused the data, focusing only on the first part of the equation. They told the president that nearly 60 percent of the public favored continuing to bomb North Vietnam, which was true but also irrelevant if not matched with the reality that a majority of Americans still wanted out of Vietnam.[22] The majority of Americans wanted to bomb Hanoi *and* withdraw from Vietnam.

Kissinger was growing increasingly worried about Nixon's ever-changing positions on Vietnam. He feared that these inconsistencies would surface just as he felt he was now making major progress in Paris. This must have weighed heavily on his mind as he prepared to meet with Le Duc Tho again at the end of September. Even though Washington and Hanoi began inching closer to an agreement, he was nervous that Nixon might at any moment blow the talks up. Of course, he also was concerned that Saigon would reject the compromises he was making in its name and without consultation. On this point, however, Nixon was adamant: He would handle Saigon if Kissinger got Hanoi to bend the knee. If Hanoi made reasonable concessions, it would be he who would convince Thieu that the United States would always step in to defend South Vietnam militarily. Nixon even suggested to Kissinger, "How about getting [Ellsworth] Bunker over and letting him do the brutalizing of Thieu,"[23] just in case there was progress in Paris? Kissinger begged Ambassador Bunker to make sure that Thieu understood that "the appearance of differences between Washington and Saigon could have practical consequences of influencing Hanoi toward a rapid settlement in the secret talks so as to exploit what the [sic] might perceive as a split between the United States and GVN [South Vietnam] and the resulting political disarray in Saigon." It was essential that Thieu "stay close to us," Kissinger told Bunker, "so that we demonstrate solidarity to Hanoi."[24]

Thieu did just the opposite. He went on record in the Saigon press stating that he "resented" Kissinger's private overtures in Paris on important political matters and claimed that he had not been fully consulted. Sven Kraemer, one of Kissinger's NSC staff, reported shortly after the September meetings that if Thieu was forced to resign as a result of any negotiated settlement the national security adviser made in Paris, it could only "be interpreted in Vietnam as a betrayal."[25] The Kraemer report further suggested that Thieu's support in South

Vietnam actually improved when "he has tried to beat back manifest US pressure."[26] Kissinger was not negotiating Thieu's resignation in Paris, but because he did not consult Saigon, there was much speculation about what was being said to Tho among the political elite in South Vietnam. On September 26, Thieu cautioned Bunker that he would defend his views on negotiations in an international press conference if Kissinger went beyond the terms Thieu had outlined during their August meeting.[27] Perhaps Thieu had been bolstered by the fact that the ARVN had recaptured Quang Tri City and had performed well throughout the summer. Perhaps, too, he wanted to issue a warning that he was not simply an American puppet.

This time, Nixon weighed in with a warning of his own. Changing his mind yet again, he sent Thieu a note suggesting that the time was right to seek a negotiated settlement. Unbelievably, he threatened Thieu that he had better be on board with an agreement because there may be a coup against his government if he did not support the US position: "I would urge you to take every measure to avoid the development of an atmosphere which could lead to events similar to those which we abhorred in 1963 and which I personally opposed so vehemently in 1968."[28] Meanwhile, in private, Nixon called Thieu and those in Saigon opposed to the peace talks "bastards" and "little assholes." "I am not going to let the United States be destroyed in this thing," he assured Kissinger. Whether Saigon liked it or not, the United States had to be "getting out." The president warned, "We cannot have this cancer eating at us at home, eating on us abroad."[29] He was disturbed that the ARVN had not, in his mind, turned all that American aid into a stable military footing. "We've got to remember," Nixon confided to Kissinger, "we cannot keep this child sucking at the tit when the child is four years old. You know what I mean?"[30] Kissinger assured the president that he did. Still, he remained optimistic about his upcoming meetings with

Tho, reporting to Nixon that Hanoi's demands were not entirely inconsistent with the US position.

Finalizing an Agreement

Kissinger met Tho again for two consecutive days at the end of September. He reported to Nixon that the "sessions both narrowed our differences in some areas, and demonstrated how far we have to go in others."[31] He saw "major movement" in the political issues that had been at the heart of disagreements in past sessions. Kissinger believed that Hanoi was finally "stripping away" its control and power over the electoral commission.[32] This was something the United States could work with, Kissinger told Nixon. The new commission was just what he wanted, an "irrelevant committee" that would provide a "face-saving cover" to a cease-fire and a divided government in South Vietnam.[33] Hanoi seemed to backtrack on Thieu, however. Tho insisted that Thieu resign immediately after an overall agreement was signed, but it now appeared that his South Vietnamese political forces would have a one-third voice in the provisional government and the ability to supervise and sanction all of the commission's decisions. Kissinger liked that the commission had very limited advisory power as it mediated between the PRG and the exiting South Vietnamese government. But he also thought Thieu and his followers would appreciate that Hanoi still had to consider the former Saigon government when thinking about the political future in the South. Although the proposal was still clearly unacceptable, Kissinger did see less daylight between the United States and North Vietnamese positions on the most fundamental issues. He remained perplexed, however, over Hanoi's insistence that the agreement be concluded by the October 15 deadline he had established earlier.

He gave Nixon three possible reasons as to why Hanoi wanted a settlement so quickly. The first was that the North Vietnamese were actually presenting their final offer. "They may find it impossible," Kissinger surmised, "to water down their political position any further after twenty years of struggle." The second was that Hanoi believed the United States would "cave in at the last moment" to secure a peace before the election. Kissinger hinted to Nixon that the Hanoi Politburo had told Moscow that this was their strategy all along. It would have been a foolish move, Kissinger concluded, given Nixon's standing in the polls and the American public's support for increased military operations in North Vietnam. Finally, and probably a bit closer to the reality in Hanoi, Kissinger suggested that the compromises made at the September meetings on political issues were the result of some of Hanoi's leaders trying "to prove to their hawks" that the United States would not make any further concessions and that North Vietnam had to give a little to get a lot.[34]

Indeed, this last scenario makes the most sense. At this point in the negotiations, Hanoi had three main military objectives. It wanted a standstill cease-fire that allowed the North Vietnamese who had infiltrated during the Easter Offensive to stay in South Vietnam along with other PAVN units that had already come south. It also insisted on a complete withdrawal of all US troops shortly after signing an agreement. And, finally, it desired the release of all political prisoners. This issue is usually most associated with the US cause, but there were rumors circulating in Hanoi that Saigon's military police were executing Communist prisoners in South Vietnam.[35] If Tho could get Kissinger to commit to an agreement covering these basic requirements, Hanoi concluded that it would quickly change the balance of forces in South Vietnam and then it would be able to meet its political objectives. In other words, it was willing to concede on some political points—in particular, the requirement that the Saigon government be dismantled before Hanoi would sign an agreement— so as to secure its three primary military objectives. If the negotiations produced a coalition government or a three-party electoral commission that recognized Saigon's role in a postwar south, it really did not matter. That concession would be quickly overrun by the military realities on the ground.[36]

Reading the transcripts of the meetings makes clear just how far apart on substantial issues Kissinger and Le Duc Tho actually were. They disagreed on the fundamental makeup of the political bodies that would oversee the political transition in Saigon and the development of an interim constitution. These are the basic building blocks of any peace agreement with legal standing and a necessity for transitional justice. The repeated formulations of an oversight committee gained no traction in Hanoi or Washington. Kissinger repeatedly rejected North Vietnam's proposed political proposals because he claimed they created a de facto coalition government in South Vietnam. Hanoi insisted that the Saigon government would have full participation, but only without Thieu.[37] After the September 27 meeting, it was difficult to see how Kissinger and Tho could meet their self-imposed October 15 deadline and just what would happen if they did not come to agreement by then. It was even more difficult to see how Kissinger was going to subdue his recalcitrant ally in Saigon.

Following the September 27 meeting, Kissinger sent Nixon a message outlining the strategy needed to move the discussions in Paris toward a final agreement. "Our immediate task," he informed the president, "is to convince Thieu of the importance of public solidarity with us as we continue the negotiating process through at least one more round."[38] Kissinger decided to send his deputy, General Al Haig, a longtime admirer of Thieu's, to Saigon to review the various proposals being put forward in Paris. He told Haig to reemphasize the continuing US commitment to Saigon, "the major efforts we have made in his behalf the last four years," and to explain the US strategy in Paris in such a way that would move Thieu to show an "understanding of our problems."[39] Privately, Kissinger and Nixon agreed that Thieu needed to help them end the war now, and then later Hanoi and Saigon could "go after each other"[40]—a remarkable admission, given all that the Americans and the Vietnamese had sacrificed.

Haig met with Thieu on October 2, reporting that the meeting had gone well and that Thieu seemed to understand what the United States was trying to accomplish in Paris. He wrote Kissinger that Thieu was reassured by their meeting and that he "will be inclined to be more cooperative" now that Haig had explained the US position clearly.[41] But the very next day, Thieu canceled his meeting with Haig. He refused to meet with Bunker as well. Instead, he now insisted that he would not support any of the US negotiating positions in Paris. Haig and Thieu did meet again on October 4, just three days before Kissinger was scheduled to begin talks in Paris with Le Duc Tho. Thieu called the US counterproposals in Paris tantamount to surrender, claiming that "he himself has no problem on whether he should remain since his government is wiped out." Furthermore, he insisted that "Saigon can only assume that everything will disappear" as a result of Kissinger's compromises in Paris. "The President, the constitution, and the General Assembly" will all be gone as a result of the proposed agreement, "even the government itself" was to be dissolved. For good measure, Thieu's vice president, Tran Van Huong, added that "the Communists have always wanted to make the US accept their demands," and that Kissinger seemed content to fulfill Hanoi's wishes.[42]

With Haig still in Saigon, Thieu told the South Vietnamese National Assembly that the United States was getting ready to sell Saigon out to the Communists. He warned, "A political solution is a domestic affair of the South. It is a right and responsibility of the southern people to settle it among themselves."[43] He cautioned that there were sinister, outside forces prepared to determine South Vietnam's future without consultation or appreciation for all that the nation had been through.

Kissinger was outraged. He instructed Haig to tell Thieu that the US president was "extraordinarily disappointed by his reaction to our various proposals and strategy" that his criticisms made it "immensely more difficult" to get a meaningful settlement in Paris, and urged the general to assure Thieu that "a public confrontation with the US would lead to complete disaster." In addition, Haig was to warn Thieu that if he continued to be insolent (Kissinger constantly called the South Vietnamese leadership "insolent"), the only option left for the United States would "be a unilateral disengagement." Kissinger concluded with a plea, "The movement toward confrontation between us must end if we are not to throw away ten years of effort and the lives of thousands which have been devoted to securing the future we have both sought."[44]

Thieu was not wrong, however; even Kissinger admitted that. In a phone conversation with Nixon shortly after reading Haig's report from his Saigon meetings with the South Vietnamese president, Kissinger said that Thieu was right, that "our terms will eventually destroy him."[45] Nixon understood clearly that the settlement Kissinger was negotiating was going to end the war, on US terms, "but not theirs [Saigon's].[46] His national security adviser was indeed negotiating away the future of South Vietnam. With each successive proposal from Hanoi, he inched closer to a deal that sealed Saigon's fate. Thieu was deeply concerned that his government would only be allowed to participate in public life as part of a three-party arrangement that gave political legitimacy to the Communists. Since official recognition of the PRG/NLF had been one of Hanoi's first principles and deeply embedded in the rationale and justification for the war in South Vietnam in the first place, it was difficult for Thieu to understand how destroying the existing government and constitution was a win.[47] He wondered how the United States could agree to allow North Vietnamese troops to remain in South Vietnam. Stopping Hanoi's war of aggression was what had brought the United States to Vietnam in 1954. Why was Hanoi getting to negotiate the political future of South Vietnam at all? That Kissinger thought Thieu could easily be dealt with *after* he secured a deal in Paris, was just one of many reckless mistakes he made during the war.

Kissinger headed to Paris on October 7 for what were supposed to be his final meetings with Le Duc Tho. The two met the next morning, Sunday, October 8, to discuss the new proposals both sides were to bring to Paris. Kissinger opened the morning session by summarizing Hanoi's position on political matters. Hanoi insisted that Thieu resign upon signature of an agreement, that the South Vietnamese constitution be abolished, and that new quasi-governmental organs be established from the national to the local level. Kissinger claimed that "the cumulative impact of these various elements" of the North Vietnamese proposal was clear. "Even if any particular one would not necessarily prove decisive, the combination of them all occurring simultaneously has to give us concern."[48] But he added, "I have been sent here by the President to try for a decisive breakthrough to a negotiated settlement."[49]

Kissinger then outlined some of the positive aspects that he saw in Hanoi's proposals submitted during the September meetings. He was particularly pleased that the principle of unanimity would guide the tripartite body and would guarantee that no single force could dominate that body while it carried out its duties. He then listed a series of remaining concerns for the US side: the provisions for a cease-fire, the stipulations on the replacement of arms, and problems arising from the influence of foreign powers. Kissinger then allowed that the United States accepted Hanoi's political position that "there are two administrations, two armies, and three political forces in South Vietnam." He also suggested that the United States was fine with calling the central postwar institution the Provisional Government of National Concord (GNC). To emphasize this point, he repeated to Tho that "we accept the essence of your September 26 position" that the new commission "can serve as mediator and advisor to the two sides which can contribute to the implementation of the signed agreement."[50] Given Saigon's veto power, it was not likely that there would be much implementation of the peace agreement, and Kissinger must have known this as he met with Tho.

In essence, Kissinger was not offering anything new. He was, however, agreeing with Tho to delay the important political questions on South Vietnam. Supporting Hanoi's proposal was simply a way for Kissinger to concede to political terms that left the Saigon government holding some political power after an agreement. It would then be up to Thieu to make the best of it against Hanoi. Was this a decent interval? Perhaps, but it also represented Kissinger's frustration with his Saigon allies and his hope to get the negotiations settled before the 1972 US presidential elections, whether Nixon thought he needed that or not. It was what Kissinger thought was necessary and he told his staff this repeatedly. When John Negroponte, one of Kissinger's closest NSC advisers on Vietnam, questioned the US acceptance of provisions contained in the DRV proposal regarding the PAVN and the GNC, Kissinger apparently exploded, "You don't understand, I want to meet their terms. I want to reach an agreement. I want the war to end before the election. It can be done, and it will be done."[51]

Throughout the morning conversations, it became clear that the sticking point to the entire agreement was still Saigon. Kissinger confessed that "we have not yet succeeded in gaining South Vietnam's approval for an electoral formula," but he was willing to "return immediately to Saigon" if there could be agreement in Paris "to work out a proposal on the remainder of Point 4 which takes into account the views of both sides."[52] Kissinger then surrendered Thieu. He suggested that he did not want Hanoi to give up on the idea of presidential elections in South Vietnam, but he also hinted that this would not be an obstacle to the agreement: "If I could bring back a solution here next week that should conclude a complete agreement between us."[53] Kissinger went through the remaining military and political issues rather quickly, hoping that Tho understood that this was about as far as the United States could go, given its need to keep some remnant of the Saigon government in place after the signing of an agreement. What happened after that was purely up to the parties inside South Vietnam, including the North Vietnamese army.

Kissinger expected that Tho would once again raise serious objections to the US position. Instead, Tho asked for a lunch recess and then after lunch asked for a longer intermission to study Kissinger's proposals. When the meeting resumed at four p.m., Kissinger was stunned when Tho presented a new proposal "regarding the content as well as the way to conduct negotiations, a very realistic and very simple proposal."[54] Hanoi's new proposal included an immediate standstill cease-fire, a prisoner exchange, a complete US troop withdrawal, and the creation of an Administration of National Concord (ANC) composed of the three parties. The newly proposed political commission would resolve all political matters in the south, but it would not have any police powers. There would also be a standstill cease-fire in South Vietnam, allowing the Saigon government and the PRG/NLF to control the areas that they now occupied. The question of North Vietnamese troops' operating inside South Vietnam was not to be addressed, only that the "question of Vietnamese armed forces in South Vietnam will be settled by the South Vietnamese parties themselves."[55] This provision gave Kissinger some political cover with conservatives back home and in Saigon, but it still left Hanoi's troops in South Vietnam. Surprisingly, Tho now dropped his demand that the United States stop replacement of armaments to South Vietnam. But this stipulation also meant that Hanoi could resupply the PAVN in South Vietnam. There was also a vague commitment to a cease-fire in Laos and Cambodia. Finally, the new proposal again insisted on postwar reconstruction aid for Vietnam, though it need not be specified in the language of the agreement.

In short, Tho's proposal was not that far apart from Nixon's May 8 proposal or what Kissinger had agreed to in their August meetings. It seemed that Hanoi was now willing to accept a military settlement separate from the political one. The new commission would handle the political problems after an agreement was signed. It would also be the forum for discussions on the armed forces operating inside South Vietnam. This arrangement allowed Thieu to stay in power until the cease-fire went into effect and the new commission began its deliberations. This, Kissinger concluded, was an agreement that Nixon could support. "We have done it," Kissinger and his assistant Winston Lord proclaimed.[56] An emotional Al Haig, who had served in Vietnam, said that this pending agreement had "saved the honor of the military men who had served, suffered, and died there [in Vietnam]."[57]

Kissinger quickly reported to Nixon that it appeared an agreement was imminent even though he did not want to go into the specifics, which were "complex and sensitive."[58] He wondered why, though, after a "decade of exertion and suffering by the North Vietnamese," they conceded so many of their conditions.[59] It now seems clear, from sources inside the government in Hanoi, that the Politburo was convinced that it could achieve its overall objectives in the negotiations—its first principles—after the agreement was signed. The Politburo sent Tho a letter of instruction on October 4, just before his meeting with Kissinger. The letter was not a surrender document as Kissinger has claimed. Instead, it was an appraisal of the balance of forces in

South Vietnam and the need to settle the war immediately to take advantage of the current military and political situation.

The letter was the result of two days of consultations at the foreign ministry in Hanoi. The North Vietnamese foreign minister, Nguyen Duy Trinh, supervised a small working group that concluded that the time had come to separate the military and political issues in order to "foil Nixon's scheme to prolong the negotiations and to win the election, to continue Vietnamization and to negotiate from a position of strength." Specifically, Tho's instructions from Hanoi were to seek agreement that quickly ended the US military presence in South Vietnam and establish a political commission that would in effect "lead to the de facto recognition of the existence of two administrations, two armies, and two areas in SVN [South Vietnam]." Such an agreement would naturally lead to a Communist victory in South Vietnam, the foreign ministry concluded, because the "new balance of forces" would be to Hanoi's "great advantage."[60] The letter stated that whatever Hanoi could not win at the bargaining table in Paris, "conditions to obtain these objectives [would evolve] later in the struggle with the Saigon clique and win bigger victories."[61]

By agreeing in principle to Le Duc Tho's October 8 proposals, Kissinger allowed Hanoi to achieve its major political and military objectives outside of the negotiations. This is something a good negotiator should never do. Sustainable peace agreements require that important political and military matters be addressed specifically in the cease-fire agreement. Kissinger left it for the Communists to overthrow the Saigon government as a practical outgrowth of the agreement. He had said as much when he told Tho in September that the US was "prepared to start a process in which, as a result of local forces, change can occur."[62] The proposals Tho put forward in Paris on October 8 recognized that Hanoi could achieve its goals by force after an agreement and that the important matter was simply getting US agreement on the military matters, especially the cessation of hostilities against North Vietnam. Kissinger reasoned that after ten years of war, the United States had no choice but to acquiesce to continued North Vietnamese presence in South Vietnam because a PAVN withdrawal had been "unobtainable" by force and therefore could not be a "condition for a final settlement."[63] Hanoi's diplomats were surprised that he did not demand more of them in Paris.[64]

The seasoned North Vietnamese leadership had negotiated with the French, the British, the Chinese, and now the Americans. They had spent most of their adult lives negotiating asymmetrical conflicts to their favor. They understood that a comprehensive peace agreement could work against them if it contained enforcement mechanisms and implementation levers that were embedded in a new South Vietnamese constitution or other framework. Their job in Paris was to make sure that the political questions had vague solutions. Ironically, this was the approach Kissinger favored as well. Both sides understood that the most important aspect of any peace agreement is the implementation phase, and yet this was the weakest part of the proposal. In effect, Kissinger and Tho were about to leave the oversight and implementation responsibilities of the peace agreement to a loosely defined commission with no capacity or legal authority to press violations and to a three-party committee made up of appointed southern Vietnamese, each with a veto power. This was a recipe for disaster. Furthermore, the proposals put forward in October 1972 contained few resources for the implementation phase and no mention whatsoever of decommissioning any armed forces.

It now seems clear that Hanoi and Washington, exhausted by major war, wanted to move as quickly as possible to the next stage of the conflict. The proposals put forward guaranteed that the political matters that they refused to address in Paris would be settled militarily in South Vietnam after a peace agreement between Washington

and Hanoi. That was precisely what Kissinger wanted. He told Mc-
George Bundy, Presidents Kennedy and Johnson's former national
security adviser, that with the proposed agreement, "we are the hell
out of South Vietnamese politics."[65] But the meaning of this agreement also raises serious questions about the efficacy and morality of
pursuing a war for political means that are then surrendered.

Kissinger continued to comply with Tho's general framework
when they met over the next three days. In lengthy negotiating sessions, the two sides hammered out the last remaining issues.[66] They
agreed to further water down the responsibilities of the political
commission, now stipulating that it was no longer required to settle all political matters in South Vietnam within ninety days of the
agreement but, rather, to "do their utmost" to reach a compromise
by the deadline. There were some significant changes in how to re-
plenish and replace military equipment inside South Vietnam, a tacit
admission by both sides of the military conflict that they knew this
agreement would engender.[67] Tho agreed to a cease-fire in Laos and
Cambodia, though there were no enforcement mechanisms built
into the agreement. And finally, the two sides established a timetable
for the cessation of US bombing of North Vietnam (October 21),
the initialing of the final agreement in Hanoi (October 22), and the
signing of the final agreement in Paris (October 30). They concluded
their four days of meetings in Paris by agreeing that with their efforts
"we will reach our objective of peace."[68]

An elated Kissinger recalled that this was his "most thrilling moment in public service."[69] After four years of hard negotiations in Paris,
he had achieved what most thought impossible, a negotiated settlement to the Vietnam War. He returned to Washington to brief Nixon,
declaring, "Well Mr. President, it looks like we've got three out of
three [China, Moscow, Vietnam]." A confused but nonetheless pleased
Nixon replied, "You got an agreement. Are you kidding? Did you

agree on it? Three out of three?"[70] Nixon then turned to Haig for confirmation. "I'm going to ask Al, because you're too prejudiced, Henry. You're so prejudiced to the peace camp that I can't trust you."[71] Haig agreed that the deal was set. Oddly, Haig then told the president that Thieu wanted this deal and that he was indeed "aboard." Nothing could have been further from the truth. Trying to cover his tracks, Kissinger then told Nixon that he had to go to Saigon to explain the agreement to Thieu, but that it was a better deal "than anything we dreamt of. I mean it was absolutely, totally hard-line with them." Nixon asked whether the agreement would "totally wipe out Thieu." Kissinger's response was again deceptive at best: "Oh no. It's far better than anything we discussed. He won't like it because he thinks he's winning."[72] He was right that Thieu would not like the agreement.

Thieu Objects

After a return trip to Paris on October 17 to go over the final drafting of the agreement, Kissinger flew directly to Saigon to meet with Thieu,[73] and spent five days going over the treaty with him point by point. On the first day, the South Vietnamese president assembled his entire national security staff and Saigon's representatives to the avenue Kléber talks in Paris. Haig called the meeting "tense" and "emotional," but Kissinger told Nixon that Thieu and his colleagues did not reveal their reaction to the proposed agreement and instead sat quietly, "coolly reserving any judgments." When Thieu asked whether the agreement was part of Nixon's reelection campaign, Kissinger pulled out a handwritten note from the president assuring Saigon's leaders that there were no "electoral considerations" in the draft agreement and that "we could not miss the chance for an honorable peace."[74]

During subsequent meetings, Kissinger continued to stress that the agreement was good for South Vietnam. Incredibly, he told Thieu that the National Liberation Front's (NLF) cadres would be totally demoralized by the peace pact (maybe implying that they still had military and political work ahead of them?) and that Nixon would respond with ferocious force if North Vietnam violated the agreement. He reported to Nixon that Thieu was coming around to support the agreement—another of his major misstatements of fact—but that South Vietnam was still having "great psychological difficulty with cutting the American umbilical cord." Kissinger wondered whether Saigon's leaders were a little too fixated on the North Vietnamese and their cunning. He claimed that what South Vietnam needed was a good dose of self-confidence to face the political and military challenges ahead of it. Still, he was sympathetic to the idea that Saigon simply wanted more time. "They know what they have to do and it is painful," he told Nixon. He lamented the fact that if the US could have lasted two more years, Saigon would "have it made." Still, Kissinger expected Thieu to get on board with the agreement if he wanted to continue to receive American military aid. The time had come, he warned, for Thieu to show his full support for "the agreement."[75] Privately, Kissinger confided that the United States "never said that we were committed to preserving him."[76]

Once again, Kissinger had badly miscalculated Thieu's willingness to do what the United States told him. Thieu leaked his conversation with Kissinger to the South Vietnamese government and he spread the rumor around Saigon that he had not been consulted about the progress in Paris. He also told supporters that he was disgusted that Kissinger presented him such a flawed agreement. Thieu told his National Assembly that he was not going to accept this surrender document, and on October 24, the day after Kissinger left Saigon, he went on the radio to announce in specific detail what was wrong with the proposal. He charged that Kissinger wanted him to participate in a coalition government (not entirely accurate) and that

North Vietnamese troops would be allowed to stay in South Vietnam (entirely accurate). He called for direct negotiations between Saigon and Hanoi and direct talks between the PRG and South Vietnam. For the next several days, Thieu and his staff examined the proposal and wrote to Kissinger with sixty-nine major changes that they required. Former ambassador to the United States Bui Diem suggested that Kissinger had "chosen to treat the South Vietnamese as secondary players in the negotiating game" and that he and Nixon had "formulated their strategies without us and had pursued their objectives with the least possible reference to us."[77] This arrogant approach to the war only made Thieu more vulnerable. He was not consulted as the fate of his country was being discussed in Paris. His only recourse was to object to the proposal and to keep the US national security adviser waiting before meeting him in the Presidential Palace in Saigon. Kissinger's predictable response was that "no ally had a right to treat an emissary of the President of the United States this way...We felt the impotent rage so cunningly seeded in foreigners by the Vietnamese."[78] Kissinger practiced his own special version of orientalism.

Thieu's fears about the PAVN and the flawed proposed agreement were justified. Allowing North Vietnamese troops to remain in South Vietnam meant that he had to orchestrate a two-front war with diminishing US resources while Hanoi continued to enjoy military support from China and the Soviet Union. This allowed local PRG/NLF forces to make rapid advances because Saigon needed to spend its resources combating the heavily mechanized PAVN infantry forces. This was not an idle concern. A top-secret CIA assessment of Communist military strength, given to Kissinger on October 16, claimed that "the enemy was inching closer to Saigon than at any time since the spring of 1968." Most military regions in South Vietnam saw significant levels of enemy troops that were now leaving their base areas and preparing to attack urban centers. Particularly crucial were

Communist advances in Military Region 4, where they threatened the important delta city of My Tho and the entire "rice bowl" of the Mekong Delta. A military freeze in place, the report warned, "could be depicted as entailing a loose Communist encirclement of Saigon with the GVN's [South Vietnam] capital technically describable...as an enclave island more or less surrounded by PRG territory."[79]

Thieu thought that Hanoi was also getting an American troop withdrawal without any requirement that it remove its own troops from South Vietnam. He had always envisioned the war in South Vietnam ending as the Korean War had, with an armistice that created a heavily guarded demilitarized zone with massive US support, including American troops. What Kissinger was negotiating instead was a unilateral American withdrawal that left the PAVN in South Vietnam and the PRG/NLF in a shared oversight arrangement as its forces marched on Saigon. It was almost too much for Thieu to bear. He reportedly told his close colleagues that he would resist the October agreement with every fiber of his being, even in the face of American pressure.[80]

Kissinger assured Thieu that the specifics of the agreement did not matter because if North Vietnam violated the peace pact, "the US would act to enforce the agreements."[81] After the war, Kissinger's critics charged that he and the president did not have the constitutional authority to make such pledges, that only Congress could make such explicit authorizations. Since Congress was not likely to make such an approval, it stood to reason that Kissinger was making empty promises and that he should have known better. Yet he defended his assurances to Thieu, explaining that he thought it was "inconceivable that the United States should fight for ten years and lose over 55,000 men and then stand by while the peace treaty, the achievement of their sacrifice, was flagrantly violated." A refusal to enforce the agreement would have turned the negotiations "into a subterfuge for abandonment."[82] That was precisely Thieu's point. He claimed that Kissinger was betraying Saigon. Kissinger's plan was more than a betrayal of a corrupt Saigon government, however; it was the abandonment of all of South Vietnam.

To make matters worse, Hanoi broke a promise to Kissinger by announcing that North Vietnam and the United States had reached a tentative peace agreement. The announcement came while he was still in Saigon. There was some political advantage to Nixon that North Vietnam had announced that an agreement was close just before the US presidential election, but it did Kissinger no favors in Saigon. Sensing that he was getting nowhere with Thieu, Kissinger instructed Haig to contact Hanoi's representatives in Paris to tell them of the difficulties he and Nixon were having with the Saigon government. Haig's cable explained that the United States could not proceed in the negotiations unilaterally, and since Saigon had so many objections to the October draft, it had to sort out the complex details further. Haig informed Hanoi that the president had also requested that "Kissinger return to Washington immediately to consult on what further steps to take." The cable also warned that the serious obstacles in Saigon were caused in part, by the "breach of confidence committed by the DRV" when it went public with the contents of the proposal. Still, Haig's cable assured Hanoi that the US remained committed to finding a solution to the war at the earliest opportunity.[83] But, Haig added, there would be no more negotiations until after the US presidential election.

To make sure that the negotiations stayed on track and that Saigon did not completely halt the progress made in Paris, Kissinger went on a publicity campaign of his own. On October 26, shortly after his return from Saigon, he held a press conference where he claimed that "peace is at hand." He suggested that Saigon had some objections to the proposal, but in a thinly veiled threat added that the United States "will make our own decisions as to how long we believe a war should be continued." To make sure that Hanoi realized what he was saying, Kissinger told the gathered reporters on the record that he believed the entire negotiations could be wrapped up in "one more negotiating session with the North Vietnamese."[84] South Vietnam was noticeably absent from this assurance. Saigon's intransigence would not stop the negotiations from moving forward.

Kissinger's press conference also served as damage control just before the November 7 presidential election. Hanoi's public announcement had put some pressure on Nixon to secure a deal before that date, but Kissinger's statements to the press gave the United States options. It was, in a sense, the best of both worlds for Nixon. He could point to supposedly substantial progress in the peace talks, but did not have to defend the specifics of an agreement that Saigon thought was a suicide pledge. Others noticed Kissinger's skill, too. Chuck Colson, one of Nixon's closest aides, called him shortly after his press conference to say that it was "a masterful performance . . . but more importantly, you put it across in such a way that now what happens now for the next 10 days, the election is settled. You've settled it."[85] Even Secretary of State Rogers applauded Kissinger's skill at turning a bad situation into a political bonanza for Nixon, telling him that his press conference "covered the ground as well as could possibly be covered. I don't know how you could have been better."[86]

Nixon, however, ever sensitive to his own light, did not like Kissinger's grandstanding just before the election. Kissinger explained it this way: "No chief executive would take kindly to an appointee who is cast by the media as the fount of all constructive actions."[87] Even though he was somewhat dissatisfied with his landslide win over McGovern (it was not as big as Johnson's margin of victory over Goldwater in 1964), Nixon mustered enough conviction to make sure Thieu supported the peace process.

Nixon sent Thieu a letter shortly after his reelection victory, explaining that the United States needed to move forward in Paris. He was resigned to settle, Nixon wrote Thieu, and he did not appreciate Saigon's "self-defeating" public "distortions" about the "sound" and "excellent" agreement that his national security adviser had negotiated. Nixon promised Thieu that he would make revisions in the language for the electoral commission and demand a North Vietnamese troop withdrawal and the decommissioning of the PLAF. He warned Thieu that he should be under "no illusions" that the United States would go beyond these requests and that Saigon had better comply or Nixon would be forced "to take brutal action" against South Vietnam. To soften the blow, Nixon promised that he would retaliate immediately if North Vietnam violated the agreement, and he offered to meet with Thieu after the agreement was signed, to symbolize their unity.[88]

Thieu still had many objections, but Nixon instructed Kissinger to get the talks in Paris moving again. The president desperately wanted to get the war behind him before the start of his second term. Luckily for Nixon, Hanoi agreed to another meeting beginning on November 20, and a timetable for two other sessions was established. During the first meeting, Kissinger presented Thieu's list of sixty-nine demands. Even Kissinger thought that this was a mistake. "The list went so far beyond what we had indicated both publicly and privately that it must have strengthened Hanoi's already strong temptation to dig in."[89] There were other reasons why Hanoi was in no mood for renegotiation on the key points of the proposal. The Politburo were careful watchers of American politics. Hanoi's leaders expected that Kissinger would soon face a deadline of his own. When the new Congress was sworn in the first week of January 1973, Nixon would be facing an even more hostile US Senate. Republicans had lost two seats and conservative Democrats who occasionally supported Nixon's Vietnam policy lost their leadership positions on a number of important committees. More important, this new Congress promised to pass a war powers resolution limiting the president's ability to take the nation to battle. It was also very likely, Laird warned, that Congress would not continue to fund the war.

Against this backdrop, Le Duc Tho now made new demands of his own. During the second day of their meetings, he insisted that the PRG/NLF and the Saigon government sign and support the proposal. He also demanded that areas now under PRG/NLF control in South Vietnam had to be carefully delineated. There would be no North Vietnamese troop withdrawal, even though Nixon had just given Thieu an assurance that Hanoi would be required to withdraw all of its troops from South Vietnam. Finally, Tho reiterated that the peace agreement must specifically state that the South Vietnamese people had the right to determine their own future. In a letter to the Politburo, Tho explained that during the meeting he had "criticized Kissinger's suggested changes to the Agreement and raised...matters of principle" for our side.[90]

Kissinger sent word to Nixon that things were not going well in Paris, but that it was still obvious that "the North Vietnamese do want a settlement." He confirmed that Hanoi had accepted a few insignificant changes that Thieu had demanded, but overall, they "drastically hardened their position." In several important areas, Kissinger complained, they had "returned to pre–October 8 negotiating positions." He said he thought that he could save the agreement, but it would take days of hard negotiations and would depend primarily on Saigon dropping "their petty demands."[91] Haig was shuttling back and forth to South Vietnam to get Thieu on board, but Kissinger feared that was not enough. After six days of negotiations with Tho, he believed that the United States had improved its position, but only slightly. He reminded the president that the United States had "come into this round of talks with an agreement that we already considered excellent." The time had come, Kissinger argued, to get a settlement.[92] The next talks were scheduled for December 4 in Paris.

When Kissinger and Tho met on the morning of December 4, there was a heated exchange. Tho began on the offensive, accusing the American of breaking his promises. He also charged that Kissinger had not responded to any of Hanoi's proposals and instead had issued threats. Tho recalled that Kissinger had sent a message saying that if there was no settlement at these December meetings, "the consequences would be unforeseeable." In a statement that proved prescient, Tho wondered whether the United States "would even use B-52 bombing raids perhaps even to level Hanoi and Haiphong," and was probably considering using nuclear weapons, a position that he claimed Nixon had supported while vice president to bail the French out at Dien Bien Phu.[93] He then ran through the litany of changes Kissinger had passed along from Thieu, refuting them one by one and concluding that the United States was using the negotiations as a ploy simply to buy Saigon more time. "If you want to negotiate and settle the problems, you must respond to our proposals," Tho demanded.[94]

Over the next several days, Kissinger and Tho closed the gap that had been created by Thieu's intervention. They made substantial progress on a number of important areas in the agreement, and Tho even agreed to advance the deadline for the cease-fire in Laos and Cambodia. Tho also dropped his demand that civilians be released from South Vietnamese jails as part of the prisoner-of-war exchange. This would leave nearly thirty thousand cadres in Thieu's jails, a concession that Tho thought Kissinger should have appreciated more. But Tho still rejected some of Kissinger's other demands. He would not change the definition of the reconciliation commission, allow the terms *North Vietnam* and *South Vietnam* to be used in the territorial claims clauses of the agreement, nor agree that

North Vietnamese troops would be withdrawn from South Vietnam, and he rejected a three-month target date for the demobilization of forces. Since most of these issues had already been dealt with in the October and November draft proposals, none of them seemed insurmountable.

During the December 9 meeting, Tho and Kissinger made compromises that moved the two sides closer together. The United States agreed to restore the PRG in the preamble of the agreement (this Tho insisted upon because it recognized the political legitimacy of the southern revolution). The United States pledged to return to the original language of Article I, agreeing to respect the independence, sovereignty, and unity of Vietnam even though Thieu had objected strongly to this provision. Kissinger also agreed to restore Article 4 over Thieu's opposition, which pledged that the United States would not interfere in the internal affairs of South Vietnam following its withdrawal. In return, Tho made several concessions of his own. He no longer insisted on the phrase "administrative structure" to describe the electoral commission. He conceded on the levels of replacement provisions for military equipment and he agreed to include a sentence requiring that North Vietnam and South Vietnam respect the Demilitarized Zone (DMZ).[95]

The only two remaining sticking points were the status of the DMZ and Hanoi's insistence that the PRG be mentioned in the text—not just the preamble—of the agreement. Both sides had returned to the spirit of the October proposal, and each had sharpened the agreement to its liking. It appeared by the December 12 meeting that Kissinger and Tho were close to handing the proposed agreement over to the avenue Kléber meetings to work out the technical aspects of the treaty. Spirits were further lifted when Kissinger brought along Ambassador William Sullivan, the assistant secretary of state, and Ambassador William Porter, chief of the US delegation in Paris.[96] Their experience and expertise would certainly help at this stage of the negotiations, Kissinger claimed. After the meeting, Kissinger told Nixon that Hanoi agreed to strengthen the language on the DMZ, and therefore, "our requirements I indicated publicly on October 26 have been essentially met." He informed the president that the only US concessions "have been to drop other changes we were requesting in an agreed text which Hanoi considered sacrosanct to start with."[97] Kissinger implied that Thieu would accept the agreement if the proposal included the tougher language on the DMZ. Once again, as he had throughout the process of negotiation, he was overstating Saigon's acceptance to compromises he had made in its name in Paris without consulting the South Vietnamese.

Kissinger was not giving Nixon the full picture. He failed to mention that the revised proposals that he claimed were major concessions from Hanoi still included the proviso that allowed the PAVN to stay in South Vietnam. Thieu never would agree to this clause unless coerced and threatened. Nixon, through Haig, instructed Kissinger to "hold tough on the DMZ issue" and said that he should expect Moscow to pressure Hanoi to accept this deal soon if they were going to have any influence over their allies at all. Nixon told Kissinger that if Tho was still intransigent, "you should try our compromise [on the DMZ issue] as the final US concession."[98] Going into the final two days of the meetings, December 11 and 12, therefore, an agreement seemed imminent. This is what makes the events that followed so puzzling and controversial.

Unexpected Escalation

Reporting to Haig following his afternoon meeting with Tho on December 11, Kissinger characterized the day's discussions as being composed "of equal parts of insolence, guile, and stalling by the North Vietnamese." He concluded that it was still possible that the two sides would reach an agreement during the next day's session, but "nothing in their behavior suggests any urgency and much in their manner suggests cock-sure insolence." He then suggested that he return to Washington in the evening after the December 12 meeting. He would not call off the negotiations altogether, but rather would inform Tho that "the two sides are close enough to continue work through diplomatic channels."[99] Kissinger feared that Hanoi was simply stalling for time, thinking that Congress would soon cut off funding for the war or that the contradictions between Washington and Saigon would precipitate a total US withdrawal. In either case, he found Hanoi's negotiating posture intolerable, even though either scenario seemed likely. Nixon agreed. That evening, he instructed Haig to cable Kissinger, telling him he should come home if he found Hanoi "unmanageably intransigent," but Nixon agreed that his national security adviser should not break off the talks. He even suggested that if Kissinger thought there was significant progress in the negotiations on December 12, he should be prepared "to extend your stay" if a "day or two more labor will resolve the matter."[100] In typical Nixon fashion, he called Haig almost hourly with updated positions—some contrary to instructions just sent to Kissinger. Eventually, the president told Kissinger that if there was no progress on December 12, he was prepared to "move immediately with the around-the-clock bombing of the Hanoi area" and the reseeding of mines near Haiphong.[101] Haig had long been a proponent of the sustained bombing of North Vietnam above the twentieth parallel, so he must have been relieved to relay Nixon's message to his boss in Paris.

At the same time, Tho was having problems with his superiors in the Politburo. According to Vietnamese sources, Xuan Thuy and Tho urged Hanoi to soften its position on the DMZ, realizing that if they continued to stick to the proposed vague language, the United States would certainly reject the entire agreement. "It is possible that the talks may be suspended for a period of time and the war will continue." Tho further warned that the United States faced many obstacles to its plans to continue the war indefinitely, but it could certainly "make massive concentrated attacks for a time and then request the resumption of talks. If we refuse to meet with them the war will continue and the US will place the blame on us."[102] Tho recommended that he agree to tougher language on the DMZ and sign the proposal. "Right now the US needs a settlement," Tho informed the Politburo, "but if we leave things too long we will miss this opportunity and then our pressure on them will have little effect, because everything has its limits."[103]

It is clear from the transcript of the December 12 meeting that the Politburo refused Tho's recommendation. There would be no compromise on the DMZ, Tho informed Kissinger, who immediately rejected the language as written. Kissinger told Haig that Hanoi was simply "playing for time," that the North Vietnamese diplomats could have "settled in three hours any time these past few days if they wanted to, but they have deliberately avoided this." Kissinger felt that "we have no leverage with Hanoi or Saigon, and we are becoming prisoners of both sides' internecine conflicts. Our task," he concluded, "is to get some leverage on both of them."[104] Accordingly, Kissinger then recommended that the United States should "reseed the mines" and "take off all restrictions on bombing south of the 20th parallel." He also recommended "a two or three day strike including B-52s north of the 20th parallel for early next week." He then issued a strong warning to Haig, who was about to be promoted to a four-star general in the US Army: "It is essential that the military perform effectively for once in the above tasks." Oddly, he concluded his cable to Haig by confirming that Hanoi has "reduced the issues to a point where a settlement can be reached with one exchange of telegrams. I do not think they will send this telegram, however, in the absence of strong pressures."[105] Kissinger's response here is puzzling. On the one hand, he recognized that the two sides were close to an agreement, but on the other he believed that Hanoi would give up its last remaining objections only if the United States unleashed the wrath of its powerful military against North Vietnamese cities.

But Kissinger had made up his mind. If he did not make progress on December 12, he would support a massive US military escalation in North Vietnam. The discussions did not resolve the remaining issue of the DMZ or the PRG, but he agreed to one final meeting on December 13. As that meeting began, he informed Tho "we will be separating tomorrow and afterwards be in touch by messages." Incredibly, Kissinger then asked Tho when he would return to Hanoi. Tho replied that he would be back in his capital on December 18. "On the 18th you are back in Hanoi," Kissinger confirmed. He then told Tho, "We will communicate with you after you are back in Hanoi, or you can communicate with us, and then we can decide whether we can settle it by messages or whether we should meet again."[106] The day Tho returned to Hanoi would see the beginning of some of the most intense bombing in the war, Operation Linebacker II. Apparently, Kissinger wanted to make sure that his negotiating counterpart was back in Hanoi to personally feel the full impact of the bombing.

It now seems clear from recently released archival sources that Kissinger and much of his staff had concluded that Hanoi "has no intention to meet any of the basic requirements that we made clear to them at the end of October," and that its tactics have been "clumsy, blatant, and fundamentally contemptuous of the United States."[107] Kissinger left Paris that afternoon for Washington and met with

Nixon and Haig the next morning to explore US options after the impasse in Paris. If Hanoi did not respond soon and positively to the latest US amendments, Kissinger recommended that "we start bombing the bejeezus out of them within 48 hours of having put the negotiating record out."[108] After the bombing raids, he argued that the US then needed to simply "offer withdrawal in exchange for our prisoners," and let the Vietnamese fight it out among themselves. "Let them settle their problems among each other," he concluded. "The South is strong enough to defend itself."[109] Kissinger did not believe this, but it solved a problem for the United States.

Nixon agreed that he had no choice but to resume the bombing of North Vietnam. "The North Vietnamese figure that they have us where the hair is short," he wrote in his diary, they "are going to continue to squeeze us. That is why we had to take our strong action."[110] The president approved Operation Linebacker II on December 18, the day Tho was scheduled to arrive back in Hanoi from Paris, and for the next eleven days, US warplanes dropped approximately 40,000 tons of bombs. The huge American B-52 bombers, built primarily for carrying large nuclear payloads, flew over seven hundred sorties. In his memoirs, Nixon wrote that this was "the most difficult decision he had to make during the war," but that it was also "clear-cut" and "necessary."[111] Before the air strikes began, he warned Admiral Moorer, chair of the Joint Chiefs of Staff, that he did not want "any more of this crap about the fact that we could not hit this target or that one. This is your chance to win this war, and if you don't, I'll hold you responsible."[112]

The bombing produced devastating results. Nearly two thousand civilians were killed and much of the Kham Thien district of Hanoi was destroyed. The bombs also hit targets in the heavily populated Bach Mai district, including the region's largest hospital. The United States lost fifteen B-52s and eleven other aircraft, but the US raids had also destroyed Hanoi's air defense cover. Intelligence reports suggested that "virtually all industrial capacity [of the DRV] was gone. Power generating plants and their transmitting grids were smashed." Gas and oil storage dumps were also destroyed and most military vehicles were hit in their storage facilities. According to one report, 80 percent of North Vietnam's electrical power was knocked out and 25 percent of the nation's petroleum supplies were destroyed.[113] Reports circulated in the US military command that North Vietnam was running dangerously low on Soviet-supplied surface-to-air missiles (SAMs) and therefore could only offer a limited defense of its major cities.

Nixon had hoped that the bombing would show Saigon that the United States was serious about its commitment to South Vietnam, but also to a negotiated settlement to the war. He wrote Thieu a letter as the Linebacker II raids started, explaining that the bombing was designed to get Hanoi back to the bargaining table and not a sign that the US president had given up on negotiations. He sent Haig to Saigon again with the letter that read, "I have asked General Haig to obtain your answer on this absolutely final offer for us to work together in seeking a settlement along the lines I have approved or to go our separate ways." Nixon informed Thieu that Haig was not coming to South Vietnam to negotiate; he was coming to get an answer from Saigon. There would be no changes in text to what the United States had agreed to in Paris, and Thieu had better support the final document or Nixon would "seek a settlement with the enemy which serves US interests alone."[114]

Of course, Haig reported, Thieu waffled. He agreed to meet with Haig and Bunker because, he told them, he generally agreed that he would go along with negotiations because this was his "pragmatic recognition that this would be the only way to retain US assistance." Still, he demanded that the United States insist on the "total and verified" withdrawal of all North Vietnamese troops from South Vietnam at the same time of the total US troop withdrawal. Haig informed Thieu that the troop question had already been settled— the North Vietnamese troops would be allowed to stay in South Vietnam—and that it was now time to signal his approval of the proposed agreement. Haig agreed with Kissinger that "Thieu is more than capable of handling the North Vietnamese threat given the necessary will to do so." Although Thieu was "irrational" and "self-serving," Haig concluded that Saigon was ready to reach a settlement and that "now makes our options very clear."[115]

Kissinger's problems extended far beyond Thieu, however, as reaction to the Christmas bombings challenged the Nixon administration's global standing and his own credibility. Whatever rationale Kissinger could claim for advocating the attacks against North Vietnam, his cause suffered tremendously. Public opinion polls showed that nearly two thirds of all Americans were against the attacks. Nixon's popularity ranking dropped to 39 percent, his lowest numbers before the Watergate scandal undid his presidency.[116] Pope Paul condemned the "sudden resumption of harsh and massive war actions" against North Vietnam. Critics denounced the president, calling his bombing campaign "war by tantrum."[117] Several members of Congress declared that they would end the war by withholding funds after Congress reconvened on January 3. Senator William Saxbie (R-OH) wondered whether Nixon had "taken leave of his senses." Senate majority leader Mike Mansfield (D-MT) called the bombings a "stone-age tactic." Democratic senator from Massachusetts Ted Kennedy said that the bombings "should outrage the conscience of all Americans." The international press was particularly critical. The *Daily Mirror* described the bombing as an act of "insane ferocity, a crude exercise in the politics of terror." The *Times of London* said the bombing was a "particular horror because of its massive scale and its indiscriminate character." The *Guardian* reported that Nixon wanted to go down in history as the most "bloodthirsty of all American presidents."[118] There is no doubt that it would have been almost impossible for Kissinger and Nixon to continue the bombings in this environment once the new Congress was sworn in on January 3, 1973.

Therefore, on December 22, Nixon sent Hanoi a message that he would halt the bombing above the twentieth parallel if Le Duc Tho would return to Paris to resume negotiations with Kissinger. Hanoi failed to respond, so Nixon unleashed the heaviest bombings of the Linebacker II campaign. On December 26, 120 bombers hit ten targets in Hanoi, Thai Nguyen, and Haiphong. Over five hundred homes were destroyed and 215 people were killed. That afternoon, Hanoi informed Nixon that Tho would meet Kissinger on January 8 in Paris. Apparently, Tho had fallen ill during a trip to China and needed time to recover.

Nixon declared victory. He claimed that the bombings forced Hanoi to send "the first signal that they had had enough."[119] He then announced that bombing would be restricted to below the twentieth parallel. But Hanoi made it clear that an end to the bombing was not a precondition for talks in Paris. The Politburo hoped that this announcement would make it impossible for Nixon and Kissinger to claim that they had bombed North Vietnam back to the bargaining table. There is still a great deal of debate on why the talks resumed. Hanoi explains the return to Paris this way: "The Nixon administration had stopped the negotiations to bomb. Now it was stopping the bombing to resume negotiations."[120] On December 30, a White House aide announced that "negotiations between presidential adviser Dr. Kissinger and special adviser Le Duc Tho and Minister Xuan Thuy will be resumed in Paris on January 8."[121]

Back to the Bargaining Table

When the talks did resume on January 8, it was clear that neither side wanted to leave Paris without an agreement. Kissinger understood that he would have to take some heat from Tho, and so he listened silently as Hanoi's leader launched a full-scale attack on the US for its recent bombings. "You thought such activities could subdue us," Tho told Kissinger, "but you were mistaken." He scolded, "You have met with failure. Over the past ten years we have never shot as many planes and captured or killed as many pilots as in the past ten days." Such actions, he continued, "tarnished the reputation of the United States," but, he concluded, if the US wanted to negotiate a peaceful settlement, "we are prepared to do that."[122] Kissinger responded that the United States was forced to take military action because Hanoi had "no intention" of settling the conflict. But, he quickly added that it was now time to "get down to business" because he was fully prepared to "come to a rapid settlement with you."[123]

Over the next four days, January 8–January 11, Kissinger and Le Duc Tho settled their remaining differences. The major breakthrough came on January 9, Nixon's birthday, when the DMZ was designated a provisional demarcation line and Hanoi agreed that the PRG were only to be recognized in the preamble, not in the text of the agreement. The phrase "South Vietnamese parties" instead of "South Vietnam" was added to the final document as well, another Kissinger concession. And, finally, the United States dropped its demand for a simultaneous cease-fire in Laos and Cambodia, agreeing to Hanoi's viewpoint on this matter. In short, the final agreement looked much like the October proposal. The claim by some that the bombing had forced Hanoi into making serious concessions during the January meetings simply is not reflected in the historical record.[124]

Kissinger called Nixon with the good news. "We celebrated the President's birthday by making a major breakthrough in the negotiations." He went on to tell Nixon that the agreement was near only because of "the President's firmness and the North Vietnamese belief that he will not be affected by either Congressional or public pressure." Not content with hyperbole, his fawning over the president soared to new levels when he assured Nixon that even Le Duc Tho recognized these positive traits.[125] He warned Nixon, however, that the major problem now facing the United States was getting Thieu on board. He suggested that Nixon tell Thieu flatly that he would "proceed, with or without him."[126]

Nixon agreed. "The main thing now, Henry, is that we have to pull this off, and it's going to be tough titty."[127] He told Kissinger that the United States must go ahead with the agreement "regardless of whether Thieu goes along or not."[128] He then sent Haig to Saigon again to make it clear to Thieu that if he continued to resist supporting the agreement, the United States would cut off all further assistance, yet he assured Thieu that he was more than willing to sign the treaty alone if necessary.[129] Thieu stalled for several days, but eventually acknowledged that he could not stop the United States from making peace in his name with his sworn enemy. "I have done all that I can for my country," Thieu told his government.[130] Kissinger and Tho scheduled a signing ceremony in Paris on January 27, 1973.

Before meeting at avenue Kléber for the signing ceremony, however, Kissinger launched a full public relations campaign to make it clear that he was responsible for bringing the war to end. He gave dozens of interviews to the press where he championed his negotiating skills but did not go into the specifics of the faulty agreement. When one reporter pressed him by asking whether, if the agreement broke down, the United States would send troops again to South Vietnam to fight the North Vietnamese troops allowed to stay there,

Kissinger flippantly replied, "I don't want to speculate on hypothetical situations that we don't expect to arise."[131]

In the End, Whose Victory?

But this was not a hypothetical situation. Within days of initialing the cease-fire agreement in Paris, North Vietnamese forces attacked more than four hundred villages in South Vietnam. In fact, over three thousand violations of the cease-fire occurred during the first three weeks of the agreement. Ambassador Bunker later concluded that the cease-fire did not end the fighting in Vietnam; instead, it initiated a new war that was more intense and brutal than the last.[132] By the end of January, the North Vietnamese and ARVN were engaged in some of the heaviest fighting of their long war in the Mekong Delta and in Kontum and Pleiku Provinces. Over 6,600 South Vietnamese soldiers were killed and more than 200,000 South Vietnamese refugees had to flee their homes while Kissinger was declaring victory in the press.[133]

The national security adviser continued his victory lap before the US House of Representatives and the US Senate. He told both groups that as a result of the agreement, all foreign forces had to be removed from South Vietnam, but then covered his tracks by skillfully stating that "whatever forces may be in South Vietnam from outside South Vietnam—specifically North Vietnamese forces—cannot receive reinforcement, replacement, or any other form of augmentation by any means whatsoever."[134] It was a forceful statement that meant nothing and hid the reality of what was already happening inside South Vietnam. From Nixon's perspective, he did not care that Kissinger was glossing over the details, only that Kissinger was taking all the credit for ending the war.

Nixon wanted to announce the peace agreement before his second inauguration, scheduled for January 20, 1972, and before Kissinger went to Congress. Kissinger warned him not to use such phrases as "lasting peace," or "guaranteed peace," because he was sure that "this thing is almost certain to blow up sooner or later."[135] Nixon was done with listening to Kissinger about Vietnam. The president felt that his national security adviser had taken all the glory for ending the war in Vietnam, and he wanted a little recognition of his own. Nixon complained that Kissinger had barely mentioned the president's name before Congress when explaining the details of the agreement.

Haldeman wrote in his diary that Nixon was angry that Kissinger "didn't make the point regarding the character of the man, how he toughed it through. We should quit worrying about defending the agreement," he recorded that Nixon said; "it either works or it doesn't, and it doesn't matter." Haldeman documented that Nixon wondered why Kissinger did not tell Congress or the press that what really mattered was "that without the P's [president's] courage we couldn't have had this"; that Nixon thought the attention on Kissinger was all wrong. "The basic line here is the character, the lonely man in the White House, with little support from government, active opposition from media and opinion leaders...the P alone held on and pulled it out." In the most telling comment of all, Nixon told Haldeman that Kissinger was "very popular," but he "did not make our points...the missing link is the Profile in Courage."[136] That was Nixon's courage, not Kissinger's. When Harry Reasoner of CBS nominated Kissinger for the Nobel Peace Prize, Nixon was outraged.

To settle the score, Nixon decided to take some of the credit for the peace agreement himself. In a January 23, 1973, address to the nation announcing the peace agreement, he claimed that the treaty will "ensure stable peace in Vietnam...and contribute...to lasting peace in Indochina and Southeast Asia." He underscored the fact he was the leader of the negotiations and that "all the conditions that I laid down then have been met." He then took considerable liberties, saying that "we have been in the closest consultation with President Thieu," and that this settlement meets "the goals and has the full support" of the South Vietnamese government. Nixon concluded his speech with the usual hyperbole, "Now that we have achieved an honorable agreement, let us be proud that America did not settle for a peace that would have betrayed our allies..."[137]

Kissinger must have cringed, hearing those words. He understood that a new war—the War of the Flags—was already under way in South Vietnam because the peace agreement he had negotiated was so terribly flawed. Despite his considerable intellect and talent, Kissinger was never able to secure a peace agreement that settled the major question of the war: the political future of South Vietnam. He allowed over 150,000 North Vietnamese troops to remain in South Vietnam as the result of the peace agreement, and all he got in exchange was the chance for South Vietnam to fight Hanoi on its own. His critics claim that he could have achieved that eventuality at any time in the war without the continued sacrifice and suffering on all sides. It's a fair point. An additional 100,000 PAVN troops were permitted to remain in Cambodia and Laos, and there was no restriction in the agreement about their resupply or movement. China and the Soviet Union continued to support Hanoi, while America's aid to South Vietnam was drying up. Kissinger had concluded that if the United States could not remove North Vietnamese troops from South Vietnam with 500,000 US troops and massive bombardment, then it was a goal that had to be sacrificed.

In a sense, Kissinger was right. There was little he could do to change reality on the ground. There were indeed limits to what he could do in Washington, Paris, or Saigon to improve the weak hand he was dealt. He had clearly recognized these severe limitations when he went to the White House in 1969. From his first trip to Vietnam in 1965 until he became national security adviser, Kissinger dispassionately explored all that had gone wrong for the United States in Vietnam. In practice, however, he made many of the same mistakes. He confused coercive power with tangible diplomatic results. When he failed to move Hanoi to his point of view, he frequently supported fierce military escalation. In doing so, he often squandered the remaining public goodwill on Vietnam, thereby narrowing his future options.

Kissinger made several other important mistakes during the negotiations. Successful negotiations to end deadly conflict often require a full spectrum of talents and resources. He squandered most of these by isolating the Defense and State Departments. By cutting Rogers and Laird out of most important strategic decisions on the war, he lost the ability to build a coalition of supportive partners. His personal ambitions and temperament led him to sometimes put political rivalries above strategic concerns. Nixon was not the kind of president to challenge his national security adviser or any of his subordinates on these issues. Therefore, Kissinger was able to secure for his small shop a monopoly on diplomacy. Finally, Kissinger's utter contempt for the South Vietnamese government meant that he never fully consulted Saigon about important matters. He was content to negotiate an end to the war on American terms, and then he coerced Saigon into accepting its fate. On April 30, 1975, Communist tanks rolled into Saigon without a US response.

The war in Vietnam was an American disaster. The loss of lives and treasure for all sides was immense. The United States suffered psychic damage from which it has never fully recovered. And yet Kissinger, despite his failures in Vietnam, has emerged as a symbol of American shrewdness in exercising power. But Kissinger was never able to strip away emotion, ego, and conventional wisdom from his handling of the Vietnam War. He therefore recklessly sought ends beyond his mean.

ACKNOWLEDGMENTS

In writing this book, I have incurred many debts, both personal and intellectual. First on any list must be my research assistants, generously funded by Burt Flickinger. Sarah Mawhinney and Lauren Stauffer provided me with a steady stream of material. Tung Vu conducted research in the Vietnamese archives in Ho Chi Minh City. Cameron Daddis and Michaela Coplen made several visits with me to the Nixon Presidential Library and Museum in Yorba Linda, California.

I owe thanks to my many wonderful students at Vassar College whose interest in the history US foreign policy is exemplary.

Special help in the form of valuable comments on draft chapters and ideas came from Pierre Asselin, Chris Appy, Larry Berman, Mai Elliott, David Elliott, Lloyd Gardner, James Hershberg, the late Luu Doan Huynh, Jeff Kimball, the late Jack Langguth, Mark Lawrence, Kyle Longley, Paul Miles, Ed Miller, David Milne, Charles Neu, John Prados, Andrew Preston, Quang Pham, Sandra Scanlon, Kathryn Statler, Heather Stur, John Prados, and James Wilson.

I owe special thanks to Colonel Greg Daddis, Colonel James Willbanks, Barbara Keys, Lien-Hang Nguyen, Fred Logevall, and the late Marilyn Young, for their friendship, support, and sound advice on this project.

For their willingness to help in various ways, large and small, I thank Richard Aldous, Joy Backer, Laura Belmonte, Tom Blanton, Jim Blight, Mark Bradley, Malcolm Byrne, Catherine Carey, Dominique Cleary, Susan Daddis, Anne Foster, Colonel Gian Gentile, Ann Heiss, Richard Immerman, Molly and Dan Katz, Liam Kennedy,

James Ketterer, Janet Lang, Scott and Marion Morrison, Mel Leffler, Terry McCarthy, Aaron O'Connell, Don Pease, Debbie Sharnak, Jerome Sherman, Ted Smyth, Jeremi Suri, Comhnall Tuohy, Eric Uuksulainen, Hannah VanDeMark, David Welch, Jackie Whitt, and David Woolner. Erin Granville helped shape this book at its early stages, and for that I am eternally grateful.

I am fortunate to be surrounded by wonderful colleagues at Vassar College. I would like to thank Nancy Bisaha, Mita Choudhury, Miriam Cohen, Andy Davison, Rebecca Edwards, Maria Hoehn, Tim Koechlin, James Merrell, Quincy Mills, Lydia Murdoch, Leslie Offutt, Justin Patch, Ed Pittman, Miki Pohl, Ismail Rashid, Steve Rock, Wayne Soon, and Michelle Whalen, who have provided such a supportive intellectual environment. I owe special thanks to President Elizabeth Bradley, Jon Chenette, Cathy Baer, John Mihaly, Natasha Brown, and Catherine Conover at Vassar, and to the late Bennett Boskey for his generous support.

I am deeply thankful to the authors whose books I have read and reread in preparation for this project. The same goes for the archivists at the Nixon Presidential Library and Museum, especially Meghan Lee-Parker. Christine Weideman helped me navigate Kissinger's papers at Yale University. I owe a great debt of gratitude to John Carland and Sahr Conway-Lanz for their advice about sources.

I have been blessed with three wonderful mentors—Steve Ireland, Frank Costigliola, and George C. Herring—who continue to offer sound advice and warm friendship.

At PublicAffairs I thank my editor, Clive Priddle, for his steadfast support and superb editing, and Peter Osnos for his friendship and undying faith in me.

My final and most important acknowledgment is to my family, especially Monica Church and Taylor Brigham, to whom this book is dedicated.

NOTES

PREFACE

1. Henry Kissinger, "The Vietnam Negotiations," *Foreign Affairs* (January 1969), accessed at https://www.foreignaffairs.com/articles/asia/1969-01-01/viet-nam -negotiations. (This online version of *Foreign Affairs* does not have page numbers.)

2. Henry Kissinger, *White House Years* (New York: Simon and Schuster, 1979), 1470.

3. Mark Atwood Lawrence, *The Vietnam War: A Concise International History* (New York: Oxford University Press, 2008), 145.

CHAPTER ONE: THE APPRENTICE

1. This is the major theme of Henry Kissinger's book *Diplomacy* (New York: Simon and Schuster, 1994).

2. As quoted in Walter Isaacson, *Kissinger* (New York: Simon and Schuster, 1992), 127.

3. As quoted in Niall Ferguson, *Kissinger, 1923–1968: The Idealist* [hereafter, *Idealist*] (New York: Penguin, 2015), 851.

4. Seymour M. Hersh, *The Price of Power: Kissinger in the Nixon White House* (New York: Summit Books, 1983), 13–14.

5. As quoted in Ferguson, *Idealist*, 828. Kissinger was frequently in Paris to consult with the US negotiating team. He had even been used in a secret peace contact, code-named PENNSYLVANIA, which showed great promise. PENNSYLVANIA began in June 1967 when two French scientists, Herbert Marcovitch and Raymond Aubrac, approached Kissinger to offer their services as go-betweens to promote negotiations between Washington and Hanoi. Aubrac was an old friend of Ho Chi Minh and promised to deliver a message to the aging DRV leader if the Johnson administration had anything new to say. Kissinger referred the proposal to Secretary of State Dean Rusk, with a copy to Defense Secretary Robert S. McNamara.

On the day that Aubrac and Marcovitch were to leave Paris for Hanoi, United States aircraft flew more than two hundred sorties against North Vietnam, more than any previous day of the war. The official explanation for the poor timing of the bombing missions was that the attacks scheduled for earlier in the month had been delayed by bad weather. Once the weather broke on August 20, the bombing resumed according to protocol and lasted for another four days. Hanoi publicized the new attacks, claiming that Johnson had used the proposed bombing pause as a diversion while he actually escalated the war. Johnson denounced these claims, but the contact fizzled and the war dragged on.

6. *Tuyen bo, Thong cao, Thong diep cua Chanh phu VNCH ve cac bien phap ngung ban nam 1968, November 1, 1968, Ho so 861* [Statement of the Government of the Republic of Vietnam on November 1, 1968, Declarations, Announcements, and Messages of the Government of the Republic of Vietnam on Ceasefires of 1968, file number 861, Second Republic of Vietnam, Vietnamese National Archives Center, Ho Chi Minh City].

7. The documentation is clear that Anna Chennault did deliver this message to the Thieu government. See for example, Memorandum, Dr. Kissinger from Richard L. Schneider, Appointment with Anna Chennault, April 7, 1969, box 810, National Security Council Files: NSC Name Files—Chennault, Anna; Richard Nixon Presidential Library and Museum, Yorba Linda, CA [hereafter, RNPLM]. For an interesting discussion of the Chennault affair, see John A. Farrell's *Richard Nixon* (New York: Doubleday, 2017) and Farrell's *New York Times* essay at https://www.nytimes.com/2016/12/31/opinion/sunday/nixons-vietnam-treachery.html. See also Ken Hughes, *Chasing Shadows: The Nixon Tapes, The Chennault Affair, and the Origins of Watergate* (Charlottesville: University of Virginia Press, 2014).

8. Bui Diem, *In the Jaws of History* (Bloomington: Indiana University Press, 1999), 234–241.

9. *Ve tinh hinh chinh tri va chinh sach ngoai gioa cua Hoa Ky, 1968–1975, Ho so 21016* [Report to the Prime Minister, June 18, 1968, On the Political Atmosphere and Foreign Policy of the United States, 1968–1975, File number 21016, Prime Minister's Palace, Vietnamese National Archives Center II, Ho Chi Minh City, Vietnam.] See also *Tuyen bo, Thong cao, Thong diep cua Chanh phu VNCH ve cac bien phap ngung ban nam 1968, October 20, 1968, Ho so 861* [The House of Representatives of the Republic of Vietnam's Resolution, October 20, 1968, file number 861, Declarations, Announcements, and Messages of the Government of the Republic of Vietnam on Ceasefires of 1968, Second Republic of Vietnam, Vietnamese National Archives Center, Ho Chi Minh City, Vietnam]. And finally, *Tuyen bo, Thong cao, Thong diep cua Chanh phu VNCH ve cac bien phap ngung ban nam 1968, November 1, 1968, Ho so 861* [Statement of the Government of the Republic of Vietnam on November 1, 1968, Declarations, Announcements, and Messages of the Government of the Republic of Vietnam on Ceasefires of 1968, file number 861, Second Republic of Vietnam, Vietnamese National Archives Center, Ho Chi Minh City].

10. Interview with Nguyen Xuan Oanh, economist and former Republic of Vietnam official, Ho Chi Minh City, Vietnam, July 1989.

11. Ken Hughes, *Chasing Shadows: The Nixon Tapes, the Chennault Affair, and the Origins of Watergate* (Charlottesville: University of Virginia Press, 2015), 8.

12. Memorandum, Dr. Kissinger from Richard L. Schneider, Appointment with Anna Chennault, April 7 1969, box 810, National Security Council Files: NSC Name Files—Chennault, Anna; RNPLM.

13. Interview with Nguyen Xuan Oanh, economist and former Republic of Vietnam official, Ho Chi Minh City, Vietnam, July 1989.

14. Henry Kissinger, *White House Years* (New York: Simon and Schuster, 1979), 10.

15. Rick Perlstein, *Nixonland: The Rise of a President and the Fracturing of America* (New York: Simon and Schuster, 2010), 393.

16. Kissinger, *White House Years*, 15.

17. Ibid., 11.

18. A reference to Johnson's "Tuesday Lunches" where he talked about Vietnam with his foreign policy associates.

19. As quoted in Gary J. Bass, *The Blood Telegram* (New York: Alfred A. Knopf, 2013), 9.

20. Kissinger, *White House Years*, 14.

21. Robert Dallek, *Nixon and Kissinger: Partners in Power* (New York: HarperCollins, 2007), 81.

22. Kissinger, *White House Years*, 27.

23. As quoted in Dallek, *Nixon and Kissinger*, 84.

24. As quoted in Dallek, *Nixon and Kissinger*, 83.

25. Kissinger, *White House Years*, 26–27.

26. Ibid.

27. Ibid.

28. Ibid.

29. Ibid., 30.

30. Ibid., 32.

31. As quoted in Isaacson, *Kissinger*, 140.

32. William P. Bundy, *Tangled Web: The Making of Foreign Policy in the Nixon Presidency* (New York: I. B. Tauris, 1998), 54–55.

33. George C. Herring, *From Colony to Superpower: U.S. Foreign Policy since 1776* (New York: Oxford, 2008), 764.

34. Ibid, 765.

35. "The Vietnam Trip, 1965—negotiations—September 24, 1965," Henry A. Kissinger Papers, Part II, Series I: Early Career and Harvard University, box 101, folder 6, Manuscripts and Archives, Yale University, New Haven, Connecticut [hereafter, Kissinger Papers, Yale].

36. "Roger Fisher, Letter to the Editor," *New Republic*, September 5, 1967, 44.

37. John T. McNaughton Papers, "June 1965, #59," box 1, file IV, Lyndon Baines Johnson Presidential Library, Austin, Texas.

38. John T. McNaughton Papers, "1964, #16 and 16a," box 8, file III, Lyndon Baines Johnson Presidential Library, Austin, Texas.

39. "The Vietnam Trip, 1965—negotiations," Part II, Series I: Early Career and Harvard University, box 101, folder 6, Kissinger Papers, Yale.

40. Ferguson, *Idealist*, 588.

41. As quoted in Ferguson, *Idealist*, 599.

42. Ferguson, *Idealist*, 621.

43. Ibid., 605.

44. Ibid.

45. Dallek, *Nixon and Kissinger*, 57.

46. "The Vietnam Trip, 1965—negotiations—Letter from John Dunn to Henry Kissinger, August 20, 1965," Part II, Series I: Early Career and Harvard University, box 101, folder 6, Kissinger Papers, Yale.

47. "The Vietnam Trip, 1965—negotiations—Meeting on Vietnam, Wednesday, August 4, 1965," Part II, Series I: Early Career and Harvard University, box 101, folder 6, Kissinger Papers, Yale.

48. Ibid.

49. Ibid.

50. Ibid.

51. Ibid.

52. Ibid.

53. Ibid.

54. Ibid.

55. Ibid.

56. "The Vietnam Trip, 1965—negotiations—Letter, September 13, 1965," Part II, Series I: Early Career and Harvard University, box 101, folder 6, Kissinger Papers, Yale.

57. Ferguson, *Idealist*, 634.

58. "The Vietnam Trip, 1965—negotiations—Letter, September 13, 1965."

59. As quoted in Ferguson, *Idealist*, 636.

60. Ibid., 635.

61. *Public Papers of the Presidents of the United States, Lyndon B. Johnson, 1965* (Washington, DC: Office of the Federal Register, 1966), 394–399.

62. "The Vietnam Trip, 1965—negotiations—October 18, 1965." Part II, Series I: Early Career and Harvard University, box 101, folder 6, Kissinger Papers, Yale.

63. Ibid.

64. Massachusetts Historical Society, Lodge Papers, Vietnam, reel 20, "Henry Kissinger to Lodge, September 14, 1965," Boston, Massachusetts.

65. "The Vietnam Trip, 1965—negotiations—October 18, 1965," Part II, Series I: Early Career and Harvard University, box 101, folder 6, Kissinger Papers, Yale.

66. "The Vietnam Trip, 1965—negotiations—October 26, 1965," Part II, Series I: Early Career and Harvard University, box 101, folder 6, Kissinger Papers, Yale.

67. "The Vietnam Trip, 1965—negotiations—November 2, 1965," Part II, Series I: Early Career and Harvard University, box 101, folder 6, Kissinger Papers, Yale.

68. Ferguson, *Idealist*, 838.

69. Henry Kissinger, "The Vietnam Negotiations," *Foreign Affairs*.

70. As quoted in Douglas Kinnard, *The War Managers: American Generals Reflect on Vietnam* (New York: Da Capo, 1977), 43.

71. Gregory A. Daddis, *Westmoreland's War: Reassessing American Strategy in Vietnam* (New York: Oxford University Press, 2014), 12.

72. Kissinger, "The Vietnam Negotiations," *Foreign Affairs*.

73. Ibid.

74. Ibid.

75. Ibid.

76. Ibid.

77. *Nhan Dan*, August 31, 1972.

78. Author interview with Luu Doan Huynh, Hanoi, Vietnam, November 1995.

79. As quoted in Hersh, *Price of Power*, 49.

80. Interview: Daniel Ellsberg Interview Transcription, May 20, 2008, with Timothy Naftali, 2008-05-20, ELLS, RNPLM.

81. "Vietnam Options, 1969," Morton Halperin Papers, box 10, folder "Vietnam Operations, January 8, 1969," Lyndon Baines Johnson Presidential Library, Austin, Texas.

82. Ibid.

83. Ibid.

84. Richard A. Hunt, *Melvin Laird and the Foundation of the Post-Vietnam Military, 1969–1973*, Secretary of Defense Historical Series (Washington, DC: Historical Office, Office of the Secretary of Defense, 2015), 94.

85. *Foreign Relations of the United States* [hereafter, *FRUS*], *1969–1974, Volume VI, Vietnam, January 1969–July 1970*, "Minutes of National Security Council Meeting, January 25, 1969," document number 10 (Washington, DC: Government Printing Office, 2006).

86. Isaacson, *Kissinger*, 163.

87. *FRUS, 1969–1974, Volume VI, Vietnam, January 1969–July 1970*, "Minutes of National Security Council Meeting, September 12, 1969," document number 120.

88. *FRUS, 1969–1974, Volume VI, Vietnam, January 1969–July 1970*, "Minutes of National Security Council Meeting, March 28, 1969," document number 49.

89. Ibid.

90. Ibid.

91. Office of the Press Secretary for the President of the United States, "Lyndon B. Johnson Speech in Akron, Ohio, October 21, 1964," at http://www.presidency.ucsb.edu/ws/?pid=26635.

92. Hunt, *Melvin Laird*, 90–95.

93. Ibid., 105.

94. Kissinger, *White House Years*, 265.

95. Memorandum for the President, Vietnam Situation and Options, undated, box 89, National Security Council Files: Vietnam Subject Files, RNPLM.

96. Memorandum for the President, Reflections on De-escalation, March 8, 1969, box 89, National Security Council Files: Vietnam Subject Files, RNPLM.

97. *FRUS, 1969–1974, Volume VI, Vietnam, January 1969–July 1970*, "Minutes of National Security Council Meeting, March 28, 1969," document number 49.

98. Ibid.

99. As quoted in Mai Elliott, *RAND in Southeast Asia: A History of the Vietnam War Era* (Santa Monica, CA: RAND Corporation, 2010), 365.

100. Hunt, *Melvin Laird*, 95.

101. Ibid., 96.

102. Memorandum, Kissinger for Laird, February 5, 1969, box 955, National Security Council Files: Haig Chronology, Feb 1–Feb 15, 1969, RNPLM.

103. As quoted in Jeffrey Kimball, *Nixon's Vietnam War* (Lawrence: University Press of Kansas, 1998), 124.

104. Ibid.

105. Ibid.

106. Memorandum, President Nixon from Kissinger, January 13, 1969, and Memorandum, President Nixon from Kissinger, January 8, 1969, box 1, National Security Council Files: Henry A. Kissinger Office Files—General Goodpaster, RNPLM.

107. Ibid.

108. Kimball, *Nixon's Vietnam War*, 127.

109. *New York Times*, February 3, 1969.

110. Conversation, Kissinger and President Nixon, March 8, 1969, 6:25–7:10 p.m., Henry A. Kissinger Telephone Conversation Transcripts [Hereafter HAK Telecon], box 1, Chronological File, RNPLM.

111. Memorandum, President Nixon from Henry Kissinger, March 10, 1969, box 175, National Security Council Files: Paris Talks/Meetings, RNPLM.

112. Memorandum, President Nixon from Henry Kissinger, January 13, 1969, box 1, National Security Council Files: Henry Kissinger Office Files—General Goodpaster, RNPLM.

113. *FRUS, 1969–1974, Volume VI, Vietnam, January 1969–July 1970*, "Memorandum from the President's Assistant for National Security Affairs (Kissinger) to President Nixon, February 19, 1969," document number 22.

114. Hunt, *Melvin Laird*, 145.

115. U.S. Air Force Oral History Interview, Office of Air Force History, Historical Research Center, "Interview with Lt. General Ray Sitton, 7–8 February 1984," Air War College, Montgomery, Alabama, 156.

116. Ibid., 159.

117. Ibid.

118. Ibid.

119. Conversation, Kissinger and President Nixon, March 15, 1969, 3:35 p.m., box 1, HAK Telecon: Chronological File, RNPLM.

120. Conversation, Kissinger and President Nixon, March 15, 1969, 3:44 p.m., box 1, HAK Telecon: Chronological File, RNPLM.

121. *FRUS, 1969–1974, Volume VI, Vietnam, January 1969–July 1970*, "Memorandum for the Record, March 15, 1969," document number 39.

122. *New York Times*, March 26, 1969.

123. Hersh, *Price of Power*, 61.

124. Hunt, *Melvin Laird*, 149.

125. See for example, William Shawcross, *Sideshow: Kissinger, Nixon, and the Destruction of Cambodia* (New York: Simon and Schuster, 1979).

126. Greg Grandin, *Kissinger's Shadow* (New York: Metropolitan Books, 2015), 55.

127. Henry Kissinger, *Ending the Vietnam War: A History of America's Involvement in and Extrication from the Vietnam War* (New York: Simon and Schuster, 2003), 61.

128. Hunt, *Melvin Laird*, 148.

129. Conversation, Kissinger and President Nixon, March 20, 1969, box 1, HAK Telecon: Chronological File, RNPLM.

130. As quoted in Barbara W. Tuchman, *The March to Folly* (New York: Random House, 1985), 382–383.

131. Luu Van Loi, *Le Duc Tho–Kissinger Negotiations in Paris* (Hanoi: Gioi Publishers, 1996).

CHAPTER TWO: THE LONE COWBOY

1. Oriana Fallaci, "Kissinger: An Interview with Oriana Fallaci," *New Republic* (December 16, 1972), 21.

2. Ibid., 20–22.

3. Henry Kissinger, *For the Record: Selected Statements, 1977–1980* (Boston: Little, Brown, 1981), 124.

4. Henry Kissinger, "Strains on the Alliance," *Foreign Affairs* (January 1963), at https://www.foreignaffairs.com/articles/cuba/1963-01-01/strains-alliance.

5. Henry Kissinger, *White House Years* (New York: Simon and Schuster, 1979), 266.

6. Kissinger wrote this memo the first day in office for Nixon to sign and send out to top officials in his administration. Kissinger, *White House Years*, 130–135. See also Bernard Kalb and Marvin Kalb, *Kissinger* (Boston: Little and Brown, 1974), 130–135; Hersh, *The Price of Power*, 66; Raymond Garthoff, *Détente and Confrontation: American-Soviet Relations from Nixon to Reagan* (Washington, DC: Brookings, 1994), 129.

7. As quoted in Gareth Porter, *A Peace Denied: The United States, Vietnam, and the Paris Peace Agreement* (Bloomington: Indiana University Press, 1975), 80.

8. Isaacson, *Kissinger* (New York: Simon and Schuster, 1992), 166.

9. Ibid., 206.

10. Ibid., 208.

11. H. R. Haldeman, *The Haldeman Diaries: Inside the Nixon White House* (New York: Putnam, 1994), March 17, 1970, 139.

12. Kissinger, *White House Years*, 263–264.

13. Memorandum, To the President from Henry A. Kissinger, March 10, 1969, box 175, National Security Council Files: Paris Talks, RNPLM.

14. Ibid.

15. Ibid.

16. Ibid.

17. Ibid.

18. Ibid.

19. Conversation, The President in Key Biscayne and Kissinger, March 8, 1969, 10:45 a.m., box 1, HAK Telecon, White House Tapes: Chronological File, RNPLM.

20. Ibid.

21. *FRUS, 1969–1974, Volume VI, Vietnam, January 1969–July 1970*, "Memorandum from the President's Assistant for National Security Affairs (Kissinger) to President Nixon, April 3, 1969," document number 52.

22. Richard Nixon, *RN: The Memoirs of Richard Nixon* (New York: Simon and Schuster, 1990), 391.

23. Kissinger, *White House Years*, 268.

24. Henry Kissinger, *Ending the Vietnam War: A History of America's Involvement in and Extrication from the Vietnam War* (New York: Simon and Schuster, 2003), 75.

25. Ibid., 76.

26. Ibid.

27. Kissinger, *White House Years*, 268. See also Nixon, *RN*, 391.

28. Ilya V. Gaiduk, *The Soviet Union and the Vietnam War* (Chicago: Ivan Dee, 1996), 207–209.

29. NLF's Ten Point Peace Plan as translated by U.S. Central Intelligence Agency, at https://www.cia.gov/library/readingroom/docs/CIA-RDP80R01720R000200160010-8 .pdf.

30. Ibid.

31. *New York Times*, May 15, 1969.

32. Speech of President Richard Nixon, May 14, 1969, Office of the Press Secretary, the White House, Washington, DC.

33. Luu van Loi, *Le Duc Tho–Kissinger Negotiations in Paris*, 85–88.

34. Kalb and Kalb, *Kissinger*, 132.

35. Porter, *A Peace Denied*, 87.

36. Ibid.

37. Harold P. Ford, "Calling the Sino-Soviet Split," US Central Intelligence Agency Library, at https://www.cia.gov/library/center-for-the-study-of-intelligence /csi-publications/csi-studies/studies/winter98_99/art05.html#rft3; see also William Taubman, "Khrushchev vs. Mao: A Preliminary Sketch of the Role of Personality in the Sino-Soviet Split." Woodrow Wilson Center, Cold War International History Project (Issues 8–9, Winter 1996/1997), 243.

38. Mao Zedong, "Second Speech to Second Session, Eighth Party Congress," May 17, 1958, as cited in Allen S. Whiting, "The Sino-Soviet Split," in *The Cambridge History of China*, vol. 14, *The People's Republic, Part I, The Emergence of Revolutionary China 1949–1965*, ed. Roderick Macfarquhar and John K. Fairbank (New York: Cambridge University Press, 1987), 488–489.

39. From Deng speech, November 14, 1960, at the Moscow conference of 81 Communist parties, as cited in CIA/Office of Current Intelligence Special Report, "The Men in the Sino-Soviet Confrontation," July 5, 1963, 2, on file in CIA's History Staff.

40. Chen Jian, "China's Involvement in the Vietnam War, 1964–1969," *China Quarterly* 142 (June 1995): 382.

41. Ibid., 382–383.

42. Jeffrey Kimball, *Nixon's Vietnam War* (Lawrence: University Press of Kansas, 1998), 142.

43. *FRUS, 1969–1974, Volume VI, Vietnam, January 1969–July 1970*, "Editorial Note," document number 84. [Editorial note captures conversation with Dobrynin.]

44. Ibid.

45. Ibid.

46. "Trends in Communist Propaganda," Foreign Broadcast Information Service, October 28, 1970, 1–2.

47. Ibid.

48. Ibid.

49. Luu van Loi, *Le Duc Tho–Kissinger Negotiations in Paris*, 94.

50. Ibid.

51. Memorandum, For President Nixon from Henry A. Kissinger—"Your meeting with Jean Sainteny," July 14, 1969, box 107, National Security Council Files: Henry A. Kissinger Office Files, Country Files, Far East—Vietnam, RNPLM.

52. Ibid.

53. Letter, To His Excellency, Ho Chi Minh, President of the Democratic Republic of Vietnam," box 107, National Security Council Files: Henry A. Kissinger Office Files, Country Files, Far East—Vietnam, RNPLM.

54. Ibid.

55. Pierre Asselin, *A Bitter Peace: Washington, Hanoi, and the Making of the Paris Agreement* (Chapel Hill: University of North Carolina Press, 2002), 20.

56. Letter, From Sainteny, July 16, 1969, box 107, National Security Council Files: Henry A. Kissinger Office Files, Country Files, Far East—Vietnam, RNPLM.

57. "President Nixon and President Thieu Meet at Midway Island, June 8 1969," Nixon Foundation, at https://www.nixonfoundation.org/2014/06/president-nixon -president-thieu-meet-midway-island-june-8-1969/.

58. Le Duan, *Thu vao Nam* [Letters to the South] (Hanoi: Nha Xuat Ban Quan Doi Nhan, Dan, 2005).

59. Kissinger, *White House Years*, 278

60. Luu Van Loi, *Le Duc Tho–Kissinger Negotiations in Paris*, 98.

61. Ibid., 102.

62. Ibid., 103.

63. Kissinger, *White House Years*, 279.

64. Ibid., 283.

65. Ibid.

66. Ibid.

67. Memorandum of Conversation, August 4, 1969, box 107, National Security Council Files: Henry A. Kissinger Office Files, Country Files, Far East—Vietnam, RNPLM.

68. Ibid.

69. Ibid.

70. Ibid.

71. Ibid.

72. Mai Van Bo, *Tan cong ngoia giao* [Diplomatic offensive and secret contacts] (Hanoi: Nhe Xuat Ban Su That, 1985), 165–168.

73. Memorandum of Conversation, August 4, 1969, box 107, National Security Council Files: Henry A. Kissinger Office Files, Country Files, Far East—Vietnam, RNPLM.

74. For a good summary of the intrigue between Kissinger, Laird, and Rogers, please see Notes, August 27, 1969, box 40, and Notes, January 14, 1972, both Haldeman Papers, White House Special Files, RNPLM.

75. In a surreal meeting among Kissinger's Senior Review Group (comprising U. Alexis Johnson, William Sullivan, David Packard, Armistead Selden, General Fred Karhos, General Richard Knowles, General William Burrows, General Robert Cushman, George Carver, Wayne Smith, John Negroponte, Admiral Robert Welander, Mark Wandler, and James Hackett), representatives from the State Department, the Defense Department, the Joint Chiefs of Staff, the Central Intelligence Agency, and the National Security Council Staff that met all too infrequently to provide meaningful and useful coordination for the secret negotiations in Paris, Kissinger asked what Hanoi was going to do after a standstill cease-fire was in place. The problem: This question came six months after the proposal was formally offered to Le Duc Tho in Paris. See *FRUS, 1969–1976, Volume VII, Vietnam, July 1970–January 1972, 1971*, "Minutes of a Meeting of the Senior Review Group, October 1" (Washington, DC: Government Printing Office, 2010), document number 266.

76. John Paul Lederach, *Building Peace: Sustainable Reconciliation in Divided Societies* (Washington, DC: United States Institute of Peace, 1998).

77. For best practices in peace negotiations, please see Chester Crocker, Fen Osler Hampson, and Pamela Aall, *Taming Intractable Conflicts* (Washington, DC: United States Institute of Peace Press, 2004); Chester Crocker, Fen Osler Hampson, and Pamela Aall, *Leashing the Dogs of War* (Washington, DC: United States Institute of Peace Press, 2007); Chester Crocker, Fen Osler Hampson, and Pamela Aall, *Herding Cats: Multiparty Mediation in a Complex World* (Washington, DC: United States Institute of Peace Press, 1999); Oliver Ramsbotham, Tom Woodhouse, Hugh Miall, *Contemporary Conflict Resolution* (Cambridge, MA: Polity, 2005); and Christine Bell, "Peace Agreements: Their Nature and Legal Status," *American Journal of International Law* 100 (April 2006): 373–412.

78. For a complete discussion of how Kissinger organized the NSC and the Senior Review Group, please see "National Security Council Structure and Functions," at https://www.nixonlibrary.gov/forresearchers/find/textual/nsc/structure.php?print=yes.

79. Ibid.

80. Letter, From Head of the Delegation to the Paris Peace Talks on Vietnam to the President's Assistant for National Security Affairs, August 9, 1969, box 861, National Security Council Files: Vietnam Negotiations, Camp David Memos, RNPLM.

81. Memorandum, For the President from the National Security Adviser, September 10, 1969, at https://www.docsteach.org/documents/document/salted-peanuts -memo-kissinger-nixon.

82. Kissinger, *White House Years*, 284.

83. *FRUS, 1969–1976, volume VI, Vietnam, January 1969–July 1970*, "Memorandum from the President's Special Adviser for National Security Affairs to President Nixon, September 11, 1969," document number 119.

84. Ibid.

85. Richard A. Hunt, *Melvin Laird and the Foundation of the Post-Vietnam Military, 1969–1973*, Secretary of Defense Historical Series (Washington, DC: Historical Office, Office of the Secretary of Defense, 2015), 120.

86. *FRUS, 1969–1974, Volume VI, Vietnam, January 1969–July 1970*, "Minutes of National Security Council Meeting, September 12, 1969," document number 120.

87. Phillip B. Davidson, *Vietnam at War: The History 1946–1975* (New York: Oxford, 1988), 598.

88. Draft, Presidential Speech, 2nd Draft, September 27, 1969, box 34, National Security Council Files: Adviser's Files, West Wing Office Series, RNPLM.

89. Isaacson, *Kissinger*, 246.

90. As quoted in Rick Perlstein, *Nixonland: The Rise of a President and the Fracturing of America* (New York: Simon and Schuster, 2010), 419.

91. Henry Kissinger, *Diplomacy* (New York: Simon and Schuster, 1994), 688.

92. Memorandum, For the President from Henry A. Kissinger, October 2, 1969, Contingency Military Operations Against North Vietnam, box 89, National Security Council Files: Vietnam Subject Files, RNPLM.

93. Conversation, Kissinger and the president, September 27, 1969, 4:40 p.m., box 3, HAK Telecon, White House Tapes, Chronological Files, RNPLM.

94. *FRUS, 1969–1974, Volume VI, Vietnam, January 1969–July 1970*, "Memorandum for the Record, October 11, 1969," document number 136.

95. Ibid.

96. As quoted in Jussi M. Hanhimaki, *The Flawed Architect: Henry Kissinger and American Foreign Policy* (New York: Oxford, 2004), 62.

97. Ibid.

98. As quoted in *New York Times*, December 10 and 11, 1968.

99. Isaacson, *Kissinger*, 237–239.

100. Robert Dallek, *Nixon and Kissinger: Partners in Power* (New York: HarperCollins, 2007), 156.

101. White House Tapes, Oval Office, number 632-2, December 8, 1971, 9:25–10:18 a.m., RNPLM; see also *Haldeman Diaries*, diary entry for December 9, 1971, 381.

102. White House Tapes, Oval Office: number 632-2, December 8, 1971, 9:25–10:18 a.m.; number 631-7, December 7, 1971, 4:33–5:05 p.m.; number 631-11, December 7, 1971, 6:28–7:04 p.m.; number 631-1, December 7, 1971, 12:57–1:58 p.m.; number 631-7, December 7, 1971, 4:35–5:05 p.m., all RNPLM; see also *Haldeman Diaries*, entry for December 7, 1971, 380, and John Ehrlichman, *Witness to Power: The Nixon Years* (New York: Simon and Schuster, 1982), 307–308.

103. White House Tapes, Oval Office, number 632-2, December 6, 1971, 12:02–12:06 p.m., RNPLM.

104. Ibid.

105. White House Tapes, Oval Office, number 309-1, December 24, 1971, 4:58–5:08 p.m., RNPLM.

106. As quoted in Barbara Keys, "Henry Kissinger: The Emotional Statesman," *Diplomatic History* 35 (September 2011): 587.

107. Ibid., 588.

108. Ehrlichman, *Witness to Power*, 297–298; see also, Isaacson, *Kissinger*, 209.

109. Keys, "Henry Kissinger," *Diplomatic History*, 587.

110. Kissinger, *Ending the Vietnam War*, 93.

111. Kimball, *Nixon's Vietnam War*, 172.

112. Gallup Poll, January 1970.

113. Dallek, *Nixon and Kissinger*, 163.

114. Isaacson, *Kissinger*, 248.

115. Dallek, *Nixon and Kissinger*, 158.

116. *Public Papers of the President, Nixon, 1969* (Washington, DC: Office of the Federal Register, 1971), 901–909.

117. Conversation, Kissinger and the President, November 3, 1969, 10:20 a.m., box 3, HAK Telecon, White House Tapes: Chronological File, RNPLM.

118. Dallek, *Nixon and Kissinger*, 166.

119. Conversation, Kissinger and the president, November 3, 1969, 10:20 p.m. and midnight, box 3, HAK Telecon, White House Tapes, Chronological File, RNPLM.

120. *FRUS, 1969–1974, Volume VI, Vietnam, January 1969–July 1970*, "Memorandum from President's Assistant for National Security Affairs (Kissinger) to the President, December 1, 1969," document number 152.

121. Ibid.

122. Ibid.

123. Isaacson, *Kissinger*, 248.

124. Ibid.

125. Memorandum, For the President from Henry A. Kissinger, December 10, 1969, box 107, National Security Council Files: Henry A. Kissinger Office Files, Country Files, Far East—Vietnam, RNPLM.

CHAPTER THREE: BOLD MOVES

1. Kissinger, *White House Years*, 436.

2. Richard A. Hunt, *Melvin Laird and the Foundation of the Post-Vietnam Military, 1969–1973*, Secretary of Defense Historical Series (Washington, DC: Historical Office, Office of the Secretary of Defense, 2015), 125–142.

3. See the work of Nguyen Viet Thanh, *Nothing Ever Dies: Vietnam and the Memory of War* (Cambridge, MA: Harvard University Press, 2016) and Nu-Anh Tran, "South Vietnamese Identity, American Intervention, and the Newspaper Chinh Luan [Political Discussion], 1965–1969," *Journal of Vietnamese Studies* 1 (February/August 2006): 169–209.

4. As quoted in Walter Isaacson, *Kissinger* (New York: Simon and Schuster, 1992), 253.

5. Memorandum, Vietnam Alternatives, Henry Kissinger to Richard Nixon, January 16, 1969, box H: 019:5, National Security Council Files: Institutional Files;

and Memorandum, From Henry Kissinger to Richard Nixon, Vietnam Situation and Options, box H: 98:7n National Security Council Files: Institutional Files, RNPLM; see also Conversation, The President and Henry Kissinger, March 8, 1969, 10:45 a m., box 1, HAK Telecon: White House Tapes, Chronological File, RNPLM.

6. Lien-Hang T. Nguyen, *Hanoi's War: An International History of the War for Peace in Vietnam* (Chapel Hill: University of North Carolina Press, 2012), 157–158.

7. Willard J. Webb, *The Joint Chiefs of Staff and the War in Vietnam, 1969–1970* (Washington, DC: Office of Joint History, Office of the Joint Chiefs of Staff, 2002), 15–19, 259.

8. Le Mau Han, *Cac Dai Hoi Dong cong san Viet Nam* [The Vietnamese Communist Party] (Hanoi: Nha Xuat Banh Chinh Tri Quoc Gia, 1995), 92.

9. As quoted in Pierre Asselin, *A Bitter Peace: Washington, Hanoi, and the Making of the Paris Agreement* (Chapel Hill: University of North Carolina Press, 2002), 25.

10. Henry Kissinger, *White House Years* (New York: Simon and Schuster, 1979), 435.

11. *FRUS, 1969–1976, Volume VI, Vietnam, January 1969–July 1970,* "Memorandum from the President's Assistant for National Security Affairs to President Nixon, January 7, 1970," document number 167.

12. *FRUS, 1969–1976, Volume VI, Vietnam, January 1969–July 1970,* "Memorandum from the President's Assistant for National Security Affairs to President Nixon, January 19, 1970," document number 170.

13. Ibid.

14. George C. Herring, *America's Longest War: The United States and Vietnam, 1950–1975,* 2nd ed. (New York: Alfred A. Knopf, 1979), 233.

15. Conversations, Kissinger and Rogers, March 19, 1971, 9:35 a.m., box 9, and The President and Henry Kissinger, March 19, 1971, 11:10 a.m., box 9, both HAK Telecon: White House Tapes: Chronological File, RNPLM; see also Douglas Brinkley and Luke Nichter, eds., *Nixon Tapes, 1971–1972* (New York: Harcourt Brace, 2014), 77.

16. Conversation, President Nixon and Kissinger, January 14, 1970, 5:40 p.m., box 3, HAK Telecon: White House Tapes, Chronological File, RNPLM; see also *FRUS, 1969–1976, Volume VI, Vietnam, January 1969–July 1970,* "Transcript of Telephone Conversation Between President Nixon and his Assistant for National Security Affairs (Kissinger), January 14, 1970," document number 169.

17. Ibid.

18. Ibid.

19. Kissinger, *White House Years*, 158.

20. *Public Papers of the President, Richard Nixon, 1970* (Washington: Office of Federal Register, 1971), 115.

21. See for example, *Haldeman Diaries*, January 27, 1970, 123; April 7, 1970, 147; and May 9, 1970, 163. For the May 9 entry Haldeman notes: "I am concerned about his condition . . . he has had very little sleep for a long time and his judgment, temper, and mood suffer badly as a result . . . He's still riding on the crisis wave, but the letdown is near at hand and will be huge."

22. Isaacson quotes Kissinger as saying that Nixon was often drunk during this period, *Kissinger*, 259.

23. As quoted in Isaacson, *Kissinger*, 249.

24. Ibid.

25. Henry Kissinger, *Ending the Vietnam War: A History of America's Involvement in and Extrication from the Vietnam War* (New York: Simon and Schuster, 2003), 111.

26. Ibid.

27. Kissinger, *White House Years*, 440.

28. Kissinger, *Ending the Vietnam War*, 113.

29. Jeremi Suri, *Henry Kissinger and the American Century* (Cambridge, MA: Harvard University Press, 2007), 48.

30. Henry Kissinger, *Years of Upheaval* (New York: Simon and Schuster, 1982), 116.

31. Suri, *Henry Kissinger and the American Century*, 14.

32. Kissinger, *White House Years* and *Years of Upheaval*.

33. Kissinger, *Ending the Vietnam War*.

34. McGeorge Bundy, "Reconsiderations: Vietnam, Watergate, and Presidential Powers," *Foreign Affairs* (December 1, 1979).

35. Nguyen Tien Hung, a Saigon official, released the Nixon-Thieu letters on April 30, 1975. He later referred to them in his book *The Palace File* (New York: Harper and Row, 1986).

36. As quoted in Isaacson, *Kissinger*, 486.

37. Ibid., 487.

38. Bundy, "Reconsiderations."

39. Stanley Hoffmann, "The Case of Dr. Kissinger," *New York Review of Books*, December 6, 1979, 1.

40. Ibid., 2.

41. Ibid.

42. Ibid.

43. Luu van Loi, *Le Duc Tho–Kissinger Negotiations in Paris*, 114–115.

44. Memorandum of a Conversation, February 21, 1970, 9:40 a.m. and 4:10 p.m., box 121, National Security Council Files: Henry A. Kissinger Office Files, Country Files, Far East—Vietnam, RNPLM.

45. Ibid.

46. Ibid.

47. Ibid.

48. Bo Ngoai Giao [Ministry of Foreign Affairs], *Dai su ky chuyen de: Dau Tranh Ngoai Giao va van dong quoc te trong nhung chien chong My, cuu nuoc* [Special chronology: the diplomatic struggle and international activities of the anti-American resistance and national salvation] (Hanoi, 1987), 249–250.

49. Ibid.

50. Memorandum of a Conversation, February 21, 1970, 9:40 a.m. and 4:10 p.m., box 121, National Security Council Files: Henry A. Kissinger Office Files, Country Files, Far East—Vietnam, RNPLM.

51. Bo Ngoai Giao [Ministry of Foreign Affairs], *Dai su ky chuyen de:* [Special chronology], 249–250; see also, Nguyen, *Hanoi's War*, 164–165.

52. Memorandum, To the President from Henry Kissinger, February 21, 1970, box 121, National Security Council Files: Henry A. Kissinger Office Files, Country Files, Far East—Vietnam, RNPLM.

53. Ibid.

54. Ibid.

55. Ibid.

56. Ibid.

57. Ibid.

58. People in attendance at the February 21, 1970, meeting included Le Duc Tho, adviser to the DRV Delegation; Xuan Thuy, chief of the DRV Delegation; Mai Van Bo, DRV delegate general in Paris; Nguyen Dinh Phuong, DRV interpreter and member of the Foreign Ministry; Luu Van Loi, DRV interpreter and member of the Foreign Ministry; Henry Kissinger, national security adviser; Major General Vernon Waters, defense attaché, US Embassy—Paris; W. Richard Smyser, National Security Council staff; and Anthony Lake, National Security Council staff.

59. Memorandum of Conversation, Morning Session, February 21, 1970, 9:40 a.m., box 121, and Memorandum of Conversation, Afternoon Session, February 21, 1970, 4:10 p.m., box 121, both National Security Council Files: Henry A. Kissinger Office Files, Country Files, Far East—Vietnam, RNPLM.

60. Luu van Loi, *Le Duc Tho–Kissinger Negotiations in Paris*, 120.

61. Ibid., 119.

62. Kissinger, *White House Years*, 444.

63. Memorandum, Current State of Vietnam Papers, February 25, 1970, box 121, National Security Council Files: Henry A. Kissinger Office Files, Country Files, Far East—Vietnam, RNPLM.

64. As quoted in David Milne, *Wordmaking: The Art and Science of American Diplomacy* (New York: Farrar, Straus, and Giroux, 2015), 368.

65. Ibid.

66. Brinkley and Nichter, *Nixon Tapes*, 717.

67. Larry Berman, *No Peace, No Honor: Nixon, Kissinger, and Betrayal in Vietnam* (New York: Simon and Schuster, 2001), 149.

68. David F. Schmitz, *Richard Nixon and the Vietnam War* (Boulder, CO: Rowman and Littlefield, 2014), 141–144.

69. Memorandum of a Conversation, March 16, 1970, box 121, National Security Council Files: Henry A. Kissinger Office Files, Country Files, Far East—Vietnam, RNPLM.

70. Ibid.

71. Kissinger, *White House Years*, 445.

72. Memorandum, Kissinger to President Nixon, December 9, 1970, box 3, National Security Council Files, POW/MIA, RNPLM.

73. Jeffrey Kimball, *Nixon's Vietnam War* (Lawrence: University Press of Kansas, 1998), 189.

74. Isaacson, *Kissinger,* 255, and Kimball, *Nixon's Vietnam War,* 190.

75. Isaacson, *Kissinger,* 254–255. See also, Memorandum of a Conversation, March 16, 1970, 9:40 a.m., box 121, National Security Council Files: Henry A. Kissinger Office Files, Country Files, Far East—Vietnam, RNPLM; see also, Memorandum for the President, My Meeting with North Vietnamese on March 16, 1970, box 121, National Security Council Files: Henry A. Kissinger Office Files, Country Files, Far East—Vietnam, RNPLM; *FRUS, 1969–1976, Volume VI, Vietnam, January 1969–July 1970,* "Memorandum of Conversation, March 16, 1970," document number 201; and Memorandum of Conversation, April 4, 1970, 9:30 a.m., box 121, National Security Council Files: Henry A. Kissinger Office Files, Country Files, Far East—Vietnam, RNPLM.

76. Kissinger, *White House Years,* 447.

77. Isaacson, *Kissinger,* 254.

78. *Haldeman Diaries,* March 13, 1970, 138.

79. *FRUS, 1969–1976, Volume VI, Vietnam, January 1969–July 1970,* "Memorandum from the President's Assistant for National Security Affairs (Kissinger) to President Nixon, February 27, 1970, document number 192.

80. Ibid.

81. Ibid.

82. Memorandum of a Conversation, March 16, 1970, box 121, National Security Council Files: Henry A. Kissinger Office Files, Country Files, Far East—Vietnam, RNPLM.

83. Ibid.

84. Ibid.

85. Ibid.

86. Memorandum, My Meeting with North Vietnamese, March 16, 1970, box 852, National Security Council Files: For the President's File, Winston Lord—China Trip, Vietnam Sensitive, Camp David, RNPLM.

87. Ibid.

88. Ibid.

89. Memorandum of Conversation, March 16, 1970, 9:40 a.m., box 121, National Security Council Files: Henry A. Kissinger Office Files, Country Files, Far East—Vietnam, RNPLM.

90. Memorandum of Conversation, April 4, 1970, 9:30 a.m., National Security Council Files: Henry A. Kissinger Office Files, Country Files, Far East—Vietnam, RNPLM.

91. Ibid.

92. Luu van Loi, *Le Duc Tho–Kissinger Negotiations in Paris,* 131.

93. Memorandum of Conversation, April 4, 1970, 9:30 a.m., National Security Council Files: Henry A. Kissinger Office Files, Country Files, Far East—Vietnam, RNPLM.

94. *FRUS, 1969–1976, Volume VI, Vietnam, January 1969–July 1970,* "Memorandum from the President's Assistant for National Security Affairs (Kissinger), April 6, 1970," document number 223.

95. Ibid.

96. Memorandum of Conversation, April 4, 1970, 9:30 a.m., National Security Council Files: Henry A. Kissinger Office Files, Country Files, Far East—Vietnam, RNPLM.

97. Ibid.

98. Kissinger, *White House Years*, 447.

99. Kissinger, *Ending the Vietnam War*, 119.

100. Richard Nixon, "Address to the Nation on Progress Toward Peace in Vietnam, April 20, 1970," at http://www.presidency.ucsb.edu/ws/?pid=2476.

101. Ibid.

102. Ibid.

103. Ibid.

104. Ibid.

105. Ibid.

106. As quoted in Gareth Porter, *A Peace Denied: The United States, Vietnam, and the Paris Peace Agreement* (Bloomington: Indiana University Press, 1975), 90.

107. *FRUS, 1969–1976, Volume VI, Vietnam, January 1969–July 1970*, "Memorandum from the President's Assistant for National Security Affairs (Kissinger) to President Nixon, March 19, 1970," document number 205.

108. *FRUS, 1969–1976, Volume VI, Vietnam, January 1969–July 1970*, "Memorandum from Senior Military Assistant (Haig) to the President's Assistant for National Security Affairs (Kissinger), April 1, 1970," document number 217.

109. *FRUS, 1969–1976, Volume VI, Vietnam, January 1969–July 1970*, "Memorandum from the President's Assistant for National Security Affairs (Kissinger) to President Nixon, April 11, 1970," document number 227.

110. *FRUS, 1969–1976, Volume VI, Vietnam, January 1969–July 1970*, "Editorial Note," document number 239.

111. Memorandum, Westmoreland to Laird, April 21, 1970, and Pursley to Kissinger, April 22, 1970, box 88, National Security Council Files: Vietnam Subject Files, RNPLM.

112. *FRUS, 1969–1976, Volume VI, Vietnam, January 1969–July 1970*, "Memorandum from the President's Assistant for National Security Affairs to President Nixon, undated," document number 253.

113. Schmitz, *Richard Nixon and the Vietnam War*, 85.

114. Hunt, *Melvin Laird*, 158.

115. Dale Van Atta, *With Honor: Melvin Laird in War, Peace, and Politics* (Madison: University of Wisconsin Press, 2008), 263.

116. *Haldeman Diaries*, April 24, 1970, 154.

117. Memorandum, From Kissinger to President Nixon, April 26, 1970, box 965, National Security Council Files: Haig Chronology Files, RNPLM; see also Conversation, Kissinger and Wheeler, April 24, 1970, 7:25 p.m., box 5, HAK Telecons: White House Tapes, Chronological File, RNPLM.

118. Memorandum, From Kissinger to President Nixon, April 26, 1970, box 965, National Security Council Files: Haig Chronology Files; and Memorandum, From Haig to Kissinger, April 27, 1970, box 965, National Security Council Files: Haig Chronology Files, RNPLM.

119. Richard Nixon, *RN: The Memoirs of Richard Nixon* (New York: Simon and Schuster, 1990), 445.

120. *Haldeman Diaries*, April 23, 1970, and April 24, 1970, 153–154; see also, Hunt, *Melvin Laird*, 158.

121. Ibid.

122. Kissinger, *Ending the Vietnam War*, 160.

123. President Nixon, "Address to the Nation on the Situation in Southeast Asia, April 30, 1970," at http://www.presidency.ucsb.edu/ws/?pid=2490.

124. Ibid.

125. Ibid.

126. Isaacson, *Kissinger*, 269.

127. *New York Times*, May 3, 1970.

128. As quoted in Harry Kopp, "The State of Dissent in the Foreign Service," September 2017, at http://www.afsa.org/state-dissent-foreign-service.

129. *FRUS, 1969–1976, Volume VI, Vietnam, January 1969–July 1970*, "Editorial Note," document number 277.

130. William Shawcross, *Sideshow: Kissinger, Nixon, and the Destruction of Cambodia* (New York: Simon and Schuster, 1979), 145.

131. Schmitz, *Richard Nixon and the Vietnam War*, 92.

132. Memorandum, Kissinger to President Nixon, May 8, 1970, box 318, National Security Council Files, RNPLM.

133. Memorandum, Kissinger to President Nixon, May 4, 1970, box 585, National Security Council Files: Cambodia Operations, 1970, RNPLM.

134. Dallek, *Kissinger and Nixon*, 210.

135. *Public Papers of the President, Richard Nixon, 1970*, 476–480.

136. Kissinger, *Ending the Vietnam War*, 171.

137. Ibid., 163.

CHAPTER FOUR: THE STANDSTILL CEASE-FIRE

1. Henry Kissinger, *Ending the Vietnam War: A History of America's Involvement in and Extrication from the Vietnam War* (New York: Simon and Schuster, 2003), 179.

2. Ibid., 175.

3. *FRUS, 1969–1976, Volume VI, Vietnam, January 1969–July 1970*, "Memorandum from the President's Deputy for National Security Affairs to President Nixon, undated," document number 346 (Washington: Government Printing Office, 2006).

4. Ibid.

5. Ibid.

6. As quoted in the *Washington Post*, December 6, 1977.

7. Kissinger, *Ending the Vietnam War*, 178.

8. Ibid., 179.

9. Conversation, Kissinger and Joseph Aslop, October 7, 1970, box 7, HAK Telecons: White House Tapes, RNPLM.

10. As quoted in Robert Dallek, *Nixon and Kissinger Nixon and Kissinger: Partners in Power* (New York: HarperCollins, 2007), 254.

11. Henry Kissinger, *White House Years* (New York: Simon and Schuster, 1979), 975–976.

12. Ibid.

13. Luu Van Loi, *Le Duc Tho–Kissinger Negotiations in Paris*, 147.

14. Ibid.

15. Ibid.

16. *FRUS, 1969–1976, Volume VII, Vietnam, July 1970–January 1972,* "Memorandum of Conversation, September 7, 1970, 9:30am–2:30pm," document number 34; see also Kissinger, *White House Years*, 976–977.

17. *FRUS, 1969–1976, Volume VII, Vietnam, July 1970–January 1972,* "Memorandum of Conversation, September 7, 1970, 9:30am–2:30pm," document number 34; see also Luu van Loi, *Le Duc Tho–Kissinger Peace Negotiations in Paris*, 149.

18. Ibid.

19. Kissinger, *Ending the Vietnam War*, 183.

20. Ibid., 182.

21. Kissinger, *White House Years*, 978.

22. Ibid.

23. Memorandum, From Kissinger to President Nixon, September 17, 1970, box 4, National Security Council Files: POW/MIA, Camp David—Sensitive, vol. 7, RNPLM.

24. Memorandum, A Longer Look at the New Communist Peace Proposal on Vietnam, September 22, 1970, box 3, National Security Council Files: Paris Talks, July–September 1970, RNPLM.

25. Charles W. Colson, *Born Again* (Grand Rapids: F. H. Revell, 1976), 41.

26. Kissinger, *Ending the Vietnam War*, 431.

27. Ibid.

28. *Haldeman Diaries*, August 18, 1970, 190.

29. *Haldeman Diaries*, August 17, 1970, 189.

30. Ibid.

31. Ibid.

32. Odd Arne Westad, Chen Jian, Stein Tonnesson, Nguyen Vu Tungard, and James Hershberg, eds., "Zhou Enlai and Pham Van Dong, September 17, 1970," 77 *Conversations Between Chinese and Foreign Leaders on the Wars in Indochina, 1964–1977*, Working Paper No. 22 (Washington, DC: Cold War International History Project, 1998), 174–178, at https://www.wilsoncenter.org/sites/default/files/ACFB39.pdf.

33. Ibid.

34. Ibid.

35. Jussi M. Hanhimaki, *The Flawed Architect: Henry Kissinger and American Foreign Policy* (New York: Oxford, 2004), 107–108.

36. Westad et al., *77 Conversations*, September 17 and September 23, 1970, 174–178.

37. Ibid., September 23, 178.

38. Memorandum, From Kissinger to President Nixon, September 28, 1970, box 4, National Security Council Files: POW/MIA, Meeting Folder, Camp David—Sensitive, vol. 6, RNPLM.

39. Kissinger, *Ending the Vietnam War*, 184.

40. Jeffrey Kimball, *Nixon's Vietnam War* (Lawrence: University Press of Kansas, 1998), 235.

41. Richard Nixon, "Address to the Nation About a New Initiative for Peace in Southeast Asia, October 7 1970," at http://www.presidency.ucsb.edu/ws/?pid=2708.

42. *New York Times*, October 9, 1970.

43. *Wall Street Journal*, October 9, 1970.

44. *Daily Citizen*, October 9, 1970.

45. *New York Times*, October 8, 1970.

46. Ibid.

47. Kissinger, *White House Years*, 980.

48. *FRUS, 1969–1976, Volume VII, Vietnam, July 1970–January 1972,* "Editorial Note," document number 46.

49. *New York Times*, October 8, 1970.

50. *Public Papers of the President, Richard Nixon, 1970*, 830.

51. "Nixon's Peace Plan," *New Republic*, October 17, 1970.

52. *New York Times*, October 9, 1970.

53. Ibid.

54. As quoted in Daniel Sargent, *A Superpower Transformed: The Remaking of American Foreign Relations in the 1970s* (New York: Oxford, 2017), 57.

55. *Haldeman Diaries*, December 15, 1970, 220–221.

56. Kissinger, *Ending the Vietnam War*, 187.

57. Ibid.

58. Kissinger, *White House Years*, 986.

59. James H. Willbanks, *A Raid Too Far: Operation Lam Son 719 and Vietnamization in Laos* (College Station: Texas A&M University Press, 2014), 24.

60. Memorandum, Meeting between President Thieu, Ambassador Bunker and General Haig, December 17, 1970, 6:00 p.m. Saigon time, box 1011, National Security Council Files: Alexander M. Haig Special Files, folder 1, RNPLM.

61. Willbanks, *A Raid Too Far*, 25–26.

62. Alexander M. Haig Jr., *Inner Circles: How America Changed the World—A Memoir* (New York: Grand Central Publishers, 1992), 273.

63. Hunt, *Melvin Laird*, 176.

64. Ibid., 177.

65. Ibid.

66. Ibid.

67. Conversation, Kissinger and President Nixon, December 9, 1970, box 8, HAK Telecons: White House Tapes, RNPLM.

68. Richard A. Hunt, *Melvin Laird and the Foundation of the Post-Vietnam Military, 1969–1973*, Secretary of Defense Historical Series (Washington, DC: Historical Office, Office of the Secretary of Defense, 2015), 177.

69. Ibid., 179.

70. Douglas Brinkley and Luke Nichter, eds., *The Nixon Tapes, 1971–1972* (New York: Harcourt Brace, 2014), 11.

71. Memorandum, From Kissinger to President Nixon, December 23, 1970, box 4, National Security Council Files: Alexander Haig Chronological Files, RNPLM; see also *FRUS, 1969–1976, Volume VII, Vietnam, July 1970–January 1972*, "Memorandum for the Record, December 23, 1970," document number 96.

72. Willbanks, *A Raid Too Far*, 57.

73. Nguyen Duy Hinh, *Lam Son 719*, Indochina Monographs (Washington, DC: US Army Center of Military History, 1979), 53–54.

74. Willbanks, *A Raid Too Far*, 50.

75. Bui Diem, *In the Jaws of History* (Bloomington: Indiana University Press, 1999), 284–285.

76. *FRUS, 1969–1976, Volume VII, Vietnam, July 1970–January 1972*, "Memorandum from the President's Assistant for National Security Affairs (Kissinger) to President Nixon, April 10, 1971," document number 176.

77. *FRUS, 1969–1976, Volume VII, Vietnam, July 1970–January 1972*, "Transcript of a Telephone Conversation Between the President's Assistant for National Security Affairs (Kissinger) and the US Army Chief of Staff (Westmoreland), April 12, 1971," document number 178.

78. Willbanks, *A Raid Too Far*, 59.

79. Kissinger, *White House Years*, 1004; see also Hinh, *Lam Son 719*, 79.

80. Willbanks, *A Raid Too Far*, 89.

81. *Washington Post*, March 9, 1971.

82. Memorandum: Henry Kissinger to the Honorable Carl Albert, March 29, 1971, box 116, National Security Council Files: Vietnam Subject Files, RNPLM.

83. Hunt, *Melvin Laird*, 185.

84. Ibid., 186.

85. Memorandum from Kissinger to President Nixon, February 26, 1971, box 116, National Security Council Files: Vietnam Subject Files, RNPLM.

86. Hunt, *Melvin Laird*, 186.

87. As quoted in Dallek, *Nixon and Kissinger*, 260.

88. *FRUS, 1969–1976, Volume VII, Vietnam, July 1970–January 1972*, "Backchannel Message from President's Assistant for National Security Affairs (Kissinger) to Ambassador to Vietnam (Bunker), March 9, 1971," document number 147.

89. As quoted in John Prados, *Vietnam: The History of an Unwinnable War, 1945–1975* (Lawrence: University Press of Kansas, 2009), 415.

90. For an excellent description of PAVN activities in Laos during Lam Son 719, please see Merle Pribbenow's translation of the PAVN's official history, *Victory in Vietnam: The Official History of the People's Army of Vietnam, 1954–1975* (Lawrence: University Press of Kansas, 2002), 271–278.

91. *FRUS, 1969–1976, Volume VII, Vietnam, July 1970–January 1972*, "Transcript of a Telephone Conversation Between the President's Assistant for National Security Affairs (Kissinger) and the US Army Chief of Staff (Westmoreland), April 12, 1971," document number 178.

92. Robert D. Sander, *Invasion of Laos: Lam Son 719* (Norman: University of Oklahoma Press, 2015).

93. *FRUS, 1969–1976, Volume VII, Vietnam, July 1970–January 1972*, "Transcript of a Telephone Conversation Between the President's Assistant for National Security Affairs (Kissinger) and the US Army Chief of Staff (Westmoreland), April 12, 1971," document number 178.

94. Richard Nixon, *RN: The Memoirs of Richard Nixon* (New York: Simon and Schuster, 1990), 499. See also Willbanks, *A Raid Too Far*, 159.

95. Richard Nixon, "Address to the Nation on the Situation in Southeast Asia, April 7, 1971, at http://www.presidency.ucsb.edu/ws/index.php?pid=2972.

96. Prados, *Vietnam*, 418.

97. For an excellent description of these events, see Willbanks, *A Raid Too Far*, p. 175.

98. *FRUS, 1969–1976, Volume VII, Vietnam, July 1970–January 1972*, "Conversation Between President Nixon and His Assistant for National Security Affairs (Kissinger), June 7, 1971," document number 211.

99. Kissinger, *White House Years*, 992.

100. Ibid., 992–994.

101. Willbanks, *A Raid Too Far*, 30.

102. As quoted in George C. Herring, *America's Longest War: The United States and Vietnam, 1950–1975*, 2nd ed. (New York: Alfred A. Knopf, 1979), 244.

103. Ibid.

104. Asselin, *A Bitter Peace*, 28.

105. *FRUS, 1969–1976, Volume VII, Vietnam, July 1970–January 1972*, "Memorandum from the President's Assistant for National Security Affairs (Kissinger) to President Nixon, April 17, 1971," document number 183.

106. Kissinger, *Ending the Vietnam War*, 209.

107. *FRUS, 1969–1976, Volume VII, Vietnam, July 1970–January 1972*, "Memorandum of Conversation, May 31, 1971, 10:00am–1:30pm," document number 207.

108. Kimball, *Nixon's Vietnam War*, 266; see also Kissinger, *White House Years*, 1018.

109. *FRUS, 1969–1976, Volume VII, Vietnam, July 1970–January 1972*, "Memorandum of Conversation, May 31, 1971, 10:00am–1:30pm," document number 207. Kissinger explained the concession this way: "The proposal sought to get away from the treadmill of demanding mutual withdrawal while in fact carrying out a unilateral withdrawal; it would, in effect, trade the residual force (PAVN troops) for an end of infiltration into South Vietnam," *Ending the Vietnam War*, 210.

110. Asselin, *A Bitter Peace*, 28.

111. Brinkley and Nichter, *Nixon Tapes*, 87.

112. Ibid., 50.

113. Memorandum, For the President's Files, March 26, 1971, box 84, National Security Council Files: Presidential Office Files, RNPLM; see also *Haldeman Diaries*, March 26 and April 26, 1971, 260–261, 279–281.

114. Ibid.

115. See especially Larry Berman, *No Peace, No Honor: Nixon, Kissinger, and Betrayal in Vietnam* (New York: Simon and Schuster, 2001).

116. Memorandum of Conversation, Kissinger and Zhou, July 10, 1971, box 90, China Visit: Record of Previous Meetings, National Security Council Files: Henry A. Kissinger Office Files, RNPLM.

117. Ibid.

118. Brinkley and Nichter, eds., *Nixon Tapes*, 87.

119. *Haldeman Diaries*, June 2, 1971, 295.

120. Ibid., June 3, 1971, 295–296.

121. As quoted in Marvin L. Kalb, *The Road to War: Presidential Commitments Honored and Betrayed* (Washington, DC: Brookings Institution Press, 2013), 144.

122. *Haldeman Diaries*, June 2, 1971, 295.

123. Memorandum, For the President's File, box 853, National Security Council Files: Vietnam Negotiations, Winston Lord—China Trip, Vietnam Sensitive, Camp David, vol. 7, April 1971–June 1971, folder 3, RNPLM.

124. Ibid.

125. *FRUS, 1969–1976, Volume VII, Vietnam, July 1970–January 1972, 1971*, "Minutes of a Meeting of the Senior Review Group, October 1," document number 266.

126. Memorandum, From Kissinger to President Nixon, June 27, 1971—My June 26 Meeting with North Vietnamese, box 4, National Security Council Files: Camp David—Sensitive, vol. 8, RNPLM.

127. Memorandum of Conversation, June 26, 1971, box 4, National Security Council Files: Camp David—Sensitive, vol. 8, RNPLM.

128. Memorandum, From Kissinger to President Nixon, June 27, 1971—My June 26 Meeting with North Vietnamese.

129. Ibid.

130. Ibid.

131. Ibid.

132. For a good summary of Big Minh's life, see his obituary in the *Los Angeles Times*, August 8, 2001.

133. Kissinger, *White House Years*, 1029.

134. Memorandum, From Kissinger to President Nixon, June 27, 1971—My June 26 Meeting with North Vietnamese.

135. Ibid.

136. Quoted in Bernard Kalb and Marvin Kalb, *Kissinger* (Boston: Little and Brown, 1974), 180.

137. Memorandum, From Kissinger to President Nixon, August 16, 1971, box 4, National Security Council Files: Camp David—Sensitive, vol. 11, RNPLM.

138. Kissinger, *White House Years*, 1035.

139. *Haldeman Diaries*, September 8, 1971, 351.

140. Ibid., June 22, 1971, 304.

141. As quoted in Dallek, *Nixon and Kissinger*, 313.

142. David Rudenstine, *The Day the Presses Stopped: A History of the Pentagon Papers Case* (Berkeley: University of California Press, 1996), 2.

143. Memorandum, From Kissinger to President Nixon, My Talks with Chou En-lai, July 14, 1971, box 1033, National Security Council Files: Miscellaneous Memoranda Relating to HAK Trip to PRC, July 1971, RNPLM.

144. Lien-Hang T. Nguyen, *Hanoi's War: An International History of the War for Peace in Vietnam* (Chapel Hill: University of North Carolina Press, 2012), 214.

145. *FRUS, 1969–1976, Volume VII, Vietnam, July 1970–January 1972*, "Message from the United States to the Democratic Republic of Vietnam, October 11, 1971," document number 269.

146. *FRUS, 1969–1976, Volume VII, Vietnam, July 1970–January 1972*, "Message from the United States to the Democratic Republic of Vietnam, October 11, 1971," document number 269; see also "Memorandum from the President's Assistant for National Security Affairs (Kissinger) to the President, September 18, 1971," document number 257.

147. Berman, *No Peace, No Honor*, 97–100.

CHAPTER FIVE: A WAR FOR PEACE

1. *Haldeman Diaries*, January 1, 1972, 391.

2. *CQ Almanac*, 1971, at: https://library.cqpress.com/cqalmanac/document.php?id =cqal72-1249975.

3. *New York Times*, January 14, 1972.

4. Gary J. Bass, *The Blood Telegram* (New York: Alfred A. Knopf, 2013), 341.

5. Robert Dallek, *Nixon and Kissinger: Partners in Power* (New York: HarperCollins, 2007), 350.

6. *Washington Post*, December 12, 1971.

7. Ibid.

8. Dallek, *Nixon and Kissinger*, 351.

9. Conversation, Kissinger and President Nixon, December 23, 1971, box 12, HAK Telecons: White House Tapes, Chronological Files, RNPLM.

10. Ibid.

11. *Haldeman Diaries*, December 30, 1971, 388.

12. On February 7, 1972, *Time* and *Newsweek* featured Kissinger on their covers under the title "Nixon's Secret Agent."

13. Conversation, Kissinger and Hugh Sidey, January 27, 1972, 6:10 p.m., box 13, HAK Telecons: White House Tapes, Chronological Files, RNPLM.

14. Conversation, President Nixon and Kissinger, January 12, 1972, 12:20 p.m., HAK Telecons: White House Tapes, Chronological Files, RNPLM.

15. Henry Kissinger, *Ending the Vietnam War: A History of America's Involvement in and Extrication from the Vietnam War* (New York: Simon and Schuster, 2003), 229.

16. Richard Nixon, "Address to the Nation Making Public a Plan for Peace in Vietnam, January 25, 1972," at http://www.presidency.ucsb.edu/ws/?pid=3475

17. Ibid.

18. Ibid.

19. *New York Times*, January 27, 1972.

20. All quotes from *New York Times*, January 26, 1972.

21. *Washington Post*, January 26, 1972.

22. *Haldeman Diaries*, January 27, 1972, 403.

23. Lien-Hang T. Nguyen, *Hanoi's War: An International History of the War for Peace in Vietnam* (Chapel Hill: University of North Carolina Press, 2012), 235.

24. Ibid.

25. Dale Andradé, *America's Last Vietnam Battle: Halting Hanoi's 1972 Easter Offensive* (Lawrence: University Press of Kansas, 1995), 51.

26. Conversation, Moorer and Kissinger, April 3, 1972, box 13, HAK Telecons: White House Tapes, Chronological Files, RNPLM.

27. James H. Willbanks, *Abandoning Vietnam: How America Left and South Vietnam Lost Its War* (Lawrence: University Press of Kansas, 2004), 133.

28. Richard A. Hunt, *Melvin Laird and the Foundation of the Post-Vietnam Military, 1969–1973*, Secretary of Defense Historical Series (Washington, DC: Historical Office, Office of the Secretary of Defense, 2015), 224.

29. As quoted in Willbanks, *Abandoning Vietnam*, 133.

30. Dallek, *Nixon and Kissinger*, 371.

31. As quoted in Dallek, *Nixon and Kissinger*, 371.

32. Ibid.

33. *FRUS, 1969–1976, Volume XIV, Soviet Union, October 1971–May 1972*, "Conversation between President Nixon and his Assistant for National Security Affairs (Kissinger), April 3, 1972," document number 79 (Washington, DC: Government Printing Office, 2006).

34. Conversation, President Nixon and Kissinger, April 19, 1972, 713-1, White House Tapes, Oval Office, RNPLM; see also *FRUS, 1969–1976, Volume XIV, Soviet Union, October 1971–May 1972*, "Conversation Between President Nixon and his Assistant for National Security Affairs (Kissinger), April 19, 1972," document number 126.

35. Henry Kissinger, *White House Years* (New York: Simon and Schuster, 1979), 1113.

36. As quoted in Willbanks, *Abandoning Vietnam*, 134.

37. As quoted in Jeffrey Kimball, *Nixon's Vietnam War* (Lawrence: University Press of Kansas, 1998), 303.

38. Hunt, *Melvin Laird*, 229–230.

39. Kimball, *Nixon's Vietnam War*, 303.

40. Conversation, Laird and Kissinger, April 3, 1972, 9:01 a.m., box 13, HAK Telecons: White House Tapes, Chronological Files, RNPLM.

41. Ibid.

42. Conversation, Kissinger and Rockefeller, April 4, 1972, 2:28 p.m., box 13, HAK Telecons: White House Tapes, Chronological Files, RNPLM.

43. Conversation, Kissinger and Laird, April 5, 1972, 7:45 p.m., box 13, HAK Telecons: White House Tapes, Chronological Files, RNPLM.

44. Ibid.

45. Ibid.

46. Conversation, Kissinger and Moorer, April 4, 1972, 9:58 a.m., box 13, HAK Telecons: White House Tapes, Chronological Files, RNPLM. See also Conversation, Kissinger and Moorer, April 5, 1972, 7:20 p.m., box 13, HAK Telecons: White House Tapes, Chronological Files, RNPLM.

47. Conversation, Kissinger and Laird, April 11, 1972, 8:18 p.m., box 13, HAK Telecons: White House Tapes, Chronological Files, RNPLM.

48. Conversation, Kissinger and Moorer, April 5, 1972, 7:20 p.m., box 13, HAK Telecons: White House Tapes, Chronological Files, RNPLM.

49. Conversation, Kissinger and Laird, April 11, 1972, 8:18 p.m., box 13, HAK Telecons: White House Tapes, Chronological Files, RNPLM.

50. Conversation, Kissinger and Laird, April 15, 1972, 11:50 a.m., box 13, HAK Telecons: White House Tapes, Chronological Files, RNPLM.

51. Conversation, Kissinger and Moorer, April 5, 1972, after 4:00 p.m., box 13, HAK Telecons: White House Tapes, Chronological Files, RNPLM.

52. Conversation, Kissinger and Laird, April 8, 1972, 12:55 p.m., box 13. HAK Telecons: White House Tapes, Chronological Files, RNPLM.

53. Ibid.

54. *Nhan Dan*, April 18, 1972.

55. Allan E. Goodman, *The Search for a Negotiated Settlement of the Vietnam War*, Indochina Monograph Series, Institute of East Asian Studies (Berkeley: University of California Press, 1986), 70.

56. Conversation, Kissinger and Buckley, April 9, 1972, 11:55 a.m., box 13, HAK Telecons: White House Tapes, Chronological Files, RNPLM.

57. Conversation, Kissinger to Rush, April 19, 1972, 12:30 p.m., box 13, HAK Telecons: White House Tapes, Chronological Files, RNPLM.

58. Goodman, *Search for a Negotiated Settlement*, 72.

59. Memorandum, Assistant for National Security Affairs (Kissinger) to Deputy Assistant for National Security Affairs (Haig), April 24, 1972, box 21, National Security Council Files: Henry A. Kissinger Office Files, RNPLM.

60. Dallek, *Nixon and Kissinger*, 378.

61. Memorandum, Assistant for National Security Affairs (Kissinger) to Deputy Assistant for National Security Affairs (Haig), April 24, 1972.

62. Memorandum, Message from General Abrams, US Force Posture in the RVN, April 21, 1972, box 113, National Security Council Files: Vietnam Subject Files, Ceasefire Vietnam, 1972, RNPLM.

63. Ibid.

64. Dallek, *Nixon and Kissinger*, 380.

65. Conversation, President Nixon and Kissinger, May 1, 1972, 7:00 p.m., box 14, HAK Telecons: White House Tapes, Chronological Files, RNPLM.

66. Conversation, President Nixon and Kissinger, May 1, 1972, 9:55 a.m., box 14, HAK Telecons: White House Tapes, Chronological Files, RNPLM.

67. Conversation, Kissinger and Laird, May 2, 1972, 10:10 p.m., box 14, HAK Telecons: White House Tapes, Chronological Files, RNPLM.

68. Conversation, Kissinger and Laird, May 2, 1972, 9:45 p.m., box 14, HAK Telecons: White House Tapes, Chronological Files, RNPLM.

69. Conversation, President Nixon and Kissinger, May 3, 1972, 6:25 p.m., box 14, HAK Telecons: White House Tapes, Chronological Files, RNPLM.

70. Luu van Loi, *Le Duc Tho–Kissinger Negotiations in Paris*, 227.

71. Ibid., 228.

72. Ibid., 229.

73. Kissinger, *Ending the Vietnam War*, 267.

74. *FRUS, 1969–1976, Volume XIV, Soviet Union, October 1971–May 1972*, "Letter from President Nixon to Soviet General Secretary Brezhnev, May 3, 1972," document number 190 (Washington, DC: Government Printing Office, 2006).

75. Conversation, President Nixon and Kissinger, May 1, 1972, 7:00 p.m., box 14, HAK Telecons: White House Tapes, Chronological Files, RNPLM.

76. Kimball, *Nixon's Vietnam War*, 315.

77. Conversation, President Nixon and Kissinger, May 6, 1972, 3:30 p.m., box 14, HAK Telecons: White House Tapes, Chronological Files, RNPLM.

78. Willbanks, *Abandoning Vietnam*, 145.

79. Richard Nixon, "Address to the Nation on the Situation in Southeast Asia, May 8, 1972," at http://www.presidency.ucsb.edu/ws/?pid=3404.

80. As quoted in Richard Reeves, *President Nixon: Alone in the White House* (New York: Simon and Schuster, 2002), 476.

81. Ibid.

82. Ibid.

83. As quoted in Geoffrey C. Ward and Ken Burns, *The Vietnam War: An Intimate History* (New York: Knopf, 2017), 501.

84. Ibid.

85. As reported in Nguyen Phu Duc, *The Viet Nam Peace Negotiations: Saigon's Side of the Story* (Christiansburg, VA: Dalley Book Service, 2005), 277.

86. Willbanks, *Abandoning Vietnam*, 145.

87. As quoted in Ilya V. Gaiduk, *The Soviet Union and the Vietnam War* (Chicago: Ivan R. Dee, 1996), 239.

88. Kimball, *Nixon's War*, 317.

89. Kissinger, *Ending the Vietnam War*, 283–284.

90. Ibid., 285.

91. Ibid., 284.

92. Pierre Asselin, *A Bitter Peace: Washington, Hanoi, and the Making of the Paris Agreement* (Chapel Hill: University of North Carolina Press, 2002), 51.

93. CIA Intelligence Memorandum, "The Overall Impact of the US Bombing and Mining Program on North Vietnam, August 1972."

94. Ibid.

95. Asselin, *A Bitter Peace*, 52–53.

96. Andradé, *America's Last Vietnam Battle*, 492.

97. Hunt, *Melvin Laird*, 246.

98. Conversation, Kissinger and Aslop, June 2, 1972, 4:02 p.m., box 14, HAK Telecons: White House Tapes, Chronological Files, RNPLM.

99. The argument is summarized quite ironically by Melvin Laird, "Iraq: Learning the Lessons of Vietnam," *Foreign Affairs* (November/December 2005), at https://www .foreignaffairs.com/articles/vietnam/2005-10-01/iraq-learning-lessons-vietnam.

100. Conversation, Kissinger to Mansfield, June 27, 1972, 10:10 a.m., box 14, HAK Telecons: White House Tapes, Chronological Files, RNPLM.

101. Ibid.

102. Goodman, *Search for a Negotiated Settlement*, 75.

103. *Washington Post*, June 19, 1972.

104. *FRUS, 1969–1976, Volume VIII, Vietnam, January–October 1972*, "Memorandum from the President's Assistant for National Security Affairs (Kissinger) to President Nixon, July 20, 1972," document number 211 (Washington, DC: Government Printing Office, 2010).

105. *FRUS, 1969–1976, Volume VIII, Vietnam, January–October 1972*, "Memorandum of a Conversation, July 19, 1972, Paris, 9:52 a.m.–4:25 p.m.," document number 207.

106. Ibid.

107. Ibid.

108. Ibid.

109. *The DRV Chronology on the Diplomatic Struggle*, entry for July 19, 1972 (Hanoi: Gioi, 1987).

110. Memorandum, Kissinger to President Nixon, August 3, 1972, My August 1 Meeting with the North Vietnamese, box 4, National Security Council Files: Camp David 1972, POW/MIA, RNPLM.

111. Luu van Loi, *Le Duc Tho–Kissinger Negotiations in Paris*, 255.

112. Ibid.

113. Ibid., 256.

114. Memorandum, Peace Proposal of the Democratic Republic of Vietnam, August 1, 1972, box 121, National Security Council Files: Henry A. Kissinger Office Files, Country Files, Far East—Vietnam, RNPLM.

115. As quoted in Asselin, *A Bitter Peace*, 56.

116. Kissinger, *Ending the Vietnam War*, 306.

117. Ibid., 306–307.

118. Memorandum, Peace Proposal of the Democratic Republic of Vietnam, August 1, 1972, box 121, National Security Council Files: Henry A. Kissinger Office Files, Country Files, Far East—Vietnam, RNPLM.

119. Ibid.

120. Kissinger, *Ending the Vietnam War*, 307.

121. Ibid., 309.

122. Ibid.

123. Ibid., 311.

124. Ibid.

125. *FRUS, 1969–1976, Volume VIII, Vietnam, January–October 1972*, "Memorandum of a Conversation, August 17, 1972, Saigon, 4:35–6:40 p.m.," document number 243.

126. Interview with Nguyen Xuan Oanh, economist and former South Vietnamese official, Ho Chi Minh City, July 1989.

127. *FRUS, 1969–1976, Volume VIII, Vietnam, January–October 1972*, "Memorandum of a Conversation, August 17, 1972, Saigon," document number 243.

CHAPTER SIX: PEACE IS AT HAND

1. *FRUS, 1969–1976, Volume XLII, Vietnam: The Kissinger–Le Duc Tho Negotiations, August 1969–December 1973*, "Memorandum of Conversation, September 15, 1972," document number 18 (Washington, DC: Government Printing Office, 2017).

2. Ibid.

3. Ibid.

4. Douglas Brinkley and Luke Nichter, *The Nixon Tapes, 1971–1972* (New York: Harcourt Brace, 2014), 622.

5. *FRUS, 1969–1976, Volume XLII, Vietnam: The Kissinger–Le Duc Tho Negotiations, August 1969–December 1973*, "Memorandum of Conversation, September 15, 1972," document number 18.

6. Ibid.

7. Ibid.

8. See Jeffrey Kimball, *Nixon's Vietnam War* (Lawrence: University Press of Kansas, 1998), 331.

9. *FRUS, 1969–1976, Volume XLII, Vietnam: The Kissinger–Le Duc Tho Negotiations, August 1969–December 1973*, "Memorandum of Conversation, September 15, 1972," document number 18.

10. Memorandum, DRVN Proposals, September 15, 1972, box 121, National Security Files: Henry A. Kissinger Office Files, Country Files, Far East—Vietnam, RNPLM.

11. Brinkley and Nichter, *Nixon Tapes*, 631.

12. "Official US Congressional Election Results, 1972," at clerk.house.gov/member_info/electionInfo/1972election.pdf.

13. The Gallup poll regularly asked Americans whether it "was a mistake to send American troops to Vietnam." From October 1967 until January 1973, more Americans agreed that it was a mistake than disagreed. By 1971–1972, 60 percent of Americans polled consistently thought it was a mistake to send American troops to Vietnam. For an interesting essay explaining this data, please see Frank Newport and Joseph Carroll, "Iraq Versus Vietnam: A Comparison of Public Opinion," *Gallup News*, August 24, 2005, at news.gallup.com/poll/18097/Iraq-versus-vietnam-comparison-public-opinion.aspx. The quotes come from Barbara J. Keys, *Reclaiming American Virtue: The Human Rights Revolution of the 1970s* (Cambridge, MA: Harvard University Press, 2014), 63.

14. *FRUS, 1969–1976, Volume XLII, Vietnam: The Kissinger–Le Duc Tho Negotiations, August 1969–December 1973*, "Memorandum of Conversation, September 15, 1972," document number 18.

15. Ibid.

16. Brinkley and Nichter, *Nixon Tapes*, 617.

17. Memorandum, General Haig to the President, Kissinger Mission, September 15, 1972, box 855, National Security Council Files: For the President's Files, Vietnam Negotiations, Winston Lord—China Trip, Vietnam Sensitive, Camp David, August–September 1972, RNPLM.

18. Memorandum, From Haig to Kissinger, September 14, 1972, box 855, National Security Council Files: For the President's Files, Vietnam Negotiations, Winston Lord—China Trip, Vietnam Sensitive, Camp David, August–September 1972, RNPLM.

19. Ibid.

20. Ibid.

21. Ibid.

22. Opinion Research Corporation, "Poll of a National Adult Sample Conducted for Richard Nixon, April 27–29, 1972." For an interesting discussion of the polls, see Patrick Hagopian, *The Vietnam War in American Memory: Veterans, Memorials, and the Politics of Healing* (Amherst: University of Massachusetts Press, 2011), 29–31 and 442.

23. Brinkley and Nichter, *Nixon Tapes*, 609.

24. Memorandum, Henry A. Kissinger to Ambassador Bunker, September 22, 1972, box 856, National Security Council Files: For the President's Files, Vietnam Negotiations, Winston Lord—China Trip, Vietnam Sensitive, Camp David, August–September 1972, RNPLM.

25. Memorandum, From Sven Kraemer to Mr. Kissinger, President Thieu and the Future of Vietnam, September 28, 1972, box 1019, National Security Council Files: Alexander M. Haig Special Files, Additional Material, Vietnam Trip, September 29–October 4, 1972, RNPLM.

26. Ibid.

27. Kimball, *Nixon's Vietnam War*, 336.

28. Ibid., 337.

29. Brinkley and Nichter, *Nixon Tapes*, 631.

30. Ibid., 628.

31. Memorandum, From Henry A. Kissinger to the President, My Meetings with the North Vietnamese, September 26–27, 1972, box 1014, National Security Council Files: Alexander M. Haig Special Files, Additional Material, Vietnam trip, September 29–October 4, 1972, RNPLM.

32. Ibid.

33. Henry Kissinger, *White House Years* (New York: Simon and Schuster, 1979), 1336–1337.

34. Memorandum, From Henry A. Kissinger to the President, My Meetings with the North Vietnamese, September 26–27, 1972, box 1014, National Security Council Files: Alexander M. Haig Special Files, Additional Material, Vietnam trip, September 29–October 4, 1972, RNPLM.

35. Ibid. Le Duc Tho made a special point of this in his meeting with Kissinger on September 26.

36. See message from the Politburo to Le Duc Tho in Paris dated October 4, 1972, and summarized in Luu van Loi, *Le Duc Tho–Kissinger Negotiations in Paris*, 302–303 (Hanoi: Gioi Publishers, 1996).

37. Memorandum, Proposal of the Democratic Republic of Vietnam, September 26, 1972, box 121, National Security Files: Henry A. Kissinger Office Files, Country Files, Far East—Vietnam, RNPLM.

38. Memorandum, From Henry A. Kissinger to the President, My Meetings with the North Vietnamese, September 26–27, 1972, box 1014, National Security Council Files: Alexander M. Haig Special Files, Additional Material, Vietnam trip, September 29–October 4, 1972, RNPLM. See also *FRUS, 1969–1976, Volume VIII, Vietnam, January–October 1972*, "Memorandum from the President's Assistant for National Security Affairs to President Nixon, September 28, 1972," document number 267; see also a summary of these dispatches in *FRUS, 1969–1976, Volume XLII, Vietnam: The Kissinger–Le Duc Tho Negotiations, August 1969–December 1973*, "Memorandum of Conversation, September 27, 1972," document number 20.

39. Ibid.

40. Brinkley and Nichter, *Nixon Tapes*, 622

41. As quoted in Henry Kissinger, *Ending the Vietnam War: A History of America's Involvement in and Extrication from the Vietnam War* (New York: Simon and Schuster, 2003), 323.

42. Memorandum of Conversation, Wednesday, October 4, 1972, Presidential Palace, Saigon, box 1018, National Security Council Files: Alexander M. Haig Special Files, Additional Material, Vietnam Trip, September 29–October 4, 1972, RNPLM.

43. Willbanks, *Abandoning Vietnam*, 167.

44. Memorandum, Henry Kissinger to Al Haig, October 4, 1972, box 1018, National Security Council Files: Alexander M. Haig Special Files, Additional Material, Vietnam Trip, September 29–October 4, 1972, RNPLM.

45. As quoted in Ken Hughes, *Fatal Politics: The Nixon Tapes, the Vietnam War, and the Casualties of Reelection* (Charlottesville, VA: University of Virginia Press, 2015), 90.

46. Ibid.

47. Memorandum, Text of Memorandum Tabled by President Thieu at Our October 4 Meeting, box 1018, National Security Council Files, Alexander M. Haig Special Files, Additional Material, Vietnam Trip, September 29–October 4, 1972, RNPLM.

48. Memorandum, Memorandum of Conversation, Sunday, October 8, 1972, Paris, box 122, National Security Council Files: Henry A. Kissinger Office Files, Country Files, Far East—Vietnam, RNPLM.

49. Ibid.

50. Ibid.

51. As quoted in Willbanks, *Abandoning Vietnam*, 169; see also Kissinger, *White House Years*, 1366.

52. Op. cit. note 48.

53. Ibid.

54. Ibid.

55. Ibid.

56. Kissinger, *Ending the Vietnam War*, 329.

57. Ibid.

58. Memorandum, Cable to President Nixon from Henry Kissinger, Paris Talks, October 10, 1972, box 856, National Security Council Files: For the President's Files, Vietnam Negotiations, Winston Lord—China Trip, Vietnam Sensitive, Camp David, October 1972, RNPLM.

59. Kissinger, *Ending the Vietnam War*, 328.

60. Luu van Loi, *Le Duc Tho–Kissinger Negotiations in Paris*, 302–303.

61. Ibid.

62. *FRUS, 1969–1976, Volume XLII, Vietnam: The Kissinger–Le Duc Tho Negotiations, August 1969–December 1973*, "Memorandum of Conversation, September 26, 1972," document number 19.

63. Kissinger, *White House Years*, 1347–1348.

64. Interviews with Luu van Loi and Nguyen Dinh Phuong, Ministry of Foreign Affairs, Hanoi, Vietnam, June 1997 and February 1998.

65. Conversation, McGeorge Bundy and Henry Kissinger, October 26, 1972, 2:34 p.m., box 16, HAK Telecons: White House Tapes, Chronological Files, RNPLM.

66. Memorandum, Memorandum of Conversation, Monday, October 9, 1972, Paris, box 122, National Security Council Files: Henry A. Kissinger Office Files, Country Files, Far East—Vietnam, RNPLM.

67. Memorandum, Memorandum of Conversation, Tuesday, October 10, 1972, Paris, box 122, National Security Council Files: Henry A. Kissinger Office Files, Country Files, Far East—Vietnam, RNPLM.

68. Memorandum, Memorandum of Conversation, Wednesday, October 11, 1972, Paris, box 122, National Security Council Files: Henry A. Kissinger Office Files, Country Files, Far East—Vietnam, RNPLM.

69. Kissinger, *White House Years*, 1345–1346.

70. Brinkley and Nichter, *Nixon Tapes*, 629.

71. Ibid.

72. Brinkley and Nichter, *Nixon Tapes*, 629–630.

73. Memorandum, Memorandum of Conversation, Tuesday, October 17, 1972, Paris, box 122, National Security Council Files: Henry A. Kissinger Office Files, Country Files, Far East—Vietnam, RNPLM.

74. Memorandum, From General Haig for the President, Meeting with President Thieu, October 19, 1972, box 857, National Security Council Files: For the President's Files, Vietnam Negotiations, Winston Lord—China Trip, Vietnam Sensitive, Camp David, October 1972, RNPLM.

75. Memorandum, From Haig to the President, Second Day Meeting with President Thieu, October 20, 1972, box 857, National Security Council Files: For the President's Files, Vietnam Negotiations, Winston Lord—China Trip, Vietnam Sensitive, Camp David, October 1972, RNPLM. The report from Haig is a cover letter attached to the longer report from Kissinger to the White House dated October 20, 1972.

76. Conversation, McGeorge Bundy and Henry Kissinger, October 26, 1972, 2:34 p.m., box 16, HAK Telecons: White House Tapes, Chronological Files, RNPLM.

77. Bui Diem, *In the Jaws of History*, 307.

78. Kissinger, *White House Years*, 1379–1380.

79. Memorandum, For Kissinger from the Central Intelligence Agency, The Security Aspects of the Settlement Package—"Could the GVN Accept a Cease-fire in Place," October 16, 1972, box 113, National Security Council Files: Vietnam Subject Files, Ceasefire—Vietnam, 1972, RNPLM.

80. Author interview with Nguyen Xuan Oanh, economist and former South Vietnamese official, Ho Chi Minh City, Vietnam, July 1989.

81. Kissinger, *Ending the Vietnam War*, 352.

82. Ibid., 352–353.

83. Cable, From General Haig at the White House to Col. Quay in Paris, October 22, 1972, box 119, National Security Council Files: Henry A. Kissinger Office Files, Country Files, Far East—Vietnam, RNPLM.

84. Transcript, News Conference of October 26, 1972, Dr. Henry Kissinger, Assistant to the President for National Security Affairs, box 119, National Security Council Files: Henry A. Kissinger Office Files, Country Files, Far East—Vietnam, RNPLM.

85. Conversation, Chuck Colson and Henry Kissinger, October 26, 1972, 7:26 p.m., box 16, HAK Telecons: White House Tapes, Chronological Files, RNPLM.

86. Conversation, William Rogers and Henry Kissinger, October 26, 1972, 12:45 p.m., box 16, HAK Telecons: White House Tapes, Chronological Files, RNPLM.

87. Kissinger, *Ending the Vietnam War*, 383.

88. Kimball, *Nixon's Vietnam War*, 349.

89. Kissinger, *Ending the Vietnam War*, 389.

90. *FRUS, 1969–1976, Volume XLII, Vietnam: The Kissinger–Le Duc Tho Negotiations, August 1969–December 1973*, "Memorandum of Conversation, November 21, 1972," document number 27 [passage in footnotes].

91. Ibid. [passage in footnotes].

92. Memorandum, From Henry A. Kissinger to the President, Changes Obtained in the Draft Agreement, November 25, 1972, box 110, National Security Files: Henry A. Kissinger Office Files, Country Files, Far East—Vietnam, RNPLM.

93. *FRUS, 1969–1976, Volume XLII, Vietnam: The Kissinger–Le Duc Tho Negotiations, August 1969–December 1973*, "Memorandum of Conversation, December 4, 1972," document number 32.

94. Ibid.

95. *FRUS, 1969–1976, Volume XLII, Vietnam: The Kissinger–Le Duc Tho Negotiations, August 1969–December 1973*, "Memorandum of Conversation, December 9, 1972," document number 37.

96. *FRUS, 1969–1976, Volume XLII, Vietnam: The Kissinger–Le Duc Tho Negotiations, August 1969–December 1973*, "Memorandum of Conversation, December 12, 1972," document number 40.

97. *FRUS, 1969–1976, Volume IX, Vietnam, October 1972–January 1973*, "Message from the President's Assistant for National Security Affairs (Kissinger) to President Nixon, December 9, 1972," document number 152 (Washington, DC: Government Printing Office, 2010).

98. *FRUS, 1969–1976, Volume IX, Vietnam, October 1972–January 1973*, "Message from the President's Deputy Assistant for National Security Affairs (Haig) to the President's Assistant for National Security Affairs (Kissinger), December 10, 1972," document number 155.

99. *FRUS, 1969–1976, Volume IX, Vietnam, October 1972–January 1973*, "Message from the President's Assistant for National Security Affairs (Kissinger) to the President's Deputy Assistant for National Security Affairs (Haig), December 11, 1972," document number 156.

100. *FRUS, 1969–1976, Volume IX, Vietnam, October 1972–January 1973*, "Message from the President's Deputy Assistant for National Security Affairs (Haig) to the President's Assistant for National Security Affairs (Kissinger), December 12, 1972," document number 158.

101. Ibid.

102. As quoted in the excellent footnotes by John Carland and Merle Pribbenow to *FRUS, 1969–1976, Volume XLII, Vietnam: The Kissinger–Le Duc Tho Negotiations, August 1969–December 1973*, "Memorandum of Conversation, December 12, 1972," document number 40.

103. Ibid.

104. *FRUS, 1969–1976, Volume IX, Vietnam, October 1972–January 1973*, "Message from the President's Assistant for National Security Affairs (Kissinger) to the President's Deputy Assistant for National Security Affairs (Haig), December 12, 1972," document number 163.

105. Ibid.

106. Memorandum, Memorandum of Conversation, December 13, 1972, Paris, box 119, National Security Council Files: Henry A. Kissinger Office Files,

Country Files, Far East—Vietnam, RNPLM; see also *FRUS, 1969–1976, Volume XLII, Vietnam: The Kissinger–Le Duc Tho Negotiations, August 1969–December 1973,* "Memorandum of Conversation, December 13, 1972, Paris," document number 41, and *FRUS, 1969–1976, Volume IX, Vietnam, October 1972–January 1973,* "Message from the President's Assistant for National Security Affairs (Kissinger) to the President's Deputy Assistant for National Security Affairs (Haig), December 12, 1972, Paris," document number 163.

107. *FRUS, 1969–1976, Volume IX, Vietnam, October 1972–January 1973,* "Message from John D. Negroponte of the National Security Council Staff to the President's Assistant for National Security Affairs (Kissinger), December 14, 1972," document 174.

108. *FRUS, 1969–1976, Volume IX, Vietnam, October 1972–January 1973,* "Conversation Among President Nixon, the President's Assistant for National Security Affairs (Kissinger), and the President's Deputy Assistant for National Security Affairs (Haig), December 14, 1972," document 175.

109. Ibid.

110. Willbanks, *Abandoning Vietnam,* 180.

111. Nixon, *RN,* 733–734.

112. Ibid.

113. Willbanks, *Abandoning Vietnam,* 181.

114. Kissinger, *White House Years,* 1459–1460; see also Nixon, *RN,* 737.

115. Memorandum, Haig to Kissinger, December 20, 1972, box 1020, National Security Council Files: Alexander M. Haig Special Files, General Haig's Vietnam Trip and Miscellany, December 17–22, 1972, RNPLM.

116. James H. Willbanks, ed., *Vietnam War: A Topical Exploration and Primary Source Collection* (Santa Barbara: ABC-CLIO, 2017), 352.

117. Nixon, *RN,* 738.

118. All of these criticisms of the bombings are captured by the Richard Nixon Presidential Library and Museum at https://www.nixonlibrary.gov/exhibits/decbomb/chapter-v.html.

119. Nixon, *RN,* 738.

120. Luu van Loi, *Le Duc Tho–Kissinger Negotiations in Paris,* 422.

121. *New York Times,* December 30, 1972.

122. *FRUS, 1969–1976, Volume XLII, Vietnam: The Kissinger–Le Duc Tho Negotiations, August 1969–December 1973,* "Memorandum of Conversation, January 8, 1973," document number 42.

123. Ibid.

124. Memorandum, Key Points to Be Made with Respect to Vietnam Agreement, Vietnam Peace Reaction, box 178, White House Special Files: Alpha Names Files, H. R. Haldeman, RNPLM.

125. *FRUS, 1969–1976, Volume IX, Vietnam, October 1972–January 1973,* "Message from the President's Assistant for National Security Affairs (Kissinger) to President Nixon, January 9, 1973," document number 256.

126. *FRUS, 1969–1976, Volume IX, Vietnam, October 1972–January 1973*, "Message from the President's Assistant for National Security Affairs (Kissinger) to President Nixon, January 11, 1973," document number 263.

127. Brinkley and Nichter, *Nixon Tapes*, 726.

128. *FRUS, 1969–1976, Volume IX, Vietnam, October 1972–January 1973*, "Message from Richard T. Kennedy of the National Security Council Staff to the President's Assistant for National Security Affairs (Kissinger) in Paris, January 11, 1973," document number 264.

129. Nixon, *RN*, 737.

130. *New York Times*, December 13, 1972.

131. Conversation, Roland Evans and Henry Kissinger, January 24, 1973, 4:26 p.m., box 18, HAK Telecons: White House Tapes, Chronological Files, RNPLM.

132. As reported in Willbanks, *Abandoning Vietnam*, 191.

133. Ibid., 192.

134. Full transcript of Kissinger's remarks reprinted in *New York Times*, January 25, 1973.

135. As quoted in Dallek, *Nixon and Kissinger*, 453.

136. *Haldeman Diaries*, January 27, 1973, 573.

137. Richard Nixon, "Address to the Nation Announcing the Conclusion of an Agreement on Ending the War and Restoring Peace in Vietnam," January 23, 1973," at www. Presidency.ucsb.edu/ws/?pid=3808.

INDEX

INDEX

Kissinger, Henry *(continued)*
memoirs of, 93–95
military escalations championed by,
33–34, 41–42, 70–77, 85, 109,
137–138, 182, 233–235, 244
misrepresentation by, 91–95
Nazi Germany experiences shaping,
92–93
as new national security adviser, 7–10
in 1965 negotiations meeting with
Harvard colleagues, 16–18
1968 October peace talks of, 2–5
1969 peace talks of, 57–70
1969 Vietnam policy of, 80–81
1970 April peace talks of, 107–109
in 1970 Cambodia military offensive,
109–120
1970 March peace talks of, 100–107
1970 September peace talks of, 124–132
1971 peace talks of, 148–159
1972 anxiety over Nixon, 160–161
1972 China visit of, 168
in 1972 December military escalation in
North Vietnam, 231–238
1972 December peace talks of, 229–233
1972 May peace talks of, 179–187
1972 November peace talks of, 227–229
in 1972 October meeting with Thieu,
221–231
1972 October peace talks of, 214–221
1972 October press conference of,
225–226
1972 September peace talks of, 200–212
1972 summer peace talks of, 189–199
1973 January peace talks of, 239–241
Nixon comments made by, 2
Nixon's doubts about, 88–89, 129–130,
157, 161–164, 195
Nixon's emotional state worries of, 90,
129
in Nixon's 1968 presidential campaign,
2–5
on Nixon's 1970 October standstill
cease-fire speech, 134

as "Nixon's Secret Agent," 164–167
Nobel Peace Prize awarded to, 91, 242
Pakistan war response of, 161–163
peace agreement announcement by,
220–221, 240–241
peace agreement finalization by,
209–221, 227–233, 239–241
peace talks of. *See* peace talks
in Pierre Hotel meeting with Nixon,
1–2, 6–7
on reality, 44–45
resignation threats of, 76
revisionism by, 91–95
Rogers shutting out by, 47–49, 65, 67,
76, 139, 201, 244
secrecy love of, 8, 10, 47, 102–103
secret back-channel of, 57–70
secret Cambodia bombings by, 36–42,
116
secretary of state appointment of, 68
Soviet cooperation plan of, 45–57
strategy for ending Vietnam War on
acceptable terms, 21–36
victory declarations of, 241–244
White House Years, 5, 94
on world role of US, 44–45, 92
Kosygin, Alexei, 55–56
Kraemer, Sven, 207–208
Kraft, Joe, 75
Ky. *See* Nguyen Cao Ky

Laird, Melvin, 9
Easter Offensive response of, 169–174,
179–180
Kissinger's memos against, 79–80
Kissinger's shutting out of, 65, 67, 76,
114, 139–140, 144, 201, 244
Kissinger's troop withdrawal
confrontation with, 28–33
in Laos invasion, 139–144
military escalation opposed by, 34,
74, 76
in 1970 Cambodia military offensive,
113–116

INDEX

People's Army of Vietnam (PAVN, North
Vietnamese Army)
Cambodia bombings targeting, 36–42,
116
Easter Offensive of, 168–179
Laos attacks targeting, 136–145
in South Vietnam after peace
agreement, 201–202, 215–217, 219,
223–224, 228, 236–237
South Vietnam's 1969 gains against, 86
People's Liberation Armed Forces (PLAF),
South Vietnam's 1969 gains against,
86
Pham Van Dong
1970 meeting with China, 130–131
rejection of Nixon's 1969 peace
proposals, 51–52
Phnom Penh, 112, 203
PLAF. *See* People's Liberation Armed
Forces
Pocket Money, 183–186
port mining, 1972 North Vietnam,
183–186
Porter, William, 230
postwar reconstruction aid
DRV's demand for, 153, 155
as possible option in negotiations, 84,
87, 155
power
Kissinger's and Nixon's shared views
on, 5–6
Kissinger's childhood experiences with,
92–93
Kissinger's concentration of, 46–49,
65–68, 114
POWs. *See* prisoners of war
presidential elections
1964 US, 13–15
1968 US, 1–5
1971 South Vietnam, 154–156, 158
1972 US, 160–161, 177–178, 200, 204,
226
PRG. *See* Provisional Revolutionary
Government

prisoners of war (POWs)
in finalized peace agreement, 210, 229
in 1970 peace talks, 101–102
in 1971 peace talks, 148, 153, 156
in 1972 peace talks, 190–195, 198–199,
201
protests
against Cambodian invasion, 116–120
against Laos invasion, 149
May 1970 march on White House, 117
military escalation affected by, 72–74,
78, 120, 146–147, 149
against 1972 bombing of North
Vietnam, 174
against Nixon's 1972 military
escalations, 183, 187
Provisional Government of National
Concord (GNC), 203, 214
Provisional Revolutionary Government
(PRG)
DRV's demand for, 51–52, 102,
107, 125–128, 153–156, 193–195,
203–206, 209
1970 eight-point peace program of,
126–128
Soviet support of, 56–57
Pruning Knife, 71–75
Pye, Lucian, 17

Quang Tri City
North Vietnam taking of, 179
South Vietnam counteroffensive
on, 186

Raborn, William, 18–19
Radford, Charles, 163
RAND Corporation, Vietnam
contingency options study by, 25–27
Reasoner, Harry, 242
reconstruction aid
DRV's demand for, 153, 155
as possible option in negotiations, 84,
87, 155
Red Flag. *See Hongqi*

293

Republic of Vietnam (GVN, South
Vietnam)
civil society and cultural identification
developing in, 83–84
Communist 1975 victory in, 244
DRV insistence on control of, 48,
51–52, 102, 107, 125–128, 153–155,
203–204
DRV 1973 attacks on, 241
Kissinger's contempt for, 99–100, 244
Kissinger's shutting out of, 65, 67, 103,
201
map of, xviii (fig.)
1971 presidential elections in, 154–156,
158
North Vietnamese forces allowed to
remain in, 201–202, 215–217, 219,
223–224, 228, 236–237
objections to finalized peace agreement,
221–231
peace agreement over political future of,
209–220, 228–230, 239, 243
rejection of Johnson's October 1968
peace talks, 3–5
troop withdrawals from. See troop
withdrawal
urbanization of, 110–111
resignation, Kissinger's threats of, 76
revisionism, Kissinger's habit of,
91–95
Rockefeller, Nelson, 1, 7, 13–14
Rodman, Peter, 71, 201
Rogers, William, 8–9
Kissinger's memos against, 79–80
Kissinger's replacement of, 68
Kissinger's shutting out of, 47–49, 65,
67, 76, 139, 201, 244
in Laos invasion, 141
military escalation opposed by, 76
in 1970 Cambodia military offensive,
114–116
in secret Cambodia bombings, 38, 40
Rolling Thunder, 3
Roosevelt, Franklin, 92

Rostow, Walt, 19
Rusk, Dean, 16, 57

Safire, William, 77
Saigon. See Republic of Vietnam
Sainteny, Jean, 59–60
Saxbie, William, 237
Schlesinger, Arthur, Jr., 44
secrecy
of Cambodia bombings, 37–40
Kissinger's and Nixon's love of, 8, 10,
47, 102–103
secret peace talks
1969 back-channel negotiations, 57–70
1970 April, 107–109
1970 February, 91, 93, 95–100
1970 March, 100–107
1970 September, 124–132
1971, 148–159
Nixon's 1972 exposure of, 164–168
secretary of defense. See Laird, Melvin
secretary of state
Kissinger's appointment as, 68
See also Rogers, William
The Senior Review Group, 68
Sheehan, Neil, 157
Sidey, Hugh, 165
Sihanouk. See Norodom Sihanouk
Silent Majority speech, 78–81, 86
Sirik Matak, 111
Sitton, Ray, 36–37
South Vietnam. See Republic of Vietnam
Soviet Union
China rift with, 53–54
Kissinger's 1972 April visit to, 175–179
Kissinger's push for cooperation from,
45–57
1971 diplomatic breakthroughs with,
151
Nixon's 1972 May letter to, 181–182
Nixon's 1972 visit to, 176–178, 184–185
Spinoza, Baruch, 44
Stalin, Joseph, 53–54
standstill cease-fire. See cease-fire

Sean Hemmerle

Robert K. Brigham is the Shirley Ecker Boskey Professor of History and International Relations at Vassar College. He is a specialist on the history of US foreign policy. His fellowships include the Rockefeller Foundation, the Mellon Foundation, and the National Endowment for Humanities. Brigham is author or coauthor of nine books, among them *Iraq, Vietnam, and the Limits of American Power* and *Argument Without End.*

PublicAffairs is a publishing house founded in 1997. It is a tribute to the standards, values, and flair of three persons who have served as mentors to countless reporters, writers, editors, and book people of all kinds, including me.

I. F. STONE, proprietor of *I. F. Stone's Weekly*, combined a commitment to the First Amendment with entrepreneurial zeal and reporting skill and became one of the great independent journalists in American history. At the age of eighty, Izzy published *The Trial of Socrates*, which was a national bestseller. He wrote the book after he taught himself ancient Greek.

BENJAMIN C. BRADLEE was for nearly thirty years the charismatic editorial leader of *The Washington Post*. It was Ben who gave the *Post* the range and courage to pursue such historic issues as Watergate. He supported his reporters with a tenacity that made them fearless and it is no accident that so many became authors of influential, best-selling books.

ROBERT L. BERNSTEIN, the chief executive of Random House for more than a quarter century, guided one of the nation's premier publishing houses. Bob was personally responsible for many books of political dissent and argument that challenged tyranny around the globe. He is also the founder and longtime chair of Human Rights Watch, one of the most respected human rights organizations in the world.

•　　•　　•

For fifty years, the banner of Public Affairs Press was carried by its owner Morris B. Schnapper, who published Gandhi, Nasser, Toynbee, Truman, and about 1,500 other authors. In 1983, Schnapper was described by *The Washington Post* as "a redoubtable gadfly." His legacy will endure in the books to come.

Peter Osnos, *Founder*